Diplomacy in Rena

MW01195041

Diplomacy in Renaissance Rome is an investigation of Renaissance diplomacy in practice. Presenting the first book-length study of this subject for sixty years, Catherine Fletcher substantially enhances our understanding of the envoy's role during this pivotal period for the development of diplomacy. Uniting rich but hitherto unexploited archival sources with recent insights from social and cultural history, Fletcher argues for the centrality of the papal court – and the city of Rome – in the formation of the modern European diplomatic system. Part I, Chronologies, considers the shifting political context, from the 1454 Peace of Lodi to the impact of the Italian wars after 1494; the assimilation of ambassadors into the ceremonial world; the prescriptive literature; and trends in the personnel of diplomacy. Part II, Themes, takes a thematic approach, exploring travel and communication practices; the city of Rome as a space for diplomacy; and the world of gift-giving.

Catherine Fletcher is Lecturer in Public History at the University of Sheffield. She is the author of *Our Man in Rome: Henry VIII and His Italian Ambassador*.

Diplomacy in Renaissance Rome

The Rise of the Resident Ambassador

Catherine Fletcher

University of Sheffield

CAMBRIDGE
UNIVERSITY PRESS

CAMBRIDGE
UNIVERSITY PRESS

University Printing House, Cambridge CB2 8BS, United Kingdom

One Liberty Plaza, 20th Floor, New York, NY 10006, USA

477 Williamstown Road, Port Melbourne, VIC 3207, Australia

314-321, 3rd Floor, Plot 3, Splendor Forum, Jasola District Centre, New Delhi - 110025, India

79 Anson Road, #06-04/06, Singapore 079906

Cambridge University Press is part of the University of Cambridge.

It furthers the University's mission by disseminating knowledge in the pursuit of education, learning and research at the highest international levels of excellence.

www.cambridge.org
Information on this title: www.cambridge.org/9781107515789

© Catherine Fletcher 2015

First published 2015
First paperback edition 2020

A catalogue record for this publication is available from the British Library

Library of Congress Cataloging in Publication data
Fletcher, Catherine, 1975–
Diplomacy in Renaissance Rome : the rise of the resident ambassador /
Catherine Fletcher. – First edition.
    pages cm
Includes bibliographical references and index.
ISBN 978-1-107-10779-3 (Hardback) – ISBN 978-1-107-51578-9 (Paperback)
1. Diplomacy–History.   2. Diplomatic and consular service–History.
3. Diplomatic and consular service, Papal States–History.   4. Ambassadors–
Italy–Papal States–History.   5. Papacy–History–1447–1565.   6. Papal
courts.   7. Renaissance–Papal States.   8. Renaissance–Italy–Rome.
9. Rome (Italy)–History–1420–1798.   I. Title.
JZ1405.F54 2015
327.456'34009024–dc23   2015014001

ISBN 978-1-107-10779-3 Hardback
ISBN 978-1-107-51578-9 Paperback

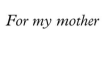

For my mother

Contents

Figures

Notes and abbreviations

When referring to the *Letters and Papers* and *Calendars of State Papers*, I have given document numbers, except in the case of unnumbered items, where a page reference is given. When citing Sanuto's diaries, I have given column numbers. The following abbreviations have been used in the notes:

ASF	Archivio di Stato di Firenze
ASMn, AG	Archivio di Stato di Mantova, Archivio Gonzaga
ASV	Archivio Segreto Vaticano
ASVe	Archivio di Stato di Venezia
BAV	Biblioteca Apostolica Vaticana
BNF	Bibliothèque Nationale de France
BL	British Library
F. Contarini	Biblioteca Nazionale Marciana, Codices Italiani VII 802 (=8219)
G. Contarini	Biblioteca Nazionale Marciana, Venice, Codices Italiani VII 1043 (=7616)
CSP Sp	*Calendar of Letters, Despatches and State Papers relating to the negotiations between England and Spain*
DBI	Dizionario Biografico degli Italiani
DNB	Oxford Dictionary of National Biography
L&P	*Letters and Papers, Foreign and Domestic, of the Reign of Henry VIII*
St P	*State Papers published under the authority of Her Majesty's Commission: King Henry the Eighth*
TNA	The National Archives
b.	busta
c.	carta (leaf)
fol.	folio

Full publication details of the works listed above are given in the Bibliography.

Introduction

In the first decade of the sixteenth century, Paride Grassi (1450~60–1528), master-of-ceremonies at the papal court, wrote a treatise on the ambassadors of the Roman curia. *De Oratoribus Romanae Curiae* was Grassi's attempt to codify a vital figure in Roman politics: the diplomat. Resident ambassadors had been tolerated in Rome for some decades, but the institutions of diplomacy were far from fully-formed. Grassi, tasked with creating order in the ceremonial world of the curia, tried to fix them but struggled. After listing the princes of Europe in order of precedence, Grassi added a marginal note: *alibi legitur* ('elsewhere, one reads') and an alternative order. His uncertainty is testimony to the effort he and his contemporaries had to make to get to grips with the new diplomacy. He left his manuscript unfinished, but, even had he completed it, the text would still have been provisional. This was a period of transition, though those powers favoured by the ceremonialists' official orders – the *Ordo Regum* and *Ordo Ducum* – preferred to claim it was not.

The shifting diplomatic practices that so taxed Grassi are the subject of this book. It tracks Rome's rise as a centre for diplomacy from the middle of the fifteenth century to the 1530s, beginning with the re-establishment of a single papacy in the city and continuing through decades, first of relative peace on the Italian peninsula and then of devastating war. This period, a little short of a century, saw a substantial expansion of permanent resident diplomacy in Europe. Rome, as the seat of the Catholic Church, attracted the largest group of envoys of any European court. As a 'supranational' centre for European diplomacy – indeed, Europe's last such centre until the twentieth century with its League of Nations, United Nations and European Community – Rome was in many ways exceptional. The popes were simultaneously spiritual overlords of Christendom and temporal princes ruling the Papal States of central Italy. That gave their diplomacy a distinct character. Yet the court of the Renaissance popes had much in common with its secular counterparts. Like other European courts, it became more settled and more magnificent in this period. Against this backdrop the popes' policy on resident diplomacy in Rome moved from unofficial toleration in the mid-fifteenth century to ceremonial assimilation in the early years of the sixteenth. My study concludes at the point when the Sack of 1527, the Reformation and the rise of Spanish power on the Italian peninsula changed the contours of European diplomacy, creating new problems and dilemmas for its personnel.

While it has long been accepted that resident diplomacy came into being in this period, the details of its development are sketchy. This book aims to explain and account for the shape of this new institution in Rome and the trends in its practices. It outlines and analyses the key elements of the resident ambassador's role, both in formal, ceremonial spheres of power and in the all-important informal arenas for diplomacy. Three paintings of ambassadors from the early decades of the sixteenth century sum up the diplomatic activities that I discuss. Vittore Carpaccio's *Stories from the Life of St Ursula* series (1495–1500) shows envoys in their ceremonial context. In *The Ambassadors Depart* (Figure 1), English ambassadors, in an imagined court environment, are taking their leave from Brittany. In Rome, the detail of such ceremonies was first codified precisely at the time Carpaccio was working. But Carpaccio does not depict only the formalities of embassy. He shows us its many informal aspects too. In the background, to the right, courtiers chat and gossip. At the centre back, a secretary takes notes. These men were important in diplomacy.

Secretaries also appear in Sebastiano del Piombo's portrait of Ferry Carondelet, Margaret of Austria's envoy to Rome (1510–12).[1] Portrayed in the canonical role of the ambassador, despatching news, Carondelet does not work alone but alongside others. Though the office of ambassador might appertain to an individual, his collaborations were all-important. In the most famous portrait of Renaissance ambassadors (Figure 2), that by Hans Holbein, Jean de Dinteville, on the left, personifies the magnificence of his prince, Francis I of France.

The Sebastiano and Holbein paintings draw our attention to the two personae of the Renaissance ambassador. In the former, he appears as his own agent, an actor in gathering news, in organising his staff, in despatching information. In the latter, he represents another: the prince who has sent him abroad. The peculiar nature of the ambassador as a figure simultaneously embodying his prince and acting on his own behalf makes him an important case-study through which to reflect on the nature of the

---

[1] Sebastiano del Piombo, *Portrait of Ferry Carondelet and His Secretaries*, 1510–12; Oil on panel, 113 × 87 cm; Museo Thyssen-Bornemisza, Madrid.

Figure 1: Vittore Carpaccio, *The Departure of the English Ambassadors*, from the *St Ursula* cycle, 1498; Oil on canvas, 280 × 253 cm, © Galleria dell'Accademia, Venice, Italy/Bridgeman Images.

early modern 'self'. It is evident from the sources that envoys made a distinction between their own 'self' and their representation of their principal. His profession and his period gave the diplomat reason to simulate and dissimulate, and when circumstances demanded, he could manipulate these two selves. The ambiguity inherent in an ambassador's dual persona allowed him to do so all the more effectively.

Most studies of early modern diplomacy focus on the diplomatic corps of a particular prince or republic. This one assesses diplomacy as it went

Figure 2: Hans Holbein the Younger, *Jean de Dinteville and Georges de Selve ('The Ambassadors')*, 1533; Oil on oak, 207 × 209 cm; © National Gallery, London.

on at a receiving court, where envoys from across Europe and beyond co-operated and conspired. As a consequence, the picture it paints is less tidy, more ad hoc than a survey of a single polity's outgoing envoys might produce. The rather chaotic terminology for diplomats – in Italian, the terms *ambasciadore* and *oratore* were used interchangeably – reflects that they were unstable, poorly-defined figures.[2] Likewise, and particularly in the early part of our period, the lines between special, resident and permanent envoys were not always clear. The diplomatic practices I explore are characterised by change and fluidity. The paradox is that they take place in a political context of European courts becoming more tightly organised, and more serious about formalities. Recent studies of court ceremony have shown its importance to early modern politics. Here, I assess the ambassador's ceremonial role alongside his negotiating and newsgathering, aiming to integrate these perspectives into a holistic picture of the diplomat's activities.

To understand the nuances of developments in Rome I have focused on practices of diplomacy. My decision to investigate the diplomatic practice of resident ambassadors rather than 'the resident ambassador' as an institution follows Daniela Frigo's argument in a wide-ranging and convincing article on the role of the ambassador in the early modern

---

[2] Gary M. Bell, 'Tudor-Stuart diplomatic history and the Henrician experience', in Robert L. Woods et al. (eds), *State, Sovereigns and Society in Early Modern England: Essays in Honour of A. J. Slavin* (Stroud: Sutton, 1998), pp. 25–43 (p. 35). The authors of the contemporary treatises on diplomacy, writing in Latin, use the classical term 'legatus'.

period that during the sixteenth century diplomacy should be regarded as a *prassi*, that is, a usual procedure, or a series of practices adopted as circumstances required.[3] While the 'instititution' of 'ambassador to Rome' came into being in a number of states during the fifteenth and sixteenth centuries, at the receiving court, the institution – of course, rather different according to the nature of the home state – was established only with reference to the world of ceremony. The remainder – indeed the majority – of the envoy's work can only be discerned through a study of his activities. In an entertaining memoir of his career, the twentieth-century Canadian diplomat Kenneth P. Kirkwood commented:

> History is normally the account of great affairs of state; and most diplomats' memoirs and reminiscences deal in part with historical episodes and affairs of state in which they had some small and passing role. But, in the way of life, there are also the sidelines of diplomatic life, the trivial and the comic, the incidentals and diversions – though each may have some unapparent significance. Dining is of importance in diplomacy, and wining; and cocktails have taken the place of the important old coffee shops.[4]

Like diplomats' memoirs and reminiscences, the traditional type of diplomatic history was concerned with 'great affairs'. However, I agree with Kirkwood that in the many sidelines of embassy life, it is possible to find details of importance. This is true to this day, but it is particularly true of the Renaissance, a period in which diplomacy was never an individual's sole occupation and a distinction between 'public' and 'private' makes little sense.

Though this is principally a book about diplomacy, through this prism, it also sheds light on society and culture in Renaissance Rome. It highlights the cosmopolitan nature of the city and its centrality to European politics, exploring its physical space as well as its symbolic world. It points to Rome's importance as a centre for the exchange of news. It shows how the development of a more princely model of papal government affected other rulers' interactions with the curia. It situates these developments in the context of the Italian wars and the shifting nature of European monarchy. In short, it emphasises Rome's importance in European political life. As a centre for diplomacy, Rome was in some ways unusual and in other ways quite typical of a European court.

---

[3] Daniela Frigo, 'Corte, onore e ragion di stato: il ruolo dell'ambasciatore in età moderna', in Frigo (ed.), *Ambasciatori e nunzi. Figure della diplomazia in età moderna* (= *Cheiron* 30 (1998)), pp. 13–55 (p. 47).

[4] Kenneth P. Kirkwood, *The Diplomat at Table: A Social and Anecdotal History Through the Looking-Glass* (Metuchen: Scarecrow Press, 1974), p. 3.

Whereas in most courts diplomats arrived to represent a principal who they regarded as equal to their host prince, the popes' spiritual and juridical role made the court of Rome distinctive. The role of ambassadors in seeking out benefices for their home country was particular to the curia, as was the figure of the cardinal-protector. Rome's liturgical ceremony did not have precise parallels elsewhere, although the competition for precedence within it certainly did. There is perhaps some resemblance to the Imperial court, where representatives of numerous princes might gather, but the number of ambassadors in Rome was substantially higher (see Chapter 1). On the other hand, as the largest diplomatic centre in Europe, Rome functioned as a meeting-place for ambassadors across the continent and as a consequence was a fulcrum for the refinement of diplomatic practices. Foreign commentators certainly thought that the Italian states were particularly developed when it came to the conduct of diplomacy, though not always in a good way. In the general functioning of resident diplomacy – through information-gathering, gift-giving, hospitality, and so forth – Rome was probably not very different from other places. Diplomacy is and was, by its nature, an international phenomenon.

In its adoption of methods from social and cultural history, this book responds to recent calls for a 'new diplomatic history' that sets out to investigate ambassadorial activity 'from below'.[5] The precise nature of the 'new diplomatic history' is still being worked out, but studies over the past twenty years have employed a variety of methodological approaches including prosopography, biography and literary history.[6] In many cases, however, these works aim to illuminate not so much diplomatic practice as a variety of other issues relating to the early modern state and political culture. Indeed, the turn in diplomatic history was foreshadowed by developments in broader scholarship on politics and the state, and the increasing attention paid by historians to what Giorgio Chittolini has described as 'privatistic' political forces.[7] Nonetheless, they collectively

---

[5] On the 'new diplomatic history', see John Watkins, 'Toward a new diplomatic history of medieval and early modern Europe', *Journal of Medieval and Early Modern Studies* 38 (2008), 1–14, the introduction to Frigo, *Ambasciatori e nunzi*, p. 7, and Lucien Bély, 'La Naissance de la Diplomatie Moderne', *Revue d'Histoire Diplomatique* 3 (2007), 271–94 (p. 272).

[6] Franca Leverotti, *Diplomazia e Governo dello Stato: I "Famigli Cavalcanti" di Francesco Sforza (1450–1466)* (Pisa: Gisem-ETS, 1992); Toby Osborne, *Dynasty and Diplomacy in the Court of Savoy: Political Culture and the Thirty Years' War* (Cambridge: Cambridge University Press, 2002); Timothy Hampton, *Fictions of Embassy: Literature and Diplomacy in Early Modern Europe* (Ithaca and London: Cornell University Press, 2009).

[7] Julius Kirshner (ed.), *The Origins of the State in Italy, 1300–1600* (Chicago and London: University of Chicago Press, 1995), especially Giorgio Chittolini, 'The "Private", the "Public", the State', pp. 34–61 (pp. 40–1).

mark an important turn away from diplomatic history as an account of high political negotiating towards a more nuanced picture of diplomacy as a social structure or practice. Alongside this shift, there has been a significant re-assessment of diplomacy in Renaissance Italy. While traditional historiography, most notably the work of Garrett Mattingly, privileged developments in the Italian republics, recent studies have emphasised the significance of Milan and the 'small states' of Mantua and Ferrara in diplomatic innovation. Mattingly's thesis (in his 1955 book, *Renaissance Diplomacy*) is that fifteenth- and early sixteenth-century Italy saw a 'modernisation' process in terms of inter-state relations, and that this was centrally driven by the city-states of Florence (in the fifteenth century) and subsequently Venice.[8] At the heart of this process lay the development of resident diplomacy. As Joseph P. Huffman has pointed out in an excellent introduction to the broader historiography of diplomacy, 'the Anglo-American historiographical tradition was built around Whig notions of state building and modernization'.[9] Mattingly was one of many American historians to work in a historiographical context that saw the republican tradition of Renaissance Italy as an ancestor of modern American republicanism, an approach now regarded as problematic.[10] At the Princeton Bicentennial Conference on The University and its World Responsibilities in 1947, he argued that North Americans were 'Western Europeans... a subsection of a great society called Western Civilization'. The history of the United States could not be detached from that of Europe.[11] Nonetheless, despite some questionable assessments of the importance of Venice and Florence in diplomatic developments, his work remains valuable.[12] In fact, he identified many of the points that later scholars have refined. His observations on the early innovations in Milan and Mantua, for example, have been elaborated into much wider studies of the diplomacy of these northern states. In particular, extensive work on the diplomacy of

---

[8] Garrett Mattingly, *Renaissance Diplomacy* (Harmondsworth: Penguin, 1973). For an appreciation of Mattingly's work and the background to the writing of *Renaissance Diplomacy*, see J. H. Hexter, 'Garrett Mattingly, Historian', in C. H. Carter (ed.), *From the Renaissance to the Counter-Reformation: Essays in Honor of Garrett Mattingly* (New York: Random House, 1965), pp. 13–28.

[9] Joseph P. Huffman, *The Social Politics of Medieval Diplomacy: Anglo-German Relations (1066–1307)* (Ann Arbor: University of Michigan Press, 2000), pp. 5–6.

[10] Anthony Molho, 'The Italian Renaissance, made in the USA', in Molho and Gordon S. Wood (eds), *Imagined Histories: American Historians Interpret the Past* (Princeton: Princeton University Press, 1998), pp. 263–94.

[11] Leo Gershoy, 'Garrett Mattingly: A personal appreciation', in C. H. Carter (ed.), *From the Renaissance*, pp. 7–12 (p. 11).

[12] For one problematic passage on Florence and Venice, see Mattingly, *Renaissance Diplomacy*, p. 76.

Francesco Sforza has emphasised the importance of the new regime in Milan in developing diplomatic practices in the middle of the fifteenth century.[13]

More generally, in recent years, there has been something of a reaction to the quest for the 'modern' in Renaissance diplomacy. Riccardo Fubini has described the 'outdatedness of the traditional approach' in terms of its focus on the resident ambassador as 'the key element in the transition from medieval to modern'.[14] In her study of the diplomacy of Mantua and Modena, Daniela Frigo has argued that the resident ambassadors employed by the rulers of these small states were not so much 'modern' as 'part of a network of relations that was feudal in character'.[15] In relation to English diplomacy, Gary M. Bell has weighed in with the conclusion that Henry VIII 'handled affairs in a most personal and "medieval" fashion'.[16] While this process of re-assessment is timely and welcome, there is a certain danger in replacing the maxim that Renaissance diplomacy was 'modern' with the maxim that it was 'medieval' (and, presumably, became 'modern' at some later stage). It may be possible to say, for example, that certain diplomatic practices of this period look more 'feudal' than others, but in general I take the view that it is more important to situate them in the context of contemporary values and understandings than to impose what is bound to be an artificial line between medieval and modern diplomacy.

Envoys' letters have been an important source for this study, but there are, of course, a number of problems in the interpretation of diplomatic correspondence.[17] The ambassadors, aware of the importance of their mission, took care to portray themselves and their work in the best possible light; the surviving letters, furthermore, tend to be those written

---

[13] The work of Ilardi, Margaroli and Leverotti on Milan has been important in this regard, as has that of Lazzarini and Frigo on Mantua and Modena. Paul M. Dover has argued for the importance of Neapolitan innovation in his 'Royal diplomacy in Renaissance Italy: Ferrante d'Aragona (1458–1494) and his ambassadors', *Mediterranean Studies* 14 (2005), 57–94.

[14] Riccardo Fubini, 'Diplomacy and government in the Italian city-states of the fifteenth century (Florence and Venice)', in Daniela Frigo (ed.), *Politics and Diplomacy in Early Modern Italy: The Structure of Diplomatic Practice, 1450–1800* (Cambridge: Cambridge University Press, 2000), pp. 25–48 (p. 25). See also, on this question, his 'L'ambasciatore nel XV secolo: Due trattati e una biografia (Bernard de Rosier, Ermolao Barbaro, Vespasiano da Bisticci)', *Mélanges de l'école française de Rome. Moyen Age* 108 (1996), 645–65.

[15] Daniela Frigo, '"Small states" and diplomacy: Mantua and Modena', in Frigo (ed.), *Politics and Diplomacy*, pp. 147–75 (p. 152).

[16] Bell, 'Tudor-Stuart diplomatic history', pp. 37–8.

[17] Filippo de Vivo, *Information and Communication in Venice: Rethinking Early Modern Politics* (Oxford: Oxford University Press, 2007), pp. 57–70.

about political developments. Nonetheless, details they provide of such things as entertainment or the role of servants, although marginal to the main content, can be exploited to provide a picture of the everyday functioning of diplomacy and its apparently minor figures. This process of 'reading across' the correspondence, as opposed to treating it in Rankean fashion as a source of information about events, has led to a variety of new insights. A series of treatises on the office of ambassador, written in the fifteenth and sixteenth centuries, such as those of Ermolao Barbaro and Étienne Dolet, have been the starting point for numerous studies of diplomatic theory.[18] They remain a useful prescriptive source; moreover, by reading between the lines, it has been possible to discern some of the authors' preoccupations and anxieties about diplomacy. An important counterpoint to these treatises has been Paride Grassi's *De Oratoribus Romanae Curiae* (On the Orators of the Roman Curia), which was written principally between 1505 and 1509, but worked on up until at least 1516, while its author was papal master-of-ceremonies.[19] While Grassi's diary is relatively well-known as a historical source (though it has never been published), this treatise has received little scholarly attention, except in relation to its comments on African ambassadors.[20] It furnishes vital keys for interpreting diplomatic conduct at the papal court, particularly in relation to questions of ceremony, precedence and gift-giving. The diary of Grassi's successor Biagio Martinelli, covering the period 1518–40, and similarly unpublished, has also been a useful source in terms of establishing the ceremonial elements of diplomatic practice

---

[18] Betty Behrens, 'Treatises on the ambassador written in the fifteenth and early sixteenth centuries', *English Historical Review* 51 (1936), 616–27. A broader but very dated survey is in J. J. Jusserand, 'The school for ambassadors', *American Historical Review* 27 (1922), 426–64. Some of the key documents are published in V. E. Hrabar, *De Legatis et Legationibus Tractatus Varii* (Dorpat, 1905). More recent analyses are in Fubini, 'L'Ambasciatore nel XV Secolo', and Maurizio Bazzoli, 'Ragion di Stato e Interessi degli Stati. La Trattatistica Sull'Ambasciatore dal XV al XVIII Secolo', *Nuova Rivista Storica* 86 (2002), 283–328.

[19] Biblioteca Apostolica Vaticana, MS Vaticani Latini 12270 is the only surviving sixteenth-century copy of the manuscript. It is in several hands, with additions by the author. There are also two seventeenth-century copies, BAV, MS Vat. Lat. 12409 and BAV, MS Barberini Latini 2452. A description of the manuscripts is contained in Marc Dykmans, "Paris de Grassi II', *Ephemerides Liturgicae* 99 (1985), 383–417 (pp. 400–3), the second part of a three-part biographical and bibliographical article on de Grassi, the other sections of which are 'Paris de Grassi', *Ephemerides Liturgicae* 96 (1982), 407–82 and 'Paris de Grassi III', *Ephemerides Liturgicae* 100 (1986), 270–333. An edition was published just as the revisions to this book were completed: Philipp Stenzig (ed.), *Botschafterzeremoniellam Papsthof der Renaissance: Der Tractatus de oratoribus des Paris de Grassi* (Frankfurt: Peter Lang, 2014).

[20] Kate Lowe, '"Representing" Africa: Ambassadors and princes from Christian Africa to Renaissance Italy and Portugal, 1402–1608', *Transactions of the Royal Historical Society*, 6th series, 17 (2007), 101–28 (p. 119).

during this period, as has the better-known Burchard.[21] The *Commentaries* of Pope Pius II and a treatise on the benefits of the Roman Curia by Lapo da Castiglionchio both give valuable insights into curia diplomacy in the mid-fifteenth century.[22] A travel account by English embassy herald Thomas Wall, records of the corruption trial of Cardinal Benedetto Accolti, maps and census returns add to our understanding of the social world of diplomats in Rome. I should note that this book grew out of research that focused in the first instance on the activities of English representatives in Rome, and I hope readers will forgive a bias towards English sources in certain chapters. A wider, comparative study of the practice of different nations in Rome (not least the Spanish, whose influence grew through this period) is certainly desirable, but must wait for another day.[23] Moreover, only from about 1490 onwards were resident ambassadors officially tolerated at the papal court, so the bulk of the discussion concerns the second half of the traditional 'Renaissance Rome' period.

The book is divided into two parts. Part I introduces the political context for the development of resident diplomacy in Rome and sets out the chronology. Chapter 1 explains the historical context: the re-establishment of a single papacy in Rome after decades of schism, the forty-year peace between the Italian states and, after 1494, the outbreak of war on the Italian peninsula, drawing in all the major European powers. Chapter 2 discusses how contemporaries understood the figure of the ambassador, and how ideas about his role developed. Against this backdrop, Chapter 3 analyses the process through which resident diplomacy was institutionalised at the papal court. Employing a detailed reading of ceremonial texts, it illustrates how diplomats were assimilated into the liturgical world of the curia as their long-term presence in Rome shifted from a source of suspicion to an accepted fact of life. It assesses this process in the context of recent discussion of performance, performativity and symbolic communication. Chapter 4 considers the men

---

[21] BAV, MS Vaticani Latini 12276: Biagio Martinelli da Cesena, *Diario 1518–1532*, and BAV, MS Barberini Latini 2799: Biagio Martinelli da Cesena, *Diario 1518–1540*. Johann Burchard, *Liber Notarum*, ed. Enrico Celani, 2 vols (Città di Castello: Lapi, 1906).

[22] Pius II (Aeneas Sylvius Piccolomini), *I Commentarii*, ed. Luigi Totaro, 2 vols (Milan: Adelphi, 1984); English references to *Secret Memoirs of a Renaissance Pope*, ed. Leona C. Gabel, trans. Florence A. Gragg (London: The Folio Society, 1988). Lapo da Castiglionchio the Younger, *De curiae commodis*, in ed. Christopher S. Celenza, *Renaissance Humanism and the Papal Curia: Lapo da Castiglionchio the Younger's* De Curiae Commodis (Ann Arbor: University of Michigan Press, 1999).

[23] Anna Maria Oliva, 'Gli oratori spagnoli a Roma tra fine Quattrocento e primo Cinquecento', in Portia Prebys (ed.), *Early Modern Rome*, pp. 706–11, proposes some lines of research in relation to Spain in this period.

who were employed as ambassadors, considering changing patterns in the personnel of diplomacy. It assesses the type of people thought appropriate to carry out diplomatic tasks, and the impact of peace and war on the choice of personnel. It considers the role of agents, secretaries and servants, as well as that of women. It discusses the employment of foreigners in diplomatic service during this period, a matter which has received only sketchy consideration in the literature.

Part II takes a thematic approach, turning to consider three aspects of diplomatic practice.Chapter 5 discusses the process of gathering and disseminating information, a central part of the ambassador's role, highlighting the importance of social networks and personal connections. Chapter 6 discusses the house, household and hospitality in diplomatic practice. Leading on from Chapter 5, this chapter continues to focus on the problematic distinction between official/unofficial and formal/informal though a consideration of the spaces in which diplomacy was practised. It analyses the symbolic and instrumental functions of diplomatic hospitality, and the importance of splendour, as well as addressing practical questions about the ambassador's house and household, assessing how contemporary writings on the general question of household management can inform our understanding of diplomatic practice. Referring to discussions on the importance of liberality and hospitality, particularly in the works of Giovanni Pontano, both Chapters 6 and 7 ask how these were expressed in the context of diplomacy. Chapter 7 investigates another key element in the working of diplomacy, gift-giving, analysing the different types of gifts given by ambassadors in the context of the extensive theoretical debates about the gift economy in the early modern period. It examines the efforts made to regulate gift-giving, and the rhetoric used to situate gifts in the context of socially-accepted norms, focusing in particular on the question of what constituted 'corruption' in this period, and highlighting the ambiguities that could arise from the ambassador's dual persona as private individual and princely representative.

My work on Renaissance diplomacy began life as a PhD thesis supervised by Sandra Cavallo at Royal Holloway, University of London, the central case-study of which became my first book, *Our Man in Rome: Henry VIII and His Italian Ambassador.* I am indebted to Sandra for her encouragement as I explored Italian archives and developed my work through doctoral and postdoctoral study. My doctoral research was funded by the Arts and Humanities Research Council and the Institute for Historical Research; fellowships at the British School at Rome and European University Institute allowed me to build on that project, as did support from the Society for Renaissance Studies, the Royal Historical

Society, Durham University and the University of Sheffield. Along the way many colleagues have offered supportive advice and comments on my work: they include Piers Baker-Bates, Susan Brigden, Sarah Cockram, Jenn DeSilva, Paul Dover, Kate Lowe, Toby Osborne, Miles Pattenden, David Rundle, Tracey Sowerby and Megan Williams. I presented aspects of my research on diplomacy at the 2008 annual meeting of the Renaissance Society of America, the Late Medieval and Early Modern Italy seminar at the IHR, the European University Institute, the University of Oxford, the Centre for Medieval and Renaissance Studies at UCLA, and the Huntington Library. I am grateful for the many helpful observations and comments. Thanks are also due to the staff of the numerous archives and libraries I visited in the course of my research, including the Archivio Segreto Vaticano, the Biblioteca Apostolica Vaticana, the state archives of Mantua, Modena, Venice and Florence, the Bibliothèque Nationale de France and the British Library.

Chapters 4 and 6 of this book incorporate material originally published in my 2010 *Renaissance Studies* essay 'Furnished with gentlemen: the ambassador's house in sixteenth-century Italy'. I am grateful for permission to reproduce it here. Further material in Chapter 6 was published in the proceedings of the conference *Early Modern Rome 1341–1667* (May 13–15, 2010). Chapter 7 includes material first published as a working paper entitled '"Those who give are not all generous": Tips and bribes at the sixteenth-century papal court' (*EUI Working Papers*, Max Weber Programme 2011/15).

1   Rome and the rise of resident diplomacy

In 1438, Lapo da Castiglionchio the Younger (1406–38) described the centrality of Rome and the papal court to the political life of Christendom:

For among Christians almost nothing of great importance is done on which the pope is not consulted or in which his authority is not in some way involved. Whether it is a deliberation concerning war, peace or striking treaties, or marriages among the greatest kings and princes of the world, or even if it concerns some controversy that occurs among these great leaders, all things are deferred to the pope, and they are all discussed in the curia as if it were a kind of public forum.[1]

Lapo, a humanist writer and curia official, expressed papal aspiration rather than reality. In 1438, when he wrote his treatise on the benefits of the Roman Curia (*De curiae commodis*), the papacy was just beginning to re-establish itself in Rome after decades of schism. Only in the years that that followed would Rome indeed become a centre for European diplomacy.

Three factors contributed to Rome's rise. The first was the juridical role of the pope. Lapo exaggerated when he said 'all things are deferred' to him, but European rulers certainly found the stamp of apostolic authority useful. When Francesco Sforza seized power in Milan, he sought diplomatic recognition from Pope Nicholas V: his efforts to secure his rule led to the creation of one of the most effective diplomatic corps in Europe. Papal bulls legitimised the Spanish conquests in the New World. Pope Alexander VI was prevailed upon to permit the marriage of Louis XII of France to his cousin's widow Anne of Brittany, allowing Louis to maintain the unity of those polities. Henry VII, who won the realm of England on the battlefield, took care to obtain recognition from Innocent VIII as its rightful ruler. In each case, representatives in Rome smoothed the way. The second factor favouring Rome was the

---

[1] Lapo, *De Curiae Commodis*, pp. 139–41.

pope's role in authorising church appointments. At the forefront of rulers' minds when they dispatched envoys to the curia was the possibility of securing benefices with which to reward loyal subjects.[2] The third factor was the Italian context. The geopolitics of Italy, a peninsula covered with small statelets often at war and as often making peace, were peculiarly conducive to the development of diplomatic relations. In the latter part of the fifteenth century, and the early part of the sixteenth, these circumstances conspired to favour the rise of Rome as a centre for European diplomacy.

With these factors in mind, this chapter explores how diplomatic representation developed in Rome in the second half of the fifteenth century. It then turns to assess the impact of three events: the end of the Great Schism, the conquest of Constantinople by Mehmet II in 1453 and the peace treaty agreed between the Italian states in 1454. These set the scene for the expansion of permanent diplomacy at the papal court in the context of a gradual Italianisation of the College of Cardinals and a parallel shift towards a more 'courtly' model of curia life. As the relative influence of non-Italian cardinals diminished, the secular rulers of Europe found alternative means of bolstering their representation in Rome through new practices of resident diplomacy and the engagement of 'cardinal-protectors'. With the outbreak of war in 1494, the dynamics of diplomacy on the peninsula shifted again. Italy became the theatre for a series of European conflicts, and the continent's rulers had new reasons to retain resident agents at its central court. By the 1520s, in the context of a more settled style of monarchy in Europe, maintaining correct diplomatic representation at the papal court had become a matter of princely honour.

a.   From Avignon to Rome

The identity of the first resident ambassador in Europe hinges on a contested definition of 'resident'. Envoys of Milan and Mantua in the late fourteenth century have good claims to the title.[3] Rome, however, was marginal to these early ambassadorial exchanges because for the latter part of the fourteenth century and the early decades of the fifteenth the Church had been split and rival popes had ruled from Rome and Avignon. The Great Schism had begun in 1378 when cardinals changed their mind about the election of Bartolomeo Prignano as Urban VI and elected Robert of Geneva as Clement VII instead. Division between the

---

[2] Leverotti, *Diplomazia e Governo*, p. 86.
[3] Mattingly, *Renaissance Diplomacy*, pp. 66–76.

successors of Urban in Rome and Robert in Avignon lasted some forty years. In 1409 the Council of Pisa deposed both the Roman pontiff, Gregory XII (r. 1406–15) and his Avignonese counterpart, Benedict XIII (r. 1394–1417), electing a third pope, Alexander V (r. 1409–10) in their place. It took the Council of Constance, convened in 1414, to settle on a single candidate. On 11 November 1417, cardinals loyal to all three of the predecessors, along with representatives of the European 'nations',[4] made Oddo Colonna, a Roman nobleman, their Pope.[5] As Martin V he ruled until 1431.

Elected largely on the basis that he was the only candidate commanding support from all five European nations present at the Council (Italy, Germany, Spain, France and England), Martin then had to establish his authority as a pope dependent on none of them in particular. While ambassadors had been a feature of the Council's proceedings, Martin was reluctant to let them become a permanent fixture. He resisted the presence of resident diplomats in Rome, establishing rules that effectively limited the tenure of an ambassador at the papal court to six months.[6] The motivation for this limitation is sometimes attributed to concerns that these new resident diplomats might be spies, but it seems equally likely that Martin wished to avoid institutionalising the representation and influence that the secular rulers of Europe had enjoyed at the Council of Constance. His cardinals, as we will see, wanted to eliminate rival bidders for the most lucrative benefices. This mistrust of diplomats had parallels elsewhere in Europe. Louis XI of France (r. 1461–83) told the Milanese ambassador Alberico Maletta that 'in these parts keeping an ambassador continually seems suspicious and not entirely friendly', though he acknowledged that in Milan the opposite was true.[7] As a consequence, much diplomacy went on through unofficial channels. The secular rulers of Europe had long employed resident agents in Rome to facilitate the transaction of church business through the complex structures of the curia. Many of these individuals also held positions as curia officials, and they gradually took on more extensive roles in

[4] The word 'nation', in this period, should be taken to refer to an ethnic group or community: it is not yet the 'imagined community' of the modern nation-state. One might speak of the 'Florentine nation in Rome', for example.

[5] Carol Richardson, *Reclaiming Rome: Cardinals in the Fifteenth Century* (Leiden: Brill, 2009), p. 74.

[6] Betty Behrens, 'Origins of the office of English resident ambassador in Rome', *English Historical Review* 49 (1934), 640–56 (p. 650).

[7] 'in queste parte a tenere continuamente uno suo ambasadore pare una cosa de suspeto e non de tuto amore et a casa vostra he il contrario', cited in Paolo Margaroli, *Diplomazia e Stati Rinascimentali: Le Ambascerie Sforzesche fino alla Conclusione della Lega Italica (1450–1455)* (Florence: La Nuova Italia, 1992), p. 273.

diplomacy. The English royal proctors are a case in point. Their principal role was to manage appointments to bishoprics, but their responsibilities often stretched wider. John Catterick, appointed in May 1413, was required in his instructions (*procuratorium*) to deal with 'any other business of ours at the apostolic see, however it arises'. This business was of great variety.[8] Certain proctors were given the title of ambassador, and some of them engaged in the type of contest over royal honour and precedence that would be central to later ambassadors' roles. They did not, however, enjoy ongoing diplomatic status. It was assumed that even if they had been dispatched as 'proctor and ambassador', the latter style was of limited duration.[9]

When Martin died in 1431, he was succeeded by Gabriele Condulmer, a Venetian, who took the name Eugenius IV. Eugenius lost control of Rome in 1434 after its citizens rebelled; he fled to Florence. In 1439 the Council of Basel deposed him and elected Amadeus VIII of Savoy as Pope Felix V instead, but this last phase of the schism was short-lived. On Eugenius' death in 1447, Pope Nicholas V (Tommaso Parentucelli, r. 1447–55) was elected. He brought a definitive end to the conciliar crisis, seeing off Felix, who abdicated in 1449. By the 1430s, there was informal toleration of longer residency at the curia. Garrett Mattingly suggests that the mission of the Venetian ambassador Zacharius Bembo to the papal court in 1435 may have established permanent representation for Venice at the curia,[10] although this seems unlikely, given the chaotic political situation that prevailed with Eugenius' absence from Rome. Yet the proscription of residency was beginning to break down. Writing in 1438, Lapo suggested that practice no longer strictly followed Martin's six-month rule:

Finally, what is more beautiful, becoming, elegant, or royal to see than the legates and orators of the greatest kings, who have been sent to the pope about the most important matters? Although some of them remain, others leave after completing the task of their legation, and others still are added. There is a great number of them every day; but although the crowd of men of this sort who dwell in the Roman curia is always enormous, still, now most of all, because of the council of union's fame, there is an even greater crowd – indeed, the number is at all all-time high.[11]

Lapo's summary here – 'some of them remain, others leave' – summed up the fluid nature of diplomatic practice at this time. There was no

---

[8] Margaret Harvey, *England, Rome and the Papacy 1417–1464: The Study of a Relationship* (Manchester: Manchester University Press, 1993), pp. 8–9.
[9] Harvey, *England, Rome and the Papacy*, p. 10.
[10] Mattingly, *Renaissance Diplomacy*, p. 74.   [11] Lapo, *De Curiae Commodis*, p. 171.

sharp distinction between a special envoy and a resident diplomat. One might simply become the other. This was one way that envoys negotiated – and undermined – the proscription of long-term residency. Nicodemo Tranchedini, the first official envoy sent by Milan's new Sforza regime to the curia, was in Rome from May 1451 to early 1453, far longer than the six months permitted. However, it was understood that his formal role was restricted to dealing with benefices: his engagement in international politics went on behind the scenes.[12] Objections to longer-term residency persisted. In March 1458, Antonio da Pistoia, secretary of Cardinal d'Estouteville and procurator of the Duke of Milan, wrote to the duke that the cardinals were insisting that after two to three months ambassadors should lose their status and be treated instead as procurators or solicitors. Their motivation, da Pistoia explained, was so that in the course of lobbying for papal favour 'the lords should go via [the cardinals], and thus be more obligated to them'.[13] Thus the princes of the church jostled for power with the representatives of secular rulers.

b. After Avignon: Constantinople

Nicholas V's grand entry to the city in 1447 marked the start of four decades of relative stability in Rome, but for Christendom more widely his papacy was far from happy. In 1453 its eastern capital, Constantinople, was conquered by the Ottoman Emperor Mehmet II (r. 1446–8 and 1451–81). The loss of Constantinople, wrote Pius II (Enea Silvio Piccolomini, r. 1458–64) in his memoirs, was 'sad news to the Christians, especially to Pope Nicholas and the [Holy Roman] Emperor Frederick III, whose reigns had been branded with no small infamy by this foul insult to the Christian religion'.[14] Nicholas' successor, Calixtus III (Alfonso Borgia, r. 1455–8), dispatched a fleet to the eastern Mediterranean, defeating a Turkish fleet off Lesbos, but Calixtus' hope that this would be followed by further victories was in vain. His successor Pius' efforts to launch a crusade against the Turks came to naught.

---

[12] Margaroli, *Diplomazia e Stati Rinascimentali*, p. 78.

[13] 'li signori andasseno per le man loro, per farseli più obligati.' Michele Ansani, 'La Provvista dei Benefici (1450–1466): Strumenti e Limiti dell'Intervento Ducale', in Chittolini (ed.), *Gli Sforza, la Chiesa Lombarda, la Corte di Roma: Strutture e Pratiche Beneficiarie nel Ducato di Milano (1450–1535)* (Naples: Liguori, 1989), pp. 1–113 (pp. 14–15, cited in Margaroli, *Diplomazia e Stati Rinascimentali*, p. 69, note 9).

[14] Pius, *Commentarii* VOL. I, 139 (*Secret Memoirs*, p. 60). Pius himself had previously been an ambassador for the Holy Roman Emperor: on his 1447 mission see Pio Paschini, 'Ambasciate e Ambasciatori a Roma dal Quattro al Cinquecento', in Ugo Ojetti (ed.), *Ambasciate e Ambasciatori a Roma* (Milan: Bestetti e Tumminelli, 1927), pp. 47–74 (pp. 47–8).

Nonetheless, the rhetoric of crusading, and of Christian unity, was important to the popes and in the diplomacy of this period.[15] The popes also used the prospect of conflict to bolster support against the conciliarists who challenged their authority with arguments for the supremacy of church councils. This was the context in which Pius issued his famous bull, *Execrabilis*, asserting papal authority and banning appeals against it to a General Council.[16]

The psychological impact of the conquest on western Europe is more difficult to quantify. Pius, writing in the third person, declared that on his election as pope in 1458, 'Among all the purposes he had at heart none was dearer than that of rousing Christians against the Turks and declaring war upon them.' That said, his commentaries recount in illuminating detail his troubles in convincing the princes of both western and eastern Europe to co-operate. Those in the west baulked at the expense; those in the east often thought it better to make peace. Some played both sides. 'The King of Bosnia,' complained Pius, 'though he had secretly come to terms with the Turks, sent ambassadors to the Pope to ask aid against them.'[17] The Venetians had agreed a peace treaty with Mehmet II within a year of Constantinople's fall (in April 1454 at Edirne), pledging 'peace and friendship'.[18] Henry VII, king of England (r. 1485–1509), ignored the papal monopoly on alum, a crucial ingredient for the textile industry, to profit from a lucrative trade smuggling it in from Ottoman territory.[19] The policy of the western princes was, in large part, 'containment and coexistence'.[20] Yet while enthusiasm for crusading was limited, an expansionist Ottoman Empire posed a genuine threat to parts of Europe, particularly in the east. There was a Turkish incursion into the Venetian *terra ferma* (mainland) in 1473, and the Turks briefly captured the city of Otranto in Puglia in 1480.[21] In alliance with the local nobility they won Hungary from the Holy Roman Emperor in the 1520s. For the rulers of

---

[15] Margaret Meserve, 'Italian humanists and the problem of the crusade', pp. 13–38, and Nancy Bisaha, 'Pope Pius II and the crusade', pp. 39–52 in Norman Housley (ed.), *Crusading in the Fifteenth Century: Message and Impact* (Basingstoke: Palgrave Macmillan, 2004).

[16] Robert Schwoebel, *The Shadow of the Crescent: The Renaissance Image of the Turk (1453–1517)* (Nieuwkoop: B. De Graaf, 1967), p. 23.

[17] Pius, *Commentarii* Vol. I, pp. 232–3, 446–7 (*Secret Memoirs*, pp. 85, 116).

[18] C. A. Frazee, *Catholics and Sultans: The Church and the Ottoman Empire* (Cambridge: Cambridge University Press, 1983), p. 10.

[19] Thomas Penn, *Winter King: The Dawn of Tudor England* (London: Penguin, 2012), pp. 201–4.

[20] Schwoebel, *Shadow of the Crescent*, p. 116.

[21] Mustafa Soykut, *The Image of the "Turk" in Italy* (Berlin: Klaus Schwarz Verlag, 2003), p. 2.

the borderlands, at least, there was force in the idea of maintaining Christian peace against an external menace: this was not solely rhetoric. Direct diplomatic contacts between the Ottoman Empire and Rome were limited. Beyazid II (r. 1481–1512) sent an ambassador to the Pope in November 1490 to seek agreement that the pope would not use the exiled Ottoman prince Djem to destabilise the Ottoman Empire. He also sent an embassy to Florence, Milan and Savoy to make alliances in the later years of the fifteenth century.[22] On the whole, however, the western powers sent envoys to Istanbul, rather than the other way about: Muslim theologians thought long residence in a non-Islamic country inadvisable. France, for example, had permanent diplomatic representation in Istanbul from the mid-1530s.[23] Until their permanent missions were established, however, European rulers needed reliable reports of conflict in eastern Mediterranean. Some had direct concerns about threats to their territory; others were more worried by the impact on trade routes.[24] While news travelled through all sorts of networks, the substantial, cosmopolitan collective of agents in Rome meant it was a particularly good place to acquire information. It became a conduit for news: in Garrett Mattingly's words, the continent's 'chief gossip shop'.[25]

c. After Avignon: Lodi

A second, related development gave further impetus to Rome's rise as a diplomatic centre. This was the Peace of Lodi and the declaration of the Italian League the following year. For decades there had been intermittent war between Venice and Milan, but events in the eastern Mediterranean concentrated minds and on 9 April 1454 Florence, Venice and Milan agreed peace.[26] An important element of the agreement was the recognition of Sforza rule of Milan. From 1454 Milan maintained stable – if perhaps not yet 'permanent' – diplomatic relations with Florence, Rome, Naples, Venice and France, and frequent contacts with Genoa, Savoy, Catalonia, the German states, England and Burgundy.[27] Naples

---

[22] Kenneth M. Setton, *The Papacy and the Levant (1204–1571)*, 4 vols (Philadelphia: American Philosophical Society, 1976–84), Vol. II, pp. 418–22.

[23] Robert Anciaux, 'Évolution de la Diplomatie de l'Empire Ottoman et de sa Perception de l'Europe aux XVIIe e XVIIIe Siècles', in Alain Servantie (ed.), *L'Empire Ottoman dans l'Europe de la Renaissance* (Leuven: Leuven University Press, 2005), pp. 151–66. Frazee, *Catholics and Sultans*, p. 27.

[24] Emilio Sola, 'La Frontera Mediterránea y la Información: Claves para el Conocimiento del Turco a Mediados del Siglo XVI,' in Servantie (ed.), *L'Empire Ottoman*, pp. 297–316.

[25] Mattingly, *Renaissance Diplomacy*, p. 151.   [26] Frazee, *Catholics and Sultans*, p. 10.

[27] Leverotti, *Diplomazia e Governo*, p. 86.

under Ferrante d'Aragona (r. 1458–94) followed a similar pattern.[28] Until 1494, the five major Italian states – Florence, Milan, Venice, the Papacy and Naples – maintained a reasonable degree of peace on the peninsula. There were some minor exceptions and a couple of major ones: the 'Salt War' of 1482–4, fought between Venice and the Papacy on one side and Ferrara, backed by the other major states, on the other, and the Neapolitan 'Barons' War' of 1485–6.[29] For the most part, however, the phrase a 'balance of power' gives a reasonable summary of the Italian situation. None of the states was large enough to defeat the others without an alliance; it was in none of their interests, for now, to start a war. The exchange of diplomats between the major states of the Italian peninsula was a means of maintaining this stability. Indeed, during the pontificate of Paul II, the curia ambassadors of the allied powers Florence, Milan and Naples wrote collective letters.[30] It is in this period of relative peace that we find the early discussions of the diplomat's role as a person going abroad to maintain friendly relations and undertake general negotiation that will be discussed in Chapter 2.

Both the negotiations for Lodi itself and the subsequent development of longer-term diplomatic relations shifted diplomatic practices in the Italian states. Franca Leverotti has shown how the *famigli cavalcanti* (literally, 'riding servants') of Francesco Sforza (r. 1450–66), who undertook diplomatic duties on an ad hoc basis, not tied to a particular city, were gradually replaced by resident ambassadors. The fourteen *famigli* listed in court records in 1450 had declined to seven by 1480 and six by 1499, while the number of permanent embassies maintained by Milan rose.[31] Their duties also shifted: in the 1450s the *famigli* had undertaken a variety of governmental and military tasks, but from 1455 they focused exclusively on diplomatic missions. At the end of the 1460s the office comprised a mix of 'resident ambassadors, messengers, and personnel qualified for particular types of negotiations'.[32] Mantua was slower to adopt resident diplomacy: it had stable representation in Milan in the second half of the fifteenth century, but in only two other cases were envoys sent to reside at other courts. Bartolomeo di Matteo Bonatti went to Rome between 1459 and 1460 to deal with Francesco Gonzaga's

---

[28] Dover, 'Royal diplomacy', p. 66.

[29] On the role of the papacy in these wars see D. S. Chambers, *Popes, Cardinals and War: The Military Church in Renaissance and Early Modern Europe* (London: I. B. Tauris, 2006).

[30] Paul M. Dover, '"Saper la Mente della Soa Beatitudine": Pope Paull II and the Ambassadorial Community in Rome (1464–71)', *Renaissance and Reformation* 31, no. 3 (2008), 3–34 (p. 21).

[31] Leverotti, *Diplomazia e Governo*, p. 21.   [32] *Ibid.*, pp. 71, 82.

promotion to the cardinalate; Antonio Donato di Giorgio de Meo was in Naples from 1466 until the renewal of the Italian League in 1470.[33] Unlike the Sforza, however, the Gonzaga of Mantua were not a new dynasty, and had no need for the careful diplomacy the former employed to secure their rule. Moreover, from 1461 the Gonzaga had a family cardinal, Francesco, able to represent their interests at the court of Rome, while the Sforza had to wait until 1484 for Ascanio Maria's promotion.[34]

There is considerable historiographical debate about the establishment of permanent resident diplomacy among the Italian states (and beyond) during the fifteenth century. The classic account – that of Garrett Mattingly in his *Renaissance Diplomacy* – concluded that by the 1450s Naples, Venice, Florence and Milan 'had established permanent embassies with each other... Thereafter only open war interrupted this reciprocal representation among the four.'[35] Subsequent debate between Riccardo Fubini and Vincent Ilardi has highlighted the difficulty of the term 'residentiality' for this early period. Fubini, working principally on diplomacy in Florence and Venice, noted the 'inherent lack of institutionality' of early resident embassies;[36] Ilardi responded that institutions evolve, and that 'it is normal for practice to precede theory'.[37] In part, the contrast here arose from the scholars' work on very different political contexts: Fubini on republics, in which offices tended to be codified, and Ilardi on the duchy of Milan, where court politics prevailed. The latter also introduced the idea of 'permanency' into the debate on residentiality: proposing that a significant change was to be found in the development of an office of ambassador that was continuously occupied.[38] The idea of the embassy as an *officium* offers a useful perspective for analysis, but it is debatable whether this is a phenomenon that can be generalised

---

[33] Isabella Lazzarini, *Fra un Principe e Altri Stati: Relazioni di Potere e Forme di Servizio a Mantova nell'Età di Ludovico Gonzaga* (Rome: Istituto Storico Italiano per il Medio Evo, 1996), pp. 77–9.

[34] Salvador Miranda, 'The Cardinals of the Holy Roman Church', www2.fiu.edu/~mirandas/consistories-xv.htm. Dover argues that Cardinal Gonzaga acted as a *de facto* Mantuan ambassador. '"Saper la Mente"', p. 17.

[35] Mattingly, *Renaissance Diplomacy*, p. 95.

[36] Fubini, 'Diplomacy and government', p. 27 and Riccardo Fubini, 'La "Résidentialité" de l'Ambassadeur dans le Mythe et dans la Réalité: Une Enquête sur les Origines', in Lucien Bély (ed.), *L'Invention de la Diplomatie. Moyen Age-Temps Modernes* (Paris: Presses Universitaires de France, 1998), pp. 27–35 (p. 29).

[37] Vincent Ilardi, 'The first permanent embassy outside Italy: the Milanese embassy at the French court, 1464–1483', in Malcolm R. Thorp and Arthur J. Slavin (eds), *Politics, Religion and Diplomacy in Early Modern Europe: Essays in Honour of De Lamar Jensen* (Kirksville: Sixteenth Century Journal Publishers, 1994), pp. 1–18 (p. 2).

[38] Ilardi, 'First permanent embassy', p. 2.

across Europe. States differed in their approach to and adoption of the new diplomacy. Venice, for example, continued to send ambassadors only on a relatively short-term basis. Individual patricians preferred to avoid long absences from domestic politics, and in turn the system helped to limit the development of overly close and potentially disloyal relationships at the host court.[39] In the context of first a prohibition on resident diplomacy, and then a rather vague toleration of it, sharp definitions of who was or was not a resident ambassador in later fifteenth-century Rome are hard to come by. Not every mission that over-ran six months should be regarded as 'resident'; some short tenures arguably had characteristics of residency, especially if the envoy was one of a series posted in turn to maintain continuous representation. Here, I concur with Ilardi that the more important criterion is that of permanence: whether the principal thought it worthwhile to maintain ongoing diplomatic representation in Rome, no matter the particular length of an individual's mission. In terms of Italian diplomacy, Daniela Frigo has argued that while the distinction between resident and special ambassadors was relatively well-defined in the political literature, the theory was not always followed through in practice, where the lines were less clear.[40] There were, she suggests, grades of ambassador, and the extent to which they were entrusted with sensitive missions, or with full knowledge of their prince's intentions, depended principally on the level of confidence that their masters placed in them. In particular, there was a significant difference between princely and republican practice: longer-term residency was in the first place a product of the former and not the latter. I assume throughout this book that a resident ambassador was posted overseas with diplomatic credentials (thus distinguishing him from an agent without formal credentials) and was responsible for managing general 'day-to-day' business (whether or not in conjunction with a specific mission). The precise length of his stay is unimportant.

In parallel with the new system of resident diplomats, foreign powers developed more structured relationships with members of the College of Cardinals through a system of national cardinal-protectors.[41] Like

---

[39] Tessa Beverley, 'Venetian ambassadors 1454–94: an Italian elite' (unpublished doctoral thesis, University of Warwick, 1999), pp. 218–26.

[40] Frigo, 'Corte, Onore e Ragion di Stato', p. 36.

[41] William E. Wilkie, *The Cardinal Protectors of England: Rome and the Tudors before the Reformation* (Cambridge: Cambridge University Press, 1974), p. 5. Marco Pellegrini, 'A turning-point in the history of the factional system in the sacred college: the power of Pope and Cardinals in the age of Alexander VI', in Gianvittorio Signorotto and Maria Antonietta Visceglia (eds), *Court and Politics in Papal Rome, 1492–1700* (Cambridge: Cambridge University Press, 2002), pp. 8–30.

resident diplomacy, this was initially controversial, and in 1425 Martin V forbade cardinals from accepting the protection of princes or other secular rulers.[42] As with his ruling on resident ambassadors, this came in the context of attempts to mend the divisions caused by decades of schism, in significant part sponsored by the secular monarchs of Europe. Yet by the end of the fifteenth century the existence of the office, like that of resident ambassador at Rome, was an established fact, though demands for reform persisted.[43] Cardinal-protectors had a formal role in relating candidates for benefices at meetings of Consistory (the assembly of pope and cardinals); this was combined with the more general task of promoting national interests and supporting the work of visiting ambassadors and agents.[44] However, the existence of a cardinal-protector did not negate the need for a resident ambassador. While cardinals had the advantage of being able to intervene directly in discussions at Consistory, in a way which ambassadors normally did not, their relationships with foreign princes were notoriously ambivalent. They were, after all, princes of the church in their own right and, as D. S. Chambers has argued, as concerned with their own protection as with that of their patron.[45] Given Rome's position as the hub of European politics, they could hardly avoid the need to forge relationships with foreign powers, but many did so with their own careers in mind.[46] A lay ambassador's relationship with his prince was different, in that he was not simultaneously tied to both royal service and church power-structures. In other words, he was less a 'servant to two masters' than the cardinal-protector. This point should not be over-stated: a lay ambassador might well have a brother or two seeking a bishopric. Some lay diplomats, as I discuss in Chapter 4, served more than one prince in the course of their careers. In the case of Rome there was the additional issue of Christian loyalty to the Pope as Vicar of Christ. Nonetheless, the structural difficulties of ensuring a diplomat's faithful service were fewer than the difficulties of ensuring such service from cardinals. The

---

[42] Josef Wodka, *Zur Geschichte der Nationalen Protektorate der Kardinäle an der Römische Kurie* (Innsbruck and Leipzig: Verlag Felizian Rauch, 1938), p. 34. On the history of the office see Olivier Poncet, 'The cardinal-protectors of the crowns in the Roman Curia during the first half of the seventeenth century: the case of France', in Signorotto and Visceglia (eds), *Court and Politics*, pp. 158–76.

[43] Wodka, *Geschichte der Nationalen Protektorate*, pp. 34–8.

[44] Wilkie, *Cardinal Protectors*, p. 6.

[45] D. S. Chambers, 'English representation at the court of Rome in the early Tudor period' (unpublished doctoral thesis, University of Oxford, 1961–62), p. 49.

[46] For an example see K. J. P. Lowe, *Church and Politics in Renaissance Italy: The Life and Career of Cardinal Francesco Soderini, 1453–1524* (Cambridge: Cambridge University Press, 1993), pp. 171–91.

combination of a capable cardinal-protector and lay ambassador, perhaps with a cleric accredited as ambassador too, was probably the most effective form of diplomatic representation in Rome around the year 1500.

d.   Reclaiming Rome

Writing in praise of the Roman curia, Lapo da Castiglionchio described it as 'the most famous place in the whole world, the grandest home of all peoples and nationalities, this most populous assembly and congress of most excellent and famous men'.[47] That was very much the image of Rome that the popes of the later fifteenth century sought to create. Ceremonials of the thirteenth century presuppose an itinerant papacy. Dykmans estimates that the popes then spent only a third of their time in Rome.[48] Subsequently, like other European monarchies, the papacy settled. Martin V, Eugenius IV and Nicholas V invested substantially in Rome's restoration, and successfully lobbied others to do likewise.[49] Their courts re-established in the city, cardinals lavished money on their titular churches. Thus the ambassadors who came to Rome in the second half of the fifteenth century found themselves in a city undergoing a substantial cultural revival. Here was a Rome discovering (and sometimes inventing) its antique past through the work of humanists like Flavio Biondo who penned such celebratory works as *Roma instaurata* (Rome Restored) and *Roma triumphante* (Rome Triumphant).[50] It was the site, in 1452, for the coronation of the Holy Roman Emperor Frederick III (r. 1452–93), an opportunity for Nicholas to show off his authority as maker of emperors.[51] Humanist scholars based elsewhere in Italy – in Florence or at the small northern courts – now found Rome an attractive source of patrons. Their ranks were swollen after 1453 with an influx of Greek-speaking refugees fleeing the Ottoman expansion. Like secular princes, the popes saw advantages in patronising the new scholarship. In 1475, Pope Sixtus IV appointed Bartolomeo Platina his librarian and transformed Nicholas' collections into the Vatican Library.

---

[47] Lapo, *De Curiae Commodis*, p. 225.
[48] Agostino Patrizi Piccolomini, *L'Oeuvre de Patrizi Piccolomini, ou Le Cérémonial Papal de la Première Renaissance*, ed. Marc Dykmans, 2 vols (Vatican City: Biblioteca Apostolica Vaticana, 1980–82), Vol. I, p. 15.
[49] Richardson, *Reclaiming Rome*, pp. 150–6.
[50] Charles L. Stinger, *The Renaissance in Rome* (Bloomington: Indiana University Press, 1998), pp. 171, 183.
[51] Aspects of Frederick's coronation are discussed in my essay, 'The altar of Saint Maurice and the invention of tradition in Saint Peter's', in Rosamond McKitterick et al. (eds), *Old Saint Peter's, Rome* (Cambridge: Cambridge University Press, 2013), pp. 371–85.

A generation later, in the reign of Julius II, a grand renovation of Saint Peter's Basilica began with the demolition of parts of the crumbling old building.[52] Some ambassadors were highly engaged with the cultural life of Rome, taking advantage of their postings to commission artworks, purchase antiquities or study in the Vatican Library. Ferry Carondelet, envoy of Margaret of Austria, commissioned a portrait of himself from Sebastiano del Piombo while on mission to Rome in 1510–12.[53]

As a bulwark against the national divisions so evident in the conciliar crisis, the early post-schism popes had created an international college of cardinals. From Paul II (r. 1464–71) onwards, however, their appointments were predominantly Italian. In particular, they promoted representatives of the Italian ruling houses.[54] Moreover, they enlarged the size of the college to do so, diminishing the power of the non-Italian cardinals who remained. Six out of ten of the new cardinals created by Paul II were Italian (or seven if Teodoro Paleologo of Montferrato, originally of Constantinople but resident in Italy, is included). Almost two-thirds of Sixtus IV's new cardinals (r. 1471–84) were Italian, and three-quarters of those promoted by Innocent VIII (r. 1484–9).[55] That is not to say that these popes had no regard at all for maintaining a cosmopolitan curia. Sixtus, for example, divided membership of the auditors of the Rota (the curia's judicial arm) between major western and Italian states. The trend was, however, Italianisation.[56] Over the course of the fifteenth century, the relationship between pope and cardinals shifted. In reaction to the years of council and schism, the popes moved to guard their authority against rivals. Whereas once the College of Cardinals had functioned as a senate, by the early sixteenth century popes were increasingly resisting efforts to defend the senatorial model: cardinals were to be 'courtiers' of the pope instead.[57] The very large elevations by Julius II (r. 1503–13; twenty-seven new cardinals) and Leo X (r. 1513–21; forty-two new cardinals) substantially diluted the power of individual members of the

[52] Bram Kempers, 'Epilogue: A hybrid history: the antique basilica with a modern dome', in McKitterick et al. (eds), *Old Saint Peter's*, pp. 386–403.

[53] Sebastiano del Piombo, *L'Opera Completa* (Milan: Rizzoli, 1980), p. 102.

[54] Stinger, *The Renaissance in Rome*, pp. 94–5.

[55] Mirandas, www2.fiu.edu/~mirandas/consistories-xv.htm. The precise figures depend on whether residency or national origin is the defining characteristic, but the trend is clear.

[56] John F. D'Amico, *Renaissance Humanism in Papal Rome: Humanists and Churchmen on the Eve of the Reformation* (Baltimore and London: Johns Hopkins University Press, 1983), p. 7.

[57] Paolo Prodi, *The Papal Prince. One Body and Two Souls: The Papal Monarchy in Early Modern Europe*, trans. Susan Haskins (Cambridge: Cambridge University Press, 1987), pp. 80–5. Jennifer M. DeSilva, 'Senators or courtiers: negotiating models for the College of Cardinals under Julius II and Leo X', *Renaissance Studies* 22 (2008), 154–73.

College.[58] Even as courtiers, however, cardinals remained princes of the Church in their own right, and indeed were encouraged to demonstrate their magnificence which would, in turn, reflect well on the pope as their patron. Rome thus accommodated not just the papal court but a collection of cardinals' courts too, often housed in palatial style.[59] Given the increasing opportunities to lobby not only the papacy itself, but members of the leading houses of Italy who held cardinals' hats – the Gonzaga of Mantua, the d'Aragona of Naples, the Sforza of Milan, the d'Este of Ferrara, and the Medici of Florence all secured promotions in the second half of the fifteenth century – there was considerable incentive to maintain diplomatic representation at the curia. Moreover, now that they could no longer rely on exercising power through national representatives within the College, the non-Italian states had to find alternative means of representation.

This diminution of relative power in the College of Cardinals was one motivating factor for the increasing use by the non-Italian states of long-term embassies and cardinal-protectorships. By the end of the fifteenth century, the restrictions on resident ambassadors' tenure had withered away. In 1490 Innocent VIII, despite threatening to do so, was in practice unable to enforce Martin V's six-month rule.[60] As Chapter 3 will show, substantial reforms to papal ceremonial during Innocent's pontificate included a thorough assimilation of ambassadors into the liturgical world of the curia. By this time, Rome was clearly the centre of European diplomacy. In May 1490, the papal master of ceremonies Johann Burchard recorded the presence in Rome of ambassadors from the Holy Roman Emperor, France, Spain, Naples, Venice, Milan, Ferrara, Mantua, the Duke of Bavaria, Scotland and Florence.[61] In the decade 1490–1500 there were over 243 diplomats accredited to Rome, but just 161 to the Holy Roman Emperor and 135 to France.[62] But this was not only a consequence of Rome's importance as a clearing-house for news, nor of changing patterns of curia appointments, nor the increasing toleration of long-term residency. It was also – and principally – the product of a new political context: the Italian Wars.

[58] DeSilva, 'Senators or courtiers', p. 164.
[59] D'Amico, *Renaissance Humanism*, p. 4. Richardson, *Reclaiming Rome*, especially Chapter 7, 'Property portfolios', pp. 263–313, for some instances of cardinals' magnificent accommodation.
[60] Behrens, 'Origins of the office', p. 651.   [61] Burchard, *Liber Notarum*, Vol. I, p. 308.
[62] Prodi, *Papal Prince*, p. 165n, citing W. Höflechner, 'Anmerkungen zu Diplomatie und Gesandtschaftswesen am Ende des 15. Jahrhunderts', in *Mitteilungen des Österreichischen Staatsarchivs* 32 (1979), 1–23.

e.   The Italian Wars and European state-building

In 1492, Innocent VIII was succeeded as pope by Cardinal Rodrigo Borgia, who took the name Alexander VI. Alexander's eleven-year reign saw the breakdown of the peace that had held since the Treaty of Lodi and the beginning of a series of wars on the Italian peninsula.[63] Involving all the major European powers, they lasted, on and off, until the conclusion of the Peace of Cateau-Cambrésis in 1559. The Peace of Lodi collapsed as a product of internal tensions in Milan, where since 1481 Lodovico Sforza had made himself the effective ruler of the city. He had initially ruled on behalf of his young nephew Gian Galeazzo, who had become duke in 1476, aged only seven. Gian Galeazzo was married to Isabella, daughter of King Alfonso II of Naples, and there were moves in Naples to ease out Lodovico in favour of his nephew. When Milan's old rival Florence backed the Neapolitans, Lodovico turned to the French, who had long-standing claims to both Milan and Naples. In 1494 Charles VIII (r. 1483–98) invaded Italy. His armies swept down the peninsula towards Naples with some ease and much destruction. Florentine opponents of Piero de' Medici's regime took the opportunity to overthrow him in Charles' wake. In response to the French descent, King Ferdinand of Aragon (r. 1479–1516), whose relatives ruled Naples, gathered his troops in Sicily. In March 1495 he formed the League of Venice against Charles with the Emperor, the Pope, Venice and Lodovico Sforza (who had now thought better of his French alliance). The claims and counter-claims of the Italian Wars were complex, involving numerous states, rulers, intra-familial disputes and accidents of inheritance. It is impossible to rehearse the entire sequence of events in the Wars here, but a short summary will give a flavour of the extensive diplomacy they entailed. The five large Italian states involved were Florence, Milan, Venice, the Papacy and Naples (which quickly fell to Spanish control). The minor powers included Ferrara, Mantua, Siena and Urbino. Even the large states included restless subject cities: the popes, for example, theoretically controlled Bologna after 1506, but had to do a good deal of negotiating with the local nobility. The wars rapidly evolved, however, into a conflict between France and the Holy Roman Empire for power on the peninsula.

A series of popes took advantage of the wars to promote both papal and family interests. Alexander VI's son Cesare Borgia tried to carve out a state in the Romagna for himself. Alexander was far from the only pope

---

[63] For a comprehensive recent account of the wars: Michael Mallett and Christine Shaw, *The Italian Wars 1494–1559* (Harlow: Pearson, 2012).

to exploit the wars in this way. Both as rulers of the Papal States, and as representatives of their families, others did so too.[64] The popes were keen to expand their territories, and used the conflict as an opportunity to assert claims to Parma and Piacenza, Reggio and Modena.[65] Envoys to Rome increasingly found themselves negotiating not only with the pope, but with his real or putative dynasty too. Pope Alexander VI died in 1503, and with him died the ambition of Cesare Borgia to establish a dynastic state. Alexander's successor, Julius II, not only took over Cesare's acquisitions in the Romagna for the papacy, but added to them the city of Bologna, whose Bentivoglio lords his armies defeated in 1506. (Julius also established his della Rovere relatives as rulers of Urbino.) In 1508, Julius joined with the Holy Roman Emperor Maximilian (r. 1508–19), Louis XII of France (r. 1498–1515) and Ferdinand of Aragon (r. 1479–1516) in the League of Cambrai, with an ambitious plan to invade Venice's mainland territories. But just as Charles VIII had found it hard to hold Naples, so the allies found the Venetian subject cities impossible to control. Venice reoccupied Padua in 1509 and in February 1510 Julius made peace with Venice. When Julius died in 1513, he was succeeded by Cardinal Giovanni de' Medici (Pope Leo X, r. 1513–21). Cardinal Giovanni had already thrown his lot in with the Spanish in order to oust his opponents from power in Florence (in 1512) and re-install his family as the city's oligarchs. The rulers of Naples and Florence – two of the five large states of the peninsula – now effectively owed their power to Spain.

In 1515 Louis XII was succeeded by his cousin Francis (r. 1515–47), who promptly decided to demonstrate his military credentials with an invasion of Italy. In alliance with Venice, his troops beat the Swiss at the Battle of Marignano. Francis proceeded to take personal control of Milan and concluded a deal with Leo X that gave him extensive powers over the Church in France. The following year Francis concluded the Treaty of Noyon with Charles of Habsburg, the new king of Spain, under which the French surrendered all claims to Naples. In 1519, Charles was elected Holy Roman Emperor (r. 1519–56), adding to his Spanish territories the Empire's historic German possessions. The Italian Wars were not the only conflict to preoccupy Charles. The Holy Roman Empire was engaged on its eastern front, with the Ottoman Empire, which was also a significant threat in the Mediterranean and north Africa. France did not

---

[64] Prodi, *Papal Prince*, pp. 38–48. Christine Shaw, 'The Papacy and the European powers', in Shaw (ed.), *Italy and the European Powers: The Impact of War, 1500–1530* (Leiden: Brill, 2006), pp. 107–26.

[65] Shaw, 'Papacy and the European powers', pp. 112–15.

have to contend with major conflicts on two fronts but on a smaller scale faced the threat of English invasion (in 1513, for example, the English took Tournai in alliance with the Holy Roman Empire). Any of these other conflicts might have a knock-on effect on the wars in Italy by diverting troops and money.

War between France and the Empire began again in 1521, now focused on and around Milan. In October 1524 Francis occupied the city, and besieged an Imperial army at nearby Pavia. The following year, an attack on the besieging troops by Spanish and German reinforcements culminated in Francis' capture and transfer to Spain. He had to offer his own sons as hostages to secure his release. The 1527 Sack of Rome by unpaid, mutinous Imperial troops prompted some rallying of the Italian powers and France against the Empire, but in the summer of 1528, when the Genoese admiral Andrea Doria switched sides to back Charles, French troops in Naples suffered a serious defeat (exacerbated by an outbreak of plague). By the 1530s, it was evident that Spain had the upper hand in the wars. Spanish envoys, as Michael J. Levin has shown, had an important role in attempting to maintain this state of affairs, though they were not always successful in their negotiations with the papacy and were constantly anxious about Italian schemes to circumvent them.[66] In practice, the Spanish 'hegemony' in Italy was not nearly as secure as Spain would have liked. Keeping up the necessary alliances required significant diplomatic effort.

The Spanish monarchy was relatively young, having come into being following the marriage of Ferdinand of Aragon and Isabella of Castile in 1469 and their subsequent accession to the two thrones.[67] The Aragonese interest in Italy lay principally in Naples, in the person of King Ferrante or Ferdinando (r. 1458–94), illegitimate son of Alfonso V of Aragon, though the Spanish also had strong interests in Rome via the Borja/Borgia family: in 1485 Ferdinand intervened in a dispute between Pope Innocent VIII and King Ferrante by means of Cardinal Rodrigo Borgia.[68] The Borgia, however, had their own interests in Italy and did not always behave as Spanish partisans.[69] Bolstered by its reconquest of

---

[66] Michael J. Levin, *Agents of Empire: Spanish Ambassadors in Sixteenth-Century Italy* (Ithaca and London: Cornell University Press, 2005).

[67] J. N. Hillgarth, *The Spanish Kingdoms 1250–1516*, 2 vols (Oxford: Clarendon Press, 1976–78), gives a helpful narrative of Spain's foreign policy in this period, Vol. II, pp. 534–84.

[68] Thomas Dandelet, *Spanish Rome 1500–1700* (New Haven and London: Yale University Press, 2001), p. 19.

[69] Michael Mallett, *The Borgias: The Rise and Fall of a Renaissance Dynasty* (London: Paladin, 1971), pp. 78, 108. For further discussion of Italian diplomats, the Borgias and Spain see my essay 'Mere emulators of Italy: The Spanish in Italian diplomatic

Granada in 1492 (ending seven hundred years of Muslim rule in the Iberian Peninsula) and by its conquests in the New World, Spain was a new power within Europe. One means through which it sought legitimacy was by resort to the papacy. Spanish rights to territories in the New World, for example, were acknowledged by a papal bull of 1493, *Inter Caetera*; in 1508 this was followed up with a grant of *Patronato Real* to Ferdinand by Julius II.[70] With Spanish control of Naples effectively established from 1504, Rome, as the capital of the neighbouring Papal States, became increasingly important to King Ferdinand. The papacy claimed Naples as its fief, and it was politic for the Spanish to respect that, but in practice many Italian leaders looked to Spanish support for their political projects. Following another overthrow of the Medici regime in 1527, Pope Clement VII (Giulio de' Medici, r. 1523–34) relied on the Spanish to defeat the last Florentine republic in 1530, finally establishing Medici government on the hereditary principle.[71] The rulers of Mantua (like many states in northern Italy an imperial fief) owed their 1530 promotion from marquises to dukes to Charles V.[72]

The period of the wars was important for the development of diplomacy in several ways. First, because they were a melting-pot for different cultures and ideas: including ideas about war, politics and diplomacy itself. Second, because the particular way they were fought – through complex alliances and with extensive use of mercenary forces – meant there had to be almost continuous negotiations between the states involved. Indeed, the princes of smaller states were often themselves *condottieri*. Third, because they were the product of a period in which some of the modern political geography of Europe took shape. Besides the emerging Spanish monarchy, probably the most significant development in the Italian context, England had acquired a new dynasty in 1485, and after decades of struggle between rival claimants to the throne was enjoying relative political stability under Henry VII. Likewise France: since the end of the Hundred Years' War its territory had been enlarged with the incorporation of Burgundy in 1477 and

---

discourse, 1492–1550', in Piers Baker-Bates and Miles Pattenden (eds), *The Spanish Presence in Sixteenth-Century Italy: Images of Iberia* (Farnham: Ashgate, 2015).

[70] Hillgarth, *Spanish Kingdoms*, Vol. 2, p. 581. For further discussion see Geo Pistarino, 'La Sede di Roma nell'Apertura del Nuovo Mondo', in Sergio Gensini (ed.), *Roma Capitale (1447–1527)* (Pisa: Pacini Editore, 1994), pp. 541–79, especially pp. 562–7.

[71] Barbara McClung Hallman, 'The "disastrous" pontificate of Clement VII: disastrous for Giulio de' Medici?', in Kenneth Gouwens and Sheryl E. Reiss (eds), *The Pontificate of Clement VII: History, Politics, Culture* (Aldershot: Ashgate, 2005), pp. 29–40.

[72] Mallett and Shaw, *Italian Wars*, p. 221.

Brittany in 1532 (though effectively from 1491 when its heiress Anne married Charles VIII).[73]

Like the papacy, the European monarchs were settling into more stable court environments. They remodelled palaces to accommodate their expanding courts and built new ones: Greenwich and Nonsuch in England; Blois and Fontainebleau in France; Brussels and the Alhambra for the Empire. All showed off their masters' magnificence.[74] These rising powers began to play out their rivalries on the Italian peninsula. Not solely there: conflicts flared up around Navarre, between Spain and France, on the borders between France and the Holy Roman Empire, and on the Empire's eastern front. By the 1520s there was a flourishing rivalry between the 'Renaissance monarchs': Charles V, Holy Roman Emperor (with territories including the German lands and Spain); Francis I, king of France; and Henry VIII, king of England. Military prowess remained a vital element in the construction of the princely persona but although actual battlefield engagement continued on occasion, increasingly it was transformed into a ritualised performance of chivalry. A rare example of the former proved disastrous for the French in 1525, when they were routed by Charles' troops at the Battle of Pavia and King Francis was taken hostage. Although outside the scope of this study, a notable diplomatic development in the period of the Italian Wars was summit peace-making.[75] There had been personal meetings between monarchs before, but the number of individual meetings between European rulers through the period of the wars is worth comment. Charles XII had met a series of Italian rulers in person in the course of his invasion of Italy. Pope Leo X met Francis I in Bologna in 1515; Pope Clement VII crowned Charles V there in 1530, the event continuing for some months as diplomatic agreements were struck not only between the two principals but with other princes. The pair met again in Bologna in 1532, and the following year Clement – rather to Charles' suspicion – met Francis I on the occasion of the marriage of Catherine de' Medici to Francis' son Henri.

Summits were generally used to make peace, and as such have a particular, but not representative, function in this period which – overall after 1494 – saw a shift on the Italian peninsula from a diplomacy of peace to the diplomacy of war and to a context of European state-

---

[73] Glenn Richardson, *Renaissance Monarchy: Monarchy: The Reigns of Henry VIII, Francis I and Charles V* (London: Arnold, 2001).

[74] Richardson, *Renaissance Monarchy*, pp. 175–80.

[75] For a detailed account of a royal summit in this period, see Glenn Richardson, *The Field of Cloth of Gold* (New Haven: Yale University Press, 2013). Joycelyne G. Russell, *Peacemaking in the Renaissance* (London: Duckworth, 1986), gives further case studies.

building. Wartime diplomacy – particularly in Italy – required very particular structures and skills. Much Italian warfare was carried out by mercenaries. A cynical description was given by Pius II, who noted that unlike the wars of the Hungarians and Turks, Italian Wars 'seldom come to a pitched battle and are aptly called by our soldiers "negotiations".'[76] It was not uncommon for ambassadors to be found following their armies, negotiating by the battlefield with mercenary commanders. In the 1528, Francesco Contarini was appointed Venetian orator to the French commander Francis de Bourbon, Count of St Pôl. His task was to convey the Venetian authorities' wishes directly to those at the French camp. Much of his correspondence deals with serious issues, but a number of letters dealing with gifts of falcons and spices for the commanders lend credence to Pius' observation that Italian warfare was not always busily warlike.[77] Chapter 4 explores the implications of warfare for the selection of diplomatic personnel. Besides those ambassadors and agents posted to commanders, men were required in Rome to collect and co-ordinate news from the front and dispatch it, post-haste, to their masters. Envoys of allied powers, gathered together in Rome, could discuss tactics. They also had informal channels of communication with hostile monarchs. Immediately after the death of Alexander VI in August 1503, when it was feared the troops of either France or Spain might enter Rome, the cardinals called in the ambassadors of France, Spain, the king of the Romans (Ferdinand of Habsburg) and Venice to discuss how to forestall a march on the city.[78] In short, the political situation made the presence of foreign powers' ambassadors in Rome a matter of practical necessity.

By the 1520s, princes were expected to have an ambassador at Rome: to fail to do so would be dishonourable. An indication of contemporary attitudes is to be found in a letter of February 1528 from Cardinal Ercole Gonzaga to his brother, the marquis of Mantua. After the Sack of Rome in 1527, the papal court was in exile at Orvieto, and the cardinal wrote:

All the ambassadors who were posted to the Pope before the ruin of Rome have come [back] to court, but no-one knows yet whether you will be sending yours, however, I thought to reply to you that it will be much to your honour to send him immediately.[79]

[76] Pius, *Commentarii* Vol. I, pp. 176–9 (*Secret Memoirs*, p. 71).
[77] Biblioteca del Museo Correr, Codice Cicogna 3473, Ducali di A. Gritti a F. Contarini.
[78] Burchard, *Liber Notarum*, Vol. II, p. 360.
[79] 'In Corte sono venuti tutti l'ambasciatori che nanti la ruina di Roma erano presso N. S. ne anchora sintende che lei vi mandi il suo perho mi e parso replicarle che sera molto suo honore a mandarlo subito.' ASMn, Archivio Gonzaga 876, c. 283r.

The use of the term 'honour' is notable, implying as it does that this was not merely a matter of strict practicality, that without an ambassador the marquis would lose out on information or negotiating clout, but rather that there were elements of duty, pride and status involved. Indeed, the repeated references to honour in diplomatic correspondence are no mere matter of courtesy but relate to a central concern in the antagonisms between Renaissance princes.

Chivalric imagery was of vital importance to the self-fashioning of rulers like Charles V, Francis I and Henry VIII. They competed for honour, sometimes metaphorically and occasionally – as at the Field of Cloth of Gold – personally.[80] Cesare Mozzarelli has argued that it was not until the end of the eighteenth century that the ideas of 'advantage' (*utile*) and 'state' fully triumphed over those of 'honour' and 'prince'.[81] The maintenance of the prince's honour in turn became a task for his ambassadors, in both symbolic and practical terms. In Behrens' phrase a king's ambassador would 'personify his dignity'.[82] She might also have written 'personify his honour'. Chapters 2 and 3 explore how this personification was understood.

---

[80] Richardson, *Field of Cloth of Gold*.

[81] Cesare Mozzarelli, 'Onore, Utile, Principe, Stato', in Adriano Prosperi (ed.), *La Corte e il "Cortegiano"*, 2 vols (Rome: Bulzoni, 1980), Vol. II, pp. 241–53.

[82] Behrens, 'Treatises', p. 620. On royal representation, see also David Starkey, 'Representation through intimacy: a study in the symbolism of monarchy and Court office in early modern England', in John Guy (ed.), *Tudor Monarchy* (New York: Arnold, 1997), pp. 42–78.

2   Conceptualising the resident ambassador

Sir Henry Wotton's famous description of an ambassador as 'an honest man sent to lie abroad for the good of his country' is as good a starting-point as any for a discussion of the Renaissance diplomat. Wotton got into trouble when his observation was put into Latin and the pun on 'lie' was lost. It is that pun, however, that sums up contemporary understandings of the sixteenth-century diplomat: he was to reside overseas and suppress the truth when necessary. In the course of the later fifteenth and early sixteenth century, the nature of the ambassador's work shifted. Though discrete, short-term missions continued, more envoys were dispatched to be resident diplomats at the court of a foreign power. While individuals came and went their office was increasingly assumed to be permanent. This chapter asks how the role of these new diplomats was understood. That they existed, there is no doubt, but what did they do from day to day? To answer that question, it considers the theory and practice of resident diplomacy, setting the scene for more detailed discussions of aspects of diplomatic practice in Chapters 4 to 7. It begins with an assessment of definitions of the ambassador in the treatises on this office (in Latin *De Officio Legati*). It then considers several key debates on the resident ambassador's role in practice, both as described in the treatises and in complementary sources. What was the balance between his respective roles as news-gatherer and negotiator? How did he relate to special ambassadors? A third section assesses how much autonomy the diplomat enjoyed. In this chapter and the next, I argue that the Renaissance ambassador had a dual, or mixed, persona, combining both official and private elements. On the one hand, he embodied his prince: on the other, he acted 'as of himself'. The functioning of these two *personae* is summed up in a case of 1463, when Pope Pius II called in the Italian ambassadors present in Rome to request their support for war against the Turks. 'The envoys,' he recorded in his memoirs, 'answered that as private individuals they approved the Pope's words but as envoys they were not empowered to answer them.'[1] In conceptualising the ambassador, I draw inspiration from Valentin Groebner's analysis of the ways that municipal office-holders received gifts in the fifteenth and sixteenth centuries. Describing the *persona mixta* of these men, he suggests that they were 'dual but insufficiently separate figures in which official and private incomes and functions overlapped in a complex manner'.[2] Redefined for the diplomat, these two *personae* – private individual and envoy – and the interplay between them have a great deal of resonance in the world of Renaissance Rome. In his official capacity, the ambassador was understood to personify the prince (or the values of the republic) he represented, and his treatment reflected this. For example, when in 1528, two English diplomats arrived in Lucca, they wrote to King Henry VIII that: 'The citizens of this citie having understanding of our commyng, presented us with a marvelous goodly and coostly present in a solempne maner and facyon, not as our personnages, but as Your Graces honnour, did requyre.'[3] In his *De Oratoribus Romanae Curiae*, Paride Grassi detailed the funeral rites to be accorded to an ambassador who dies while on a mission to Rome and said that he should be accorded the same pomp, more or less, as the prince who has sent him.[4] This is one of the clearest indications that ambassadors were conceived of as embodying their prince: further evidence for this understanding of the figure of the ambassador is presented in the chapters below. However, it is important to acknowledge the limits of this idea. As I note in Chapter 3, if both an ambassador and his prince were present at a particular ceremony, the ambassador effectively lost his status: his role was redundant. More generally, actual aristocrats outranked ambassadors in liturgical ceremony. The Duke of Albany's manoeuvrings as French ambassador (discussed below) became possible precisely because his ducal status trumped that of the Imperial ambassadors. The embodiment of princely honour could not outrank a prince in person. The process of personification worked somewhat differently for republics, but the idea that a diplomat should embody 'good' values remained. Machiavelli, for example, wrote that 'above all, a representative must strive to

[1] Pius, *Commentarii*, Vol II, pp. 2404–5 (*Secret Memoirs*, p. 342).

[2] Valentin Groebner, *Liquid Assets, Dangerous Gifts: Presents and Politics at the End of the Middle Ages*, trans. Pamela E. Selwyn (Philadelphia: University of Pennsylvania Press, 2002), p. 68.

[3] *State Papers Published under the Authority of Her Majesty's Commission: King Henry the Eighth*, 11 vols (London: Record Commission, 1832–50) (hereafter *St P*), Vol. VII, p. 60.

[4] Grassi, 'Et denique plus aut minus huiusmodi pompa [lacuna in MS] pro condicione non quidem Oratoris Legati sed Domini Legantis eundem.' MS Vat. Lat. 12270, fol. 149r.

get reputation, which he does by striking actions which show him an able man and by being thought liberal and honest, not stingy and two-faced, and by not appearing to believe one thing and say another.'[5] Ambassadors' personal qualities could redound to their principal's benefit – or to his discredit. That was possible precisely because the two aspects of their persona were indistinct.

a.   The treatises on the office of ambassador

The first treatise devoted to discussion of the resident ambassador, Ermolao Barbaro's *De Officio Legati*, was written in the latter part of the fifteenth century. Born in Venice, Ermolao (1454–93) had a considerable reputation as a humanist. His father and grandfather had been in Venetian diplomatic service, and Ermolao went as ambassador to the newly-elected Holy Roman Emperor Maximilian (in 1486–7), to the Duke of Milan (1488–9) and to Rome (1490). The treatise was most likely written sometime between the latter two missions, and certainly before 1491.[6] Although several earlier authors had discussed the role of the ambassador, Barbaro's treatise was the first to deal explicitly with those diplomats sent abroad on embassies of no fixed duration with the aim of maintaining friendly relations, in other words, residents.[7] In the sixteenth century, Étienne Dolet (1509–46) contributed a second *De Officio Legati*. Born in Orléans, Dolet studied at the University of Padua and from there was recruited by a French ambassador to Venice, Jean de Langeac, Bishop of Limoges, to act as his secretary, a post which he held in 1528–9. Jesse Reeves, editor of Dolet's treatise, suggests plausibly that it may have been composed during or shortly after this period, although it was not printed until 1541.[8] Although Dolet did not personally serve in

---

[5] Niccolò Machiavelli, 'Advice to Raffaello Girolami when he went as ambassador to the Emperor', in *The Chief Works and Others*, trans. Allan Gilbert, 3 vols (Durham: Duke University Press, 1965), Vol. I, pp. 116–19 (p. 116). All references are to this translation.

[6] Pio Paschini, *Tre Illustri Prelati del Rinascimento: Ermolao Barbaro, Adriano Castellesi, Giovanni Grimani* (= *Lateranum* new series 23 (1957)), pp. 11–39. Ermolao Barbaro, 'De Officio Legati', in ed. Vittore Branca, *Nuova Collezione di Testi Umanistici Inediti o Rari XIV* (Florence: Olschki, 1969), pp. 157–67, editor's introduction pp. 17–18. Further on Barbaro, see Douglas Biow, *Doctors, Ambassadors, Secretaries: Humanism and Professions in Renaissance Italy* (Chicago: University of Chicago Press, 2002), pp. 104–5 and Vittorio Branca, 'Ermolao Barbaro and late quattrocento Venetian humanism', in J. R. Hale (ed.), *Renaissance Venice* (London: Faber & Faber, 1973), pp. 218–43.

[7] Barbaro, 'De Officio Legati', p. 159; Behrens, 'Treatises', p. 621.

[8] Étienne Dolet, *De Officio Legati* (Lyons, 1541), published in translation as 'Étienne Dolet on the functions of the ambassador, 1541', ed. Jesse S. Reeves, *American Journal of International Law* 27 (1933), 80–95. For background, see Richard Copley Christie, *Étienne Dolet: The Martyr of the Renaissance* (London: Macmillan, 1880).

Rome, he posits his text as general advice to ambassadors and, as we will see, makes reference within it to the papal court. To Dolet's essay should be added Niccolò Machiavelli's 1522 'Advice to Raffaelo Girolami when he went as ambassador to the Emperor' and a number of relevant *Ricordi* in Francesco Guicciardini's collection. None of these texts is specific to Rome but they do tell us about theorists' approaches to the practice of diplomacy, a phenomenon that is inherently international. Very different in nature is the manual *De Oratoribus Romanae Curiae* (*On the Orators of the Roman Curia*) by Paride Grassi, discussed in more detail in Chapter 3. Intended as guidance for ceremonialists dealing with diplomats rather than advice to diplomats themselves, it provides an important counter-point to the better-known treatises and, unlike them, deals specifically with the detail of ceremonial practice in the court of Rome.

Barbaro began his treatise with the statement that an ambassador was given his mandate by his republic or prince, making clear that he intended to address diplomacy in general, rather than in any particular state.[9] His opening line, moreover, implicitly addressed the important question of who was permitted to send envoys. In the fourteenth and early fifteenth centuries, an ambassador had been almost anyone sent by almost anyone else to conclude negotiations with a third party. What distinguished him from other envoys or agents was that he carried powers to negotiate.[10] By the sixteenth century, however, an ambassador was fairly strictly defined as a representative of a foreign power. The process of definition is apparent in the ceremonial treatises of the papal court, discussed in Chapter 3. In a revision of the ceremonial dating from 1503 to 1506, Johann Burchard added the qualification that religious orders and subjects of the papacy could not send ambassadors to Rome.[11] The final decision, however, did not lie with the ceremonialists. Their rulings were overturned several times in the late fifteenth century by popes who wanted to give a formal welcome to the ambassadors of the Grand Master of the Knights Hospitallers of St John of Jerusalem (the Knights of Rhodes or from 1530, the Knights of Malta).[12] When in 1502 he tried to exclude the Bolognese envoy from the papal chapel,

---

[9] 'Legati munus est mandata Reipublicae suae vel Principis obire diligenter et ex usu eius, a quo legati nomen habuit.' Barbaro, 'De Officio Legati', p. 159.

[10] Donald E. Queller, *The Office of Ambassador in the Middle Ages* (Princeton: Princeton University Press, 1967), p. 12. John Ferguson, *English Diplomacy 1422–1461* (Oxford: Clarendon Press, 1972), pp. 148–9 and for some revisions to Ferguson's account, see Edward L. Meek, 'The conduct of diplomacy during the reign of Edward IV (1461–1483)' (unpublished doctoral thesis, University of Cambridge, 2001), pp. 20–44.

[11] Patrizi, *L'Oeuvre*, p. 205 apparatus.   [12] Burchard, *Liber Notarum*, Vol. I, p. 460.

Burchard was over-ruled by Franciscus Trochia, a papal secretary.[13] His successor, Paride Grassi, wrote that Bologna, although formally subject to the Pope, was permitted to send ambassadors, as was the Order of the Knights Hospitallers of St John of Jerusalem (the Knights of Rhodes or from 1530, the Knights of Malta).[14] The exceptions reflected the particular circumstances of Bologna (a rebellious subject city to be placated with such concessions) and the Knights of Rhodes (on the front line of the conflict with the Turks).[15] It is, however, clear that they were exceptions: they prove the general rule that only republics or sovereign princes could send embassies. Subjects could not.

Having specified who was permitted to dispatch ambassadors, the ceremonialists also sought to categorise the types of envoys who might be sent. The fluidity of practice caused them some difficulty. Patrizi Piccolomini, writing in the late 1480s or early 1490s, differentiated between ambassadors who came to Rome to pledge obedience to the pope or on some other matter of great importance pertaining to the public good (*ad prestandam obedientiam summo pontifici, sive ob aliquam rem magne importantie et spectantem ad bonum publicum*), and ambassadors who came on their masters' private business (*ob res privates suorum dominorum veniunt*).[16] Given the proscription on long-term residents in Rome, it is not surprising that he made no mention of their presence. Twenty years on, the proscription having effectively lapsed, Paride Grassi acknowledged resident diplomats as a fact of life. The king of France, he observed, 'always, or almost continuously, keeps one or two ambassadors at the Roman Curia for general and day-to-day matters'. However, he 'sends other, new ambassadors to pledge obedience, or for difficult and important matters which newly arise'.[17] Grassi's description of French practice echoes the phrase 'to deal with business that arises from day to day precisely, according to law/custom' (*negotia quae de die in diem contingent accurate ex more tractet*) appearing in a letter of 1520 from Cardinal Wolsey regarding the dispatch of Thomas Spinelly as resident ambassador to the Emperor.[18] If a summary of the resident's role is

---

[13] Burchard, *Liber Notarum*, Vol. II, p. 339.   [14] BAV, MS Vat. Lat. 12270, fols. 71–74v.

[15] On Rhodes, see Nicolas Vatin, 'The Hospitallers at Rhodes and the Ottoman Turks, 1480–1522', in Housley (ed.), *Crusading in the Fifteenth Century*, pp. 148–62.

[16] Patrizi, *L'Oeuvre*, p. 204.

[17] 'Videlicet Rex Christianissimum Franciae qui semper vel quasi continue solet tenere in Romana Curia unum aut duos Oratores pro generalibus, et occurentibus in dies negotijs mittat alios Oratores novos pro obedientia prestanda vel rebus arduis et importantibus de novo emersis.' BAV, MS Vat. Lat. 12270, fol. 28r.

[18] Betty Behrens, 'The office of the English resident ambassador: its evolution as illustrated by the career of Sir Thomas Spinelly, 1509–22', *Transactions of the Royal Historical Society*, 4th series, 16 (1933), 161–95 (p. 163, citing *Letters and Papers, Foreign and*

required, then 'deal with day-to-day business' is as good as any in encompassing its varied and contingent nature. Beyond this, the ceremonialists had little to say about the role of the resident, though their regulations shaped his participation in the ceremonial world.

As they grappled with new practices of residency, the ceremonialists in Rome also sought to distinguish between types of special ambassadors. Patrizi grouped together ambassadors who came to Rome to pledge obedience to a pope (following the coronation of a new pope or of a new ruler in their sending state) and those who came to deal with other matters of great importance, according both types a ceremonial entry to the city. Only ambassadors who came on their master's private business were treated otherwise. For example, members of a French embassy arriving in 1486 on their master's 'particular business' were greeted by the households of cardinals who were their 'particular friends'.[19] Ceremonial welcomes were gradually restricted further. In 1488, when the Venetian ambassador Domenico Trevisano arrived, a formal instruction to greet him was not sent to cardinals because he was not coming to pledge obedience; the same applied to a Florentine envoy arriving in 1505.[20] By Grassi's time, ceremonial entries were only accorded to those pledging obedience. Although he identified a type of envoy who arrived to deal with 'difficult and important matters', these men were exempt from the ceremonial welcome.[21] The context is important here. Grassi was writing after 1494, in the period of the Italian wars when many high-ranking ambassadors came and went for negotiations. Grand entrances were not always perceived to be appropriate for these men. For example, in 1529, eighteen months or so after the Emperor Charles V's mutinous troops had sacked Rome, Charles' ambassador arrived in the city, 'without pomp and without ceremony [...] the times being as they are'.[22] The Sack was an extreme case, but this letter goes some way towards explaining why ceremonial welcomes may have been curtailed.

Barbaro and Dolet agreed that the ambassador's role was to maintain friendly relations. In both cases this was a piece of rhetoric concerned with establishing the diplomat as a virtuous figure. Barbaro, active in Italy's 'balance of power' period, had a greater claim to sincerity on this

---

Domestic, of the Reign of Henry VIII, eds. J. S. Brewer, J. Gairdner and R. H. Brodie, 22 vols (London: HMSO, 1862–1932), hereafter *L&P*, Vol. iii.i, 892).

[19] Burchard, Vol. I, p. 155.

[20] Burchard, Vol. I, p. 241; Vol. II, p. 497. Patrizi, *L'Oeuvre*, p. 204.

[21] 'Oratores excipiuntur quando veniunt pro magnis, et arduis negocijs.' BAV, MS Vat. Lat. 12270, fol. 10r.

[22] 'senza pompa, et senza cirimonia [...] per essere li tempi della sorte che sono'. ASMn, Archivio Gonzaga 878, c. 48v.

point than Dolet, whose service in Venice encompassed a period of secret negotiations between France and England for a military alliance.[23] When Dolet stated that the diplomat 'should furthermore be very careful to be a promoter of peace and harmony rather than of war or discord', he contradicted his earlier, fuller, statement on ambassadors' instructions:

> Instructions, then, are the basis of an ambassadorship, and in following and executing them lies the whole duty of an ambassador. All his wits are on the alert, and all his prudence is employed to this end, whether they have to do with making a truce, concluding a war, establishing a peace, or with the formation of an alliance for war, or with arranging a marriage, or with the handling of any other important matter whatsoever.[24]

In short, an envoy's mission consisted of whatever 'important matters' his masters might choose to entrust to him, and that did not necessarily entail keeping the peace. Ambassadors posted to Rome could expect to add to this list of tasks, the processing of benefices and similar curia business. Besides, there was another sense in which resident diplomacy did little to establish peace. In providing a constant flow of news, gossip and rumour, residents aroused as many suspicions as they allayed.[25] In practice, a resident had multiple duties, contingent on his own status and relationship with his prince, the political circumstances and his place in the team of representatives in Rome that might include a cardinal, other envoys, procurators and agents.

b.   The role of the resident

It is clear from the treatises that by the turn of the fifteenth to sixteenth centuries, a resident ambassador was understood to represent a prince or republic, to hold formal credentials (thus distinguishing him from an agent) and to be responsible for managing general 'day-to-day' business (whether or not in conjunction with a specific mission). This section of the chapter explores what this quotidian business might consist of, considering three facets: the resident's role as 'fixer', newsgathering and negotiating, and his activities in Consistory (the formal assembly of pope and cardinals) and conclaves.

---

[23] *Calendar of Letters, Despatches and State Papers Relating to the Negotiations between England and Spain*, 13 vols (London: Longman, 1862–1916) (hereafter *CSP Sp*), Vol. III.I, 329.

[24] Dolet, 'De Officio Legati', pp. 89, 85.

[25] Melissa Meriam Bullard, 'The language of diplomacy in the Renaissance', in Bernard Toscani (ed.), *Lorenzo de' Medici: New Perspectives* (New York: Peter Lang, 1993), pp. 263–78.

i.   *The resident as 'fixer'*

The resident was rarely a sole agent. He might be one of a pair; he certainly interacted with visiting special envoys who came on specific missions. His many and sometimes onerous duties as 'fixer' were vital to the smooth functioning of diplomacy. He might provide hospitality, obtain safe-conducts, write letters of introduction, and counsel more generally about those customs of the court that would be unfamiliar to visitors. Nicodemo Tranchedini, an agent in Rome for the Sforza ruler of Milan from 1451 to 1453, saw Pope Nicholas V twice a week as well as discreetly preparing the ground for other embassies, maintaining personal relationships with key curia personnel, and monitoring the mood of the curia.[26] In October 1527, the English resident in Rome sent letters of introduction for an English envoy arriving in northern Italy, and the following year advised English special ambassadors how to 'use and ordre' themselves 'at our accesse unto the pope's presence'.[27] In 1529, the Mantuan envoy in Rome found himself arranging accommodation for a visiting Imperial diplomat, while in May 1530, his counterpart in Venice had to do the same for his master's mother, Isabella d'Este Gonzaga.[28] In short, the resident's activities laid the foundations for the negotiating work of others.

A resident's local knowledge should not be underestimated: it was vital for ambassadors to understand the customs of a court in order to be able to interpret events correctly, as Cardinal Giovanni Salviati pointed out in a letter of December 1527. When the French king suddenly decided to leave the court and spend a week alone at St Germain, suspicions were aroused among the diplomats present that he might be leaving to engage in secret negotiations with the Emperor. Salviati, the papal legate, dismissed the rumours, saying that neither he nor 'many others who know the custom and style of the court' had such doubts.[29] Such knowledge, along with social networks, contacts and access to the principal figures at court, was a key asset for the resident ambassador. He had to maintain

---

[26] Margaroli, *Diplomazia e Stati Rinascimentali*, p. 77.

[27] BL, Cotton MSS, Vit. B, vol. IX, fol. 177r (*L&P*, Vol. IV, 3497). BL, Harleian MS 419, fol. 71r (*L&P*, Vol. IV, 4119), cited in LukeMacMahon, 'The ambassadors of Henry VIII: the personnel of English diplomacy, c.1500–c.1550' (unpublished doctoral thesis, University of Kent, 1999), p. 43.

[28] ASMn, AG 1464 fols. 467–8, fol. 490. Marin Sanuto, *I Diarii*, eds. RinaldoFulin, Federico Stefani, Nicolò Barozzi, Guglielmo Berchet and Marco Allegri, 59 vols (Bologna: Forni, 1969), LIII, col. 229.

[29] 'a me non cade questo dubbio nella mente ne a molti altri che sanno il costume et il modo della Corte.' Archivio Segreto Vaticano, Segr. Stato, Francia 1, fol. 73v. Letter to Jacopo Salviati, 28 December 1527.

knowledge of, and links with, the leading families of Rome, sometimes for practical reasons of access to suitable accommodation, sometimes because they would be useful contacts in military operations. He had to ensure his servants got to know those of others, the better to hear gossip and rumour. He had to participate in the social circuit, both to personify his master's magnificence and to gather information himself. The curia resident of a country like England, which did not in general send resident diplomats to Italian states other than Rome or Venice, also had to be prepared to deal with English interests across the whole Italian peninsula.

The resident ambassadors of the ultramontane powers might also be required to translate on occasion. Ideally, an ambassador in Rome would have both fluent Latin and Italian. As Chapter 4 shows, in the fifteenth century, many Italian states contrived to find men so qualified, but their ultramontane powers had other priorities, especially after the onset of war. Indeed, Latin alone was insufficient: one needed to master the local pronunciation. In 1485, Burchard remarked on the 'quite barbaric' pronunciation of the Bishop of Worms, ambassador of Philip, Count Palatine, on the occasion of his pledge of obedience to Pope Innocent VIII.[30] In 1487, both Latin and Italian were used in the welcome of the Duke of Ferrara to Rome: the orators of England, Spain, Naples, Hungary, Scotland and Bohemia spoke in either of the two, while the duke gave his thanks in Italian.[31] The vernacular was becoming more important. Even earlier, when Pius II criticised the Marshal of Toulouse, a French envoy to the papal court in 1462, he described him as 'noble in his own country, though uneducated and ignorant of Italian'. The Marshal had to present his message from King Louis through an interpreter. It is notable that the criticism here is that he lacks Italian, not Latin.[32] Although Latin was the formal language of the curia, by the early sixteenth century, it was no longer assumed that its use was universal, and in the context of an Italianised curia the use of vernacular expanded. Language could also be used to make a political statement: in 1505, the king of France sent his diplomatic mandates to Rome in French, perhaps an assertion of his authority on the peninsula.[33] Paride Grassi cited cases from 1507 and 1509 in which the kings of Aragon and France respectively sent ambassadors with letters of credential in the vernacular. These had to be translated, and were read at Consistory first in the original language, by a native speaker in the papal service, and then in

[30] 'Orationem Satis Barbarice Pronunciante', Burchard, *Liber Notarum*, Vol. I, p. 118.
[31] Burchard, *Liber Notarum*, Vol. I, p. 199.
[32] Pius, *Commentarii*, Vol. I, 1588–89 (*Secret Memoirs*, p. 254).
[33] Burchard, *Liber Notarum*, Vol. I, p. 478.

Latin translation.[34] By the 1520s, Italian was the working language in Rome, though many curia officials would have spoken other tongues too.[35] Some acquaintance with Italian was undoubtedly an advantage for an ambassador. In the 1520s, Francesco Gonzaga, a Mantuan diplomat, commented that two English envoys recently posted to Rome, Edward Fox and Stephen Gardiner could not speak Italian, only Latin.[36] Unlike a substantial proportion of English envoys to Italy, Fox and Gardiner had not studied at Italian universities.[37] Yet by working in concert with the Italian residents employed by the English crown in Rome they could overcome the limitations of language.

ii.   Newsgathering and negotiation

In the days when the resident ambassador's presence was tolerated only unofficially, his role was necessarily limited to gathering information. Only later did it become possible for him to engage explicitly in formal negotiations with the pope. That role of gathering information was central to the office of ambassador, but it was not the envoy's only function. Residents in Rome, who had church business to handle, may well have spent proportionately greater time on negotiations (over appointments to benefices, for example) than counterparts at other courts. Envoys of the ultramontane powers, for whom quick consultation with the principal was impossible, may have enjoyed rather more latitude as to tactics than their Italian counterparts. All this makes generalisations about the balance between negotiating and newsgathering functions rather risky, and caution is needed in relation to assessments like that of Betty Behrens who, writing in the 1930s, summed up the traditional view of the resident diplomat: 'the resident ambassador collected the news and the special ambassadors did the negotiating'. The resident was 'invariably their inferior, and often little better than their servant'.[38] Thirty years later, Paolo Prodi concurred: the resident was almost never entrusted with the conclusion of great political negotiations, for which a special ambassador would be sent. The latter would be able to convey his

---

[34] BAV, MS Lat. 12270, fol. 42v.

[35] Joycelyne G. Russell, *Diplomats at Work: Three Renaissance Studies* (Stroud: Sutton, 1992), p. 6.

[36] ASMn, Archivio Gonzaga 877, c. 28r, 26 March 1528.

[37] MacMahon, 'Ambassadors of Henry VIII', p. 81 and Fletcher, 'Performing Henry at the court of Rome', in Thomas Betteridge and Suzannah Lipscomb (eds), *Henry VIII and the Court: Art, Politics and Performance* (Aldershot: Ashgate, 2013), pp. 179–96 (p. 188).

[38] Behrens, 'Office of the English resident ambassador', pp. 163–4.

prince's will more directly, and often more authoritatively, because the resident was 'almost always a lower-ranking agent'.[39]

While it is certainly true that high-ranking envoys were used for important business, in Rome at least, residents had significant responsibilities beyond that of obtaining news. For example, in the 1520s, an English resident ambassador at Rome, John Clerk, ran into trouble when a bull against the English royal interest was procured at the curia. Expressing his displeasure, Henry VIII wrote:

> That wee of specyall trust and confidence haud deputed yow, to be resident in that Court, as our Oratour not onelie to solicite and execute all such Causes, and matters as we have and shall Committ unto you from tyme to tyme, but alsoe vigilantlie to attend and see, that nothing should be impetrated, or obteyned there preiudiciall or hurtfull to us, or to this Realme or derrogatorie, to our dignitie Royall.[40]

This letter offers a notable early description of how the duties of a resident ambassador were understood by a prince. In contrast to the frequent suggestion in the literature that the resident's key duty was information-gathering, it describes a much more active role for the ambassador than simply gathering information: 'soliciting' and 'executing', seeing that nothing 'prejudicial' or 'hurtful' could be obtained.[41] Indeed, it suggests that Michael Mallett's observation that in the latter half of the fifteenth century 'information-gathering was only a part of diplomacy and by no means the sole function of the resident ambassador' remained true well into the next century.[42] As Paolo Margaroli has noted in relation to Milanese diplomatic missions, the majority combined information-gathering aims with political mediation.[43] While the consistent supply of news was indeed an advantage of the resident system, the importance of permanent representation lay in the development of networks that could facilitate negotiation as well as newsgathering.

---

[39] Paolo Prodi, *Diplomazia del Cinquecento: Istituzioni e prassi* (Bologna: Prof. Riccardo Pàtron, 1963), p. 57.

[40] BAV, MS Barberini Latini 3567, 'Lettere e Negotiationi del Cardinale Volsey Inglese nella Corte di Roma, in Lingua Inglese', fol. 16v. The date of this letter is not clear, but Clerk was accredited from April 1521 to September 1522 and again from March 1523 to December 1525. Gary M. Bell, *A Handlist of British Diplomatic Representatives, 1509–1688* (London: Royal Historical Society, 1990), pp. 159–60.

[41] Scholars privileging the information-gathering role include Mattingly, *Renaissance Diplomacy*, p. 104; Linda S. Frey and Marsha L. Frey, *The History of Diplomatic Immunity* (Columbus: Ohio State University Press, 1999), p. 147; Biow, *Doctors, Ambassadors, Secretaries*, p. 102.

[42] Michael Mallett, 'The emergence of permanent diplomacy in Renaissance Italy', *DSP Discussion Papers*, no. 56 (Leicester: Centre for the Study of Diplomacy, 1999), p. 7.

[43] Margaroli, *Diplomazia e Stati Rinascimentali*, p. 290.

The tendency of some literature on diplomacy to emphasise this aspect of the ambassador's work has two roots. In part it is a function of the fact that writing is the most visible trace of his practice. Yet diplomatic letter-writing was not simply about conveying information. Machiavelli's 'Advice to Raffaello Girolami' focuses on the importance for the ambassador of letter-writing, reporting and providing information. He writes, for example: 'Great honor also comes to an ambassador from the reports he writes to those who send him.'[44] Machiavelli's comments, however, are principally concerned with ensuring that the ambassador creates a positive impression back home by means of his reporting, and not with the intrinsic value of the reporting itself (there is no harm, he suggests, in repeating the same material provided it is done eloquently).[45] Beyond its basic purpose, letter-writing was about creating the impression that the ambassador was wise, prudent and well-informed, and enabling him to avoid the pitfall of subsequently discovering that he had failed to pass on some potentially important detail.[46]

A fundamental aspect of an ambassador's job was to negotiate on behalf of his prince, in line with his instructions (I discuss the question of autonomy below). This was particularly true of Rome, where there was a considerable volume of business to be done through the curial structures, but it cannot have been irrelevant elsewhere when there were treaties to agree or trade disputes to iron out.[47] As Francesco Gonzaga, the Mantuan ambassador, commented of Edward Fox and Stephen Gardiner's mission to the papal court (in exile at Orvieto) in early 1528:

In fact, these ambassadors, as far as I can gather, are here principally for the cause that I've already written about, for the dispensation of the king's marriage, although it's not admitted, and they manage the business most secretly.[48]

On the following day, Gonzaga noted that there were 'many difficulties to resolve' before the matter could be settled.[49] Those difficulties were, however, things that could – in theory at least – be resolved through a process of negotiation, and this was the principal role of these ambassadors. In this case, two special ambassadors had been sent from

---

[44] Machiavelli, 'Advice', p. 117.   [45] *Ibid.*, p. 119.

[46] Hampton, *Fictions of Embassy*, pp. 21–3.

[47] On the routine duties of Spanish ambassadors in sixteenth-century Rome, see Levin, *Agents of Empire*, pp. 134–53.

[48] 'Essi Oratori in effetto secondo posso comprendere sono qui principalmente per la causa che gia anche ho scritto per la dispensa del matrimonio del Re, pur non si confessa, è maneggiano la cosa secretissimamente.' ASMn, Archivio Gonzaga 877, c. 31v, 27 March 1528.

[49] 'Per quanto intendo vi sono di molte difficulta da asettare prima che se ne venga alo effetto.' ASMn, Archivio Gonzaga 877, c. 38r, 28 March 1528.

England with instructions for their mission. However, in their negotiations, they worked with the English resident, an Italian diplomat, Gregorio Casali:

> The English ambassadors who are here, have been two or three times with the Pope, and nothing is known about their negotiations, His Holiness having given them secret audience, where no-one was present except himself and [the ambassadors], together with the Cavalier Casali.[50]

Although Henry VIII's 'divorce'[51] – for its dramatic outcome – may seem to be a particularly special case, marriage-related negotiations were an important aspect of a sixteenth-century diplomat's role. Ambassadors in Rome were regularly tasked with obtaining the necessary papal dispensations.[52] At the time Gonzaga was writing, Clement VII had recently agreed to declare the marriage of Margaret Tudor and the Earl of Angus invalid after negotiations in which the Duke of Albany, ambassador for France, was heavily involved.[53] Gonzaga himself was extensively involved in negotiations over his own master's various betrothals.[54] The strategic significance of marriages was such that vast diplomatic effort was devoted to ensuring the successful conclusion of these alliances.

Negotiations over benefices were likewise highly politicised, not least when kings and popes disagreed on appointments to particular sees. A furious row broke out in October 1509 over the see of Provence between the Pope and the ambassadors of the king of France. According to a contemporary Venetian dispatch, the French threatened to break off diplomatic relations, to which Julius II replied, 'On you go, we know very well how to govern without you.'[55] In the 1520s, English diplomats in Rome were involved in negotiating to upgrade certain abbeys to the status of bishoprics.[56] They lobbied not only the Pope, but also the

---

[50] 'Gli ambasciadori d'Inghilterra che sono qui, sono stati per due o tre volte da Nostro Signore et della negociatione loro per anchora non s'intende altro, havendoli Sua Santita dato audienza secreta, dove non è intervenuto se non la persona di quella, et essi, insieme co'l cavaliere Casale.' ASMn, Archivio Gonzaga 877, c. 28r, 26 March 1528.

[51] Strictly speaking, Henry was seeking a declaration that his first marriage had never been valid, but contemporaries used the word 'divorce' and I see no reason to avoid it.

[52] Levin, *Agents of Empire*, pp. 144–5.

[53] This was in March 1527. See Margaret Tudor's entry in the *Oxford Dictionary of National Biography*.

[54] For an example, ASMn, Archivio Gonzaga 877, c. 151r, 1 May 1528.

[55] '"Padre sancto, poi che'l mio Re non po' impetrar cossa che'l voglia da la Beatitudine Vostra, non è mestier che'l tegni ambassator qui. Io me ne posso andar." Rispose: "Andate a la bon hora, che saperemo ben governar senza de vui."' *Dispacci Degli Ambasciatori Veneziani alla Corte di Roma Presso Giulio II, 25 Guigno 1509–9 Gennaio 1510*, ed. Roberto Cessi (Venice, 1932), p. 132.

[56] For some examples, see *L&P*, Vol. IV, 2879, 4905, 4932, 5638, 5649; LPL, MS 4434, fols. 76r, 119r.

ambassadors of other powers, to ensure broader support for their project, telling the Mantuan ambassador that certain of the abbots in possession were 'ill-living types' and the proposal would bring 'reputation and honour' to the Holy See.[57] The process of obtaining such papal bulls was, however, a long one. It required a detailed knowledge of the institutions of the curia, along with an awareness of which palms to grease and, preferably, an already-established network of friends and associates who could assist.

In short, the role of the resident diplomat was varied indeed. It might encompass tasks as diverse as obtaining information, translation, negotiation; military missions (of which more in Chapter 5), arranging accommodation (Chapter 6) and gift exchange (Chapter 7). The effective execution of all these tasks rested on the maintenance of an intricate network of contacts. Winning friends in government circles – and in Rome winning over individual cardinals – was central.[58]

iii. *Councils, Consistory and conclaves*

Resident ambassadors in Rome had specific responsibilities that counterparts elsewhere did not share. These concerned their interaction with the structures of the curia, and in particular their roles in Consistory, at church councils and during conclaves. Although Grassi says that newly-arrived ambassadors should come to Consistory, this is a prescription only for those who come to pledge obedience to the Pope.[59] For example, at the start of Clement VII's papacy, the Venetians attended Consistory to pledge obedience on 20 April 1523, the Florentines on 27 April and the Sienese on 5 June.[60] However, Consistory records and the diary of Grassi's successor Biagio Martinelli demonstrate that those who came to Rome to take up roles as residents did not attend in this way.[61] Consistory was rather more the business meeting of the cardinals than a focus for diplomatic dealings, and the references in its records to ambassadors are sparse. Most negotiation took place in private audiences

---

[57] 'Questi oratori Inglesi, per le lettere che ultimamente tengono dal loro Re, ricercano da N. S. che certe buone Abbatie, che sono nel paese là, possino essere erette in vescovadi, et privatine alcuni possessori, quali asseriscono di mala vita... Et si consenterà, che le dette abbatie siano ridotte in vescovadi, sicome si dimanda, parendo cosa laudabile, et che apporti riputatione, et honore à la Sede Apostolica.' ASMn, Archivio Gonzaga 878, c. 181r, 1 June 1529.

[58] Margaroli, *Diplomazia e Stati Rinascimentali*, p. 292. Frigo, 'Small states', pp. 152–3.

[59] BAV, MS Vat. Lat. 12270, fols. 61r-69v.

[60] ASV, Arch. Concist., Acta Misc. 31, fols. 145r, 145v, 149v.

[61] This is apparent by cross-referencing with Bell, *Handlist*, for English diplomacy.

involving the pope, ambassadors, and a handful of advisers.[62] Envoys had to meet cardinals elsewhere to find out what went on behind Consistory doors. Formal audiences were not, however, the only alternative space for diplomatic interactions. Chapter 6 will discuss the wide variety of locations where ambassadors and cardinals might interact. In 1509, Venetian orators got information about Consistory dealings from their compatriot Cardinal Grimani, who gave them an update on the business and the contents of letters that had arrived from Spain.[63] This was a two-way process: diplomatic letters raising matters of grave concern were sometimes read at Consistory. In 1523, the Hungarian ambassador came to Consistory to read letters petitioning for aid against the Turkish invasion,[64] and in 1526, letters from the Doge of Venice to his ambassador at Rome, Marco Venier, were read at Consistory.[65] On the whole, however, only special circumstances brought ambassadors to Consistory for reasons other than pledging obedience. The 1521 presentation, for example, of Henry VIII's book against Luther by the ambassador John Clerk, at which Clerk made a 'fine oration' was rather exceptional, taking place as it did at a special meeting of Consistory called for that purpose alone.[66]

Ambassadors also played significant roles in Church councils, where although far smaller as a group than the assembled prelates, they might exercise significant influence on proceedings. Even the Fifth Lateran Council, held between 1512 and 1517 and often dismissed as unrepresentative, numbered among its participants, orators from twenty-three polities: Savoy, Venice, England, the marquis of Brandenburg, Denmark, Florence, the Emperor Maximilian, several Imperial electors, Portugal, the marquis of Monferrato, the duke of Milan, the duke of Ferrara, Mantua, Lucca, Rome (the conservatores urbis), the Grand Master of Rhodes, the king of Poland, the duke of Mazioviae (Mazowsze, united with Poland in 1526), Bologna, France, Spain, the Swiss Confederation, the patriarch of Jerusalem, the order of Teutonic knights (Prussia) and Parma. The patriarch of the Maronites in Syria may have sent orators too. Other countries (for example, Scotland) were represented by bishops as bishops and there is no record of an ambassador attending on their behalf.[67] In 1513, the Lateran Council saw

---

[62] Pellegrini, 'A turning-point in the history of the factional system', pp. 27–8.
[63] *Dispacci*, p. 29.   [64] ASV, Arch. Concist., Acta Misc. 31, fol. 148v.
[65] ASV, Arch. Concist., Acta Misc. 31, fol. 200v.
[66] ASV, Arch. Concist., Acta Misc. 31, fol. 130r. 2 October 1521. *L&P*, Vol. III, 1654; Henry Ellis (ed.), *Original Letters Illustrative of English History*, 11 vols (London: Dawsons, 1969), 3rd series, Vol. I, pp. 262–9 (p. 263).
[67] Nelson H. Minnich, 'The participants at the Fifth Lateran Council', *Archivum Historiae Pontificiae* 12 (1974), 157–206, list of ambassadors on pp. 205–6, reprinted in Nelson H. Minnich, *The Fifth Lateran Council (1512–17)* (Aldershot: Ashgate Variorum, 1993).

Claude de Seyssel (for Louis XII of France), Marino Caracciolo (for Massimiliano Sforza of Milan) and the Imperial ambassador Alberto Pio da Carpi in contention over a decision to absolve Louis of responsibility for the Pisan schism.[68] The earlier councils of Basel and Ferrara/Florence had likewise involved representatives of the secular monarchs of Europe, as would the later Council of Trent.[69]

Ambassadors had a very specific role during papal conclaves. The four doors to the conclave were each allocated to a different group of guards. The first was to be secured by a great prelate or powerful nobleman, to whom two or three hundred infantrymen would be assigned, the second by the conservators [magistrates] and captains of Rome's rioni [districts], along with noble citizens, the third was to be guarded by lay orators and the fourth, by the prelates of the Roman curia, whether orators or not.[70] Patrizi emphasised that the final group should include men of several nations. This is particularly noteworthy because in the aftermath of the conciliar crisis, it suggests that importance was attached to achieving a mix of nations and to the avoidance of any impression that a single prince might gain control of proceedings. Ambassadors were not officially admitted to conclaves, but might find a means to enter in the capacity of servant to a friendly cardinal.[71] The boundaries were undoubtedly porous. To take one example, at the conclave of 1513, Christopher Bainbridge, an English cardinal, was accompanied by his nephew Roger Bainbridge and his secretary Richard Pace. Silvestro Gigli, English orator (and representative at the Lateran Council) was one of the guardians. The team snuck news of proceedings out by scratching messages into one of Bainbridge's silver plates and giving it to Gigli to pass on.[72] There were, however, limits to the power of ambassadors to influence the cardinals in the course of a conclave: just one or two defections from a faction could swiftly change a candidate's fortune.[73] A struggling candidate might throw his weight behind a third candidate to outmanoeuvre a rival: a beneficiary of such a strategy was Rodrigo Borgia, who became

---

[68] Nelson H. Minnich, 'The "Protestatio" of Alberto Pio (1513)', *Società, Politica e Cultura a Carpi ai Tempi di Alberto III Pio: Atti del Convegno Internazionale (Carpi, 19–21 maggio (1978)*, Rino Avesani et al. (eds), (*Medioevo e Umanesimo* 46), Vol. 1 (Padua: Studio Bibliografico Antenore, 1981), pp. 261–89, reprinted in Minnich, *Fifth Lateran Council*.

[69] Mandell Creighton, *A History of the Papacy from the Great Schism to the Sack of Rome*, 5 vols (London: Longmans, Green & Co, 1892–94), p. 206; John W. O'Malley, *Trent: What Happened at the Council* (Cambridge, MA: Belknap Press, 2013).

[70] Patrizi, *L'Oeuvre*, pp. 29–30.

[71] For such a proposal in relation to the 1534 conclave: BNF, MS Français 19751, fol. 116v.

[72] D. S. Chambers, *Cardinal Bainbridge in the Court of Rome* (Oxford: Oxford University Press, 1965), pp. 42–3.

[73] Shaw, 'Papacy and the European powers', pp. 124–5.

Pope Alexander VI.[74] That did not stop rulers from instructing their ambassadors on how to intervene. Often several letters of credence would be provided, giving the envoy some flexibility as favourites emerged. The Florentine ambassador was provided with promises of support for three different cardinals in 1430; anticipating the conclave of 1534, the English sent diplomatic blanks for their agent to fill in the name of the favourite.[75]

c.   The extent of the resident's autonomy

Conclaves were one occasion on which ambassadors in Renaissance Rome might have to take decisions without formal instructions from their prince. There were many other instances, particularly in the context of war, where it was impossible to wait for a response. As Francesco Guicciardini acknowledged:

It is impossible to give ambassadors instructions so detailed as to cover every circumstance; rather discretion must teach them to accommodate themselves to the end generally being pursued.[76]

Communications were simply not adequate for diplomats to wait when a matter was urgent: even in good circumstances, it took two weeks for a courier to travel from London to Rome.[77] As Christine Shaw has pointed out, in the event of a pope's death it would be extremely difficult for any ultramontane prince to receive the news and issue specific instructions to his agents in Rome on their intervention in the conclave: he would have to rely on 'good contingency plans', 'loyal cardinals' and 'an experienced ambassador with good contacts'.[78] Gary M. Bell suggests that in the absence of reliable communication 'the personalities of diplomats were crucial'.[79] It is, of course, hard to quantify the balance of factors in any given case but access to information, social connections and experience must, I think, have weighed quite as heavily as individual character. Gregorio Casali, an Italian diplomat in the service of Henry VIII, made an unusually explicit observation on the question of autonomy when he responded to criticism of his negotiations for Henry's divorce from

---

[74] Mallett, *The Borgias*, pp. 107–8.

[75] F. Petruccelli della Gattina, *Histoire Diplomatique des Conclaves*, 2 vols (Paris: Librarie Internationale, 1864), Vol. I, p. 240. *St P*, Vol. VII, p. 570 (*L&P*, Vol. VII, 1255).

[76] Francesco Guicciardini, *Maxims and Reflections of a Renaissance Statesman (Ricordi)*, trans. Mario Domandi (Gloucester, MA: Smith, 1970), p. 40.

[77] The calculation of this figure is detailed in Chapter 5.

[78] Shaw, 'The papacy and the European powers', pp. 124–5.

[79] Bell, 'Tudor-Stuart diplomatic history', p. 37.

Catherine of Aragon with the defence that he had been left to act 'as I myself should judge to be most necessary for the victory to be obtained'.[80] Casali's case, which I have discussed elsewhere, bears out the observation of Michael Mallett that even although ambassadors were obliged to seek new instructions should a 'major policy issue' arise, that nonetheless left space for 'considerable personal initiative'.[81]

The extent of an ambassador's discretion to act autonomously was a matter of concern to contemporary theorists. Giovanni Gioviano Pontano, a noted humanist and politician who undertook a number of diplomatic missions for the king of Naples, considered in his treatise on obedience (probably written in the 1460s but published in 1518) whether it was permissible for a diplomat to act autonomously if circumstances suddenly changed. He came to no statement of principle, but concluded that because rulers' attitudes on this point differed widely, being an ambassador was a difficult task.[82] Machiavelli, in his 'Advice to Raffaello Girolami', reduced the question to a matter of personal morality, with only the passing comment:

> How to carry out a commission faithfully is known to everybody who is good, but to carry it out adequately is the difficulty.[83]

In contrast, Étienne Dolet was rather more concerned about the question of instructions and possible deviation from them. The ambassador, he said, should be given 'frank, clear, and entirely unambiguous orders', the 'prudent performance' of which would be his 'whole duty'.[84] However, he recognised that even the fullest of instructions could not cover every eventuality, and advised:

> [When] a matter lying beyond the limits of your orders comes into discussion, see that you merely discuss it, and that you promise to furnish nothing until your king has been advised and his order or consent has been received [...] But it often happens that an occasion is so urgent that you can not wait for a reply. Wherefore, if anything which you see is greatly to your king's advantage depends upon quick action, you will [...] conclude it as promptly as possible.[85]

---

[80] Nicholas Pocock (ed.), *Records of the Reformation: The Divorce 1527–1533*, 2 vols (Oxford: Clarendon Press, 1870), Vol. II, p. 520 (*L&P*, Vol. VII, 86).

[81] Fletcher, *Our Man in Rome*; Mallett, 'Emergence', p. 8.

[82] Pontano (1426/9–1503) was involved in negotiations for the Peace of Bagnolo (1484) and for a treaty between King Ferdinand and the Pope (1486). *Dizionario Biografico degli Italiani* (Rome: Enciclopedia Italiana, 1960-), online at www.treccani.it/biografie. Giovanni Pontano, *Ioannis Ioviani Pontani Opera Omnia Soluta Oratione Composita* (Venice: Aldo Manuzio, 1518), pp. 37r–37v, cited with a partial translation in Carol Kidwell, *Pontano: Poet and Prime Minister* (London: Duckworth, 1991), p. 113.

[83] Machiavelli, 'Advice', p. 116.   [84] Dolet, 'De Officio Legati', pp. 85, 88.

[85] *Ibid.*, p. 88.

Given the need for an ambassador to make such decisions, Dolet concluded that the best course of action was to ensure the appointment of 'a man of prudence and acumen'.[86] His assessment echoes that of Barbaro, who likewise emphasised 'prudence' as the yardstick to be applied by the diplomat in unexpected situations. The long-serving Neapolitan orator Anello Arcamone garnered praise from his master's ally, the duke of Milan, who described him as 'full of natural and fortuitous prudence'.[87] The references to prudence draw on Aristotle, but reflect too its particular Renaissance form, which emphasised the importance, as John Martin has put it, of 'cultivating a certain ambiguity about one's beliefs'.[88] Prudence and dissimulation were closely related.[89]

Barbaro was more cautious than Dolet about the importance of consultation with the principal, stating that:

> Above all, the ambassador should take care that he never speaks either for or against anyone, or of anything, with the Prince, unless the Senators have mandated it.[90]

The difference in approach can be attributed to the particular republican context of Barbaro's writing. While representatives of republics were often tied closely to instructions, a royal diplomat who enjoyed the confidence of his sovereign might well have more latitude (in terms of tactics, at least) so long as that confidence lasted. As Daniela Frigo has argued, in the fifteenth and early sixteenth centuries, there was a 'marked distinction' between the ambassadors of princes and those of republics: in the principalities diplomacy lacked clear rules and instead relied on the reciprocal relationship of fidelity (*fidelitas*) from the ambassador and grace (*gratia*) from the prince.[91] The republics, on the other hand, had much more formalised systems: their statute books contain numerous

---

[86] *Ibid.*, p. 90.

[87] 'Pieno de Natural et Accidentale Prudentia.' Duke of Milan to Branda Castiglioni, 9 November 1482, ASMi, AS, PE-Roma, b. 241, cited in Dover, 'Royal diplomacy', p. 73.

[88] John Martin, 'Inventing sincerity, refashioning prudence: the discovery of the individual in renaissance Europe', *American Historical Review* 102 (1997), 1309–42 (p. 1325); see also the discussion in his *Myths of Renaissance Individualism* (Basingstoke: Palgrave Macmillan, 2006), p. 32.

[89] Jon R. Snyder, *Dissimulation and the Culture of Secrecy in Early Modern Europe* (Berkeley: University of California Press, 2009), pp. 8–10.

[90] 'Ante omnia cavere debet legatus ne pro se neu pro aliquo aut de aliqua re cum Principe unquam loquatur, nisi Patres mandaverint,' Barbaro, 'De Officio Legati', p. 163.

[91] Frigo, 'Corte, Onore e Ragion di Stato', p. 14. See also Francesco Senatore, *"Uno Mundo de Carta": Forme e Strutture della Diplomazia Sforzesca* (Naples: Liguori, 1998), p. 87.

injunctions relating to the conduct of ambassadors.[92] Although diplomacy was an international system and required international norms, there was sufficient flexibility to accommodate a range of local practices. Ambassadors were expected to be aware of their limits and to exercise their judgement appropriately.

d.   The diplomat's dual persona

The two different ways that an ambassador could participate in a conclave – in a formal capacity, as a guardian, or informally, as a cardinal's servant – highlight the two sides to his persona and the way that both could play a role in the conduct of diplomacy. In the case of the conclave, no-one would genuinely believe that the diplomat playing cardinal's servant was really there in only a personal capacity. Yet the fact that he could pretend to do so was important. At the start of this chapter, I discussed some situations in which the ambassador appeared to embody his prince or republic. The idea that the diplomat personified his prince is also apparent in the prescriptions for his physical type and clothing. Barbaro and Dolet agreed that the ambassador should be of middle age, observations contextualised by Da Castiglionchio's comment that prudence is acquired through 'length of age and everyday practice and experience with things.'[93] Dolet added:

Special care must be taken that the ambassador be a man suitable to his office in figure, face and stature. A handsome figure moves most persons to admiration, or at any rate it often wins us the favour of many of them. But if we are uncomely, or disfigured by some blemish, or maimed in some way, then, when we are greeted by a smile, perhaps it is not altogether a complimentary one.[94]

Evidently ambassadors were not always so favoured, because Grassi found it necessary to specify that those laymen present who were old, ill, infirm or too young would not be required to participate in the ritual papal ablutions.[95] Dress was also important in cultivating a princely image. Lay ambassadors, said Grassi, should wear cloth of gold or silver, velvet, satin or silk: 'better a cheerful red than a sorrowful black.'[96] Gold collars were to be worn, and ambassadors often adopted national symbols to underline their allegiance. Pius II described how the retinue of King Casimir of Poland's ambassador arrived in Mantua in 1459:

---

[92] Donald E. Queller, *Early Venetian Legislation on Ambassadors* (Geneva: Droz, 1966) and Giuseppe Vedovato, *Note sul Diritto Diplomatico della Repubblica Fiorentina* (Florence: Sansoni, 1946).

[93] Lapo, *De Curiae Commodis*, p. 137.   [94] Dolet, 'De Officio Legati', p. 84.

[95] BAV, MS Vat. Lat. 12270, fol. 95r.   [96] *Ibid.*, fol. 41v.

'He had a great number of attendants, all dressed alike in their national costume, wearing plumed hats, carrying quivers and slings, and mounted on very sleek horses.'[97] Indeed, sumptuous diplomatic dress was so much the standard in this period that Thomas More could use it to make a satirical point in his *Utopia*, when the Anemolian envoys, ignorant of Utopian mores, enter in precisely the standard garb of European diplomats only to appear ridiculous to their hosts:

> Thus three ambassadors made their entry with a hundred attendants, all clad in garments of different colours, and the greater part in silk; the ambassadors themselves, who were of the nobility of their country, were in cloth-of-gold, and adorned with massy chains, earrings and rings of gold; their caps were covered with bracelets set full of pearls and other gems.[98]

Visual depictions of ambassadors from this period, such as Carpaccio's *Dream of St Ursula*, Sebastiano's *Ferry Carondelet* and Holbein's *Ambassadors*, give some impression of the lavish nature of diplomatic attire. In the last of these, Jean de Dinteville, on the left, wears a national symbol, the insignia of the French chivalric Order of St Michael on the gold chain around his neck. However, that ambassadors might embody their monarchs in their dress was an idea that sometimes led to misunderstandings. In the 1520s, Girolamo Ghinucci, an ambassador for the king of England, had one hapless papal official slung into prison when the official dared to challenge him for breaching sumptuary law by wearing velvet shoes. Ghinucci claimed that as a royal ambassador he was exempt from the regulations, although I would question whether he was entirely in the right on that point, for Ghinucci was a cleric and the ceremonial roles in which ambassadors embodied their princes were by this time reserved to laymen.[99]

The confusion over Ghinucci's attire underlines that contemporaries also understood that diplomats had their own, private persona. For example, during the period of Clement VII's illness in 1529, Gasparo Contarini, Venetian ambassador, was received 'not to negotiate anything, nor as an orator, but as a private gentleman'.[100] But this private persona could come into play in ambassadors' work too: in fact, its

---

[97] Pius, *Commentarii* Vol. I, pp. 528–9 (*Secret Memoirs*, p. 128).

[98] Thomas More, *Utopia* (1516), ed. Henry Morley (London: Cassell, 1901, online at www.gutenberg.org/files/2130/2130-h/2130-h.htm).

[99] Archivio di Stato di Siena, Balia, fol. 619. I am grateful to Guido Rebecchini for drawing my attention to this reference, which I initially thought referred to one of the Casali brothers but is more likely to refer to the Sienese Ghinucci.

[100] 'non pero per negociar cosa alcuna, ne come Orator, ma come gentilhomo privato'. Biblioteca Nazionale Marciana, Codices Italiani VII, 1043 (=7616) Lettere di asparo Contarini (1528–1529) (hereafter G. Contarini), fol. 204r.

existence was essential to the functioning of diplomacy. On numerous occasions envoys raised ideas or made proposals that were understood to be on their own initiative, rather than their master's, or exploited the uncertain space between the two. The ambiguous persona of the diplomat created ample space for such dissimulation. As we have seen, when Italian envoys wanted to refuse Pius II's request for backing for a crusade, they answered that 'as private individuals they approved the Pope's words but as envoys they were not empowered to answer them'.[101] When Sir Francis Bryan and Pietro Vanni were sent to Rome as English ambassadors in late 1529, their draft instructions included the injunction that:

And the said master Peter as of hym self shall aparte say unto his holynes, Sir I being an Italyan can not, but with a more fervent zeale and mynde than an other studye and desire, the weale honour and surete of your holynes and the see Apostolique, which compellethe me to shewe unto your holynes frankly what I see in this mater.[102]

The instructions went on to set out in some detail precisely what Vanni should say to the Pope. The comments he was to make 'as of himself', pretending a personal interest as an Italian in the welfare of the Church, were in fact nothing of the sort: rather, they were an integral part of the English strategy.

The reference to the 'self' in Vanni's instructions is a further point of note in the context of the extensive debate on questions of individualism and self-fashioning in Renaissance studies.[103] John Jeffries Martin has argued that a variety of different concepts of the 'self' existed in the Renaissance, and indeed that they changed over time, with a greater emphasis, for example, on the 'sincere self' as the sixteenth century progressed.[104] His concepts of the 'prudential self', prepared to dissimulate where necessary and embodied in Castiglione's perfect courtier, and of the 'self-consciously acting' 'performative self', have particular

---

[101] Pius, *Commentarii* Vol. II, pp. 2404–5 (*Secret Memoirs*, p. 342).
[102] BL, Cotton MSS, Vit. B, vol. x, fol. 174v (*L&P*, Vol. IV, 4977).
[103] Key works include Richard C. Trexler (ed.), *Persons in Groups: Social Behavior as Identity Formation in Medieval and Renaissance Europe* (Binghamton, New York: Center for Medieval & Early Renaissance Studies, 1985) and William J. Connell (ed.), *Society and Individual in Renaissance Florence* (Berkeley: University of California Press, 2002). For a recent contribution, including surveys of the relevant literature, see Paul D. McLean, *The Art of the Network: Strategic Interaction and Patronage in Renaissance Florence* (Durham and London: Duke University Press, 2007), especially Chapter 8, pp. 193–223. The latter works, of course, pose the problem of whether or not it is appropriate to generalise from the Florentine case.
[104] Martin, *Myths of Renaissance Individualism*. McLean, *Art of the Network*, p. 210, questions Martin's periodisation, suggesting that a tension between ideas of prudence and sincerity can be discerned in letters of the 1420s and 1430s.

significance in the study of the ambassador.[105] (I return to the notions of performance and performativity in Chapter 3.) The royal diplomat would simultaneously perform the role of his prince, while maintaining a prudent silence on matters best kept secret, exploiting the ambiguity of his dual persona for political effect. An ambassador was able to present various selves as the situation demanded, exercising a certain degree of personal autonomy in that process. He could appear as the personification of his prince's dignity, or as himself: he could be sincere about his own or his prince's opinions or he could prudently dissimulate. Indeed, the diplomat could not always even be certain of his principal's preferences and on occasion, had no choice but to act on his own initiative.

Timothy Hampton has argued that the ambassador differs from the courtier: 'The courtier dissimulates in order to represent himself effectively at court. The ambassador, by contrast, represents himself *while representing another.*'[106] This formulation makes a useful distinction but it underestimates the ambassador's capacity to manipulate his two personae. This ability is apparent in numerous aspects of diplomatic practice: in his interactions with the pope, in his networking, in his home life, in his dress and in his giving and receipt of gifts. His two *personae* – his own and that of his office – were not distinct. Chapter 3 will show how, in the ceremonial world, the ambassador usually represented his prince but a high-ranking or well-connected envoy might, on occasion, leverage his own status or family ties to his master's advantage. Outside the realm of ceremony, the task of the resident envoy was to handle 'day-to-day' business. This was various but was by no means restricted to information-gathering. In the world of news and negotiation, the ambassador might make use of both personae, using the liminal space between them to achieve diplomatic ends.

---

[105] Martin, *Myths*, pp. 32–6.   [106] Hampton, *Fictions of Embassy*, p. 9.

3   The ritual world of the curia

When the papal master-of-ceremonies Paride Grassi wrote that during diplomatic audiences, no actors or jesters should be present at Consistory, his comment was more than a little ironic.[1] For much of the diplomatic ceremony at Rome was a matter of theatre: a means for the European princes to display their power and assert their precedence. It was heavily symbolic. When an ambassador acted out his role on a grand liturgical occasion, as bearer of the papal canopy or train, or of water to wash the Pontiff's hands, he was playing the part of their princes in the 'theatre of the world'. He personified his prince's honour – or, in some cases, his republic's virtues. This chapter explores the functioning of that ceremonial world. The theatrical metaphors often applied to early modern Rome (by contemporaries as well as later historians) have an obvious echo in Clifford Geertz's anthropological discussion of the 'theatre-state'.[2] Few scholars of early modern Europe would embrace the model of the theatre-state outright, recognising that the pomp of European ceremonies was firmly in the service of power rather than the other way about. There is nonetheless a growing view that ceremony should not be treated as frivolous or empty.[3] Barbara Stollberg-Rilinger, for example, has described the institutions of the Holy Roman Empire as 'an ensemble of ritual and symbolic practices'.[4] Ceremony can be said to have a performative quality: through the repetition of ritual acts, it effects

---

[1] BAV, MS Vat. Lat. 12270, fol. 42r.

[2] Clifford Geertz, *Negara: The Theatre-State in Nineteenth-Century Bali* (Princeton: Princeton University Press, 1990).

[3] There is a very useful discussion of this historiography in Toby Osborne, 'The house of Savoy and the theatre of the world: performances of sovereignty in early modern Rome', in Matthew Vester (ed.), *Sabaudian Studies: Political Culture, Dynasty and Territory, 1400–1700* (Kirksville: Truman State University Press, 2013), pp. 167–90 (especially on this point, pp. 168–70).

[4] Barbara Stollberg-Rilinger, 'Le Rituel de l'Investiture dans le Saint-Empire de l'Epoque Modern: Histoire Institutionelle et Pratiques Symboliques', *Revue d'Histoire Modern et Contemporaine* 56, no. 2 (2009), pp. 7–29 (p. 9).

what it signifies.[5] That is why participation in ceremony – or the decision
to be absent – was taken so seriously. In Rome, liturgical rituals not only
signified the commitment of European powers to the Church, but their
relative positions in a hierarchy: the orders of kings and dukes known as
the *Ordo Regum* and *Ordo Ducum*.

With this significance of ceremony in mind, this chapter explores
shifting practices of diplomacy through a close reading of ceremonial
manuals from the court of Renaissance Rome.[6] These texts provide an
excellent basis for assessing the ways in which diplomats were assimilated
into the papal court. By tracking the growing engagement of ambassadors in the ceremonial world, it is possible to identify ways that diplomacy was formalised in the later fifteenth and early sixteenth century.
Only accredited diplomats, dispatched by sovereign powers, could participate in the ceremonial world: their credentials afforded them recognition and distinguished them from agents. The chapter considers first
the ceremonial of Agostino Patrizi Piccolomini, who worked in the office
of ceremonies from about 1466 to 1488, and the subsequent elaboration
of Patrizi's text by his successor, Johannes Burchard who (literally)
annotated ambassadors into Patrizi's manuscript. Second, it considers
the work of Paride Grassi, who succeeded Burchard and between about
1506 and 1516, wrote a handbook for the office of ceremonies on dealing
with diplomats, *De Oratoribus Romanae Curiae*. It discusses a series of
broad issues regarding the assimilation of ambassadors first, and then
turns to consider questions of precedence in some detail. The chapter
concludes with an assessment of how theories of performance, performativity and symbolic communication help contextualise the ceremonial
world, and considers their connections to the conceptual approach to the
Renaissance ambassador outlined in Chapter 2.

---

[5] Barbara Stollberg-Rilinger, 'The impact of communication theory on the analysis of the
early modern statebuilding processes', pp. 313–18 in Wim Blockmans, André Holenstein
and Jon Mathieu (eds), *Empowering Interactions: Political Cultures and the Emergence of the
State in Europe 1300–1900* (Farnham: Ashgate, 2009), p. 314. The ideas here are derived
from speech act theory: see J. L. Austin, *How to Do Things with Words*, eds. J. O. Urmson
and Marina Sbisà, 2nd edition (Oxford: Oxford University Press, 1976).

[6] An excellent introduction to the papal court is Henry Dietrich Fernández, 'The
patrimony of St Peter: the papal court at Rome c.1450–1700', in John Adamson (ed.),
*The Princely Courts of Europe: Ritual, Politics and Culture under the Ancient Régime
1500–1750* (London: Weidenfeld & Nicolson, 1999), pp. 141–63. On the work of the
ceremonialists, see Jennifer Mara DeSilva, 'Ritual negotiations: Paris de' Grassi and the
office of ceremonies under Popes Julius II and Leo X' (unpublished doctoral thesis,
University of Toronto, 2007), especially Chapter 2, and Jörg Bölling, *Das
Papstzeremoniell der Renaissance: Texte, Musik, Performanz* (Frankfurt am Main: Peter
Lang, 2006).

a.   Assimilating ambassadors

Agostino Patrizi Piccolomini's career spanned several decades of the later fifteenth century, the period in which diplomatic representation at the court of Rome expanded substantially. Born in Siena around 1435, Agostino Patrizi served as secretary to his compatriot, Pope Pius II, from 1460 to 1464. Like other members of Pius' household, he was permitted to adopt the pope's family name, Piccolomini. Following Pius' death, he entered the service of Francesco Todeschini Piccolomini, a papal nephew who later became Pius III (r. 1503). By 1466, he had become a clerk of ceremonies in the papal chapel, a role in which he continued until late the following decade, when he returned to his home town. He was succeeded by Johannes Burchard in 1483, but returned to Rome the following year to take over the role of their superior, Antoine Rébiol, with the title President of the Office of Ceremonies, which he held until 1488.[7] Patrizi's ceremonial built on earlier texts from both Rome and Avignon to set out the rules for the conduct of ceremony in Rome.[8] It covered papal and imperial coronations, canonisations, the creation of cardinals, public processions, the reception of visiting princes, the conduct of general councils and the feasts of the liturgical calendar. It exists in a printed edition of 1516 (the Marcello edition), and at least twenty-five manuscript copies, the earliest of which may be dated between 1488 and 1495. In the hand of a copyist, it includes amendments by both Patrizi and Burchard. Philological analysis by Marc Dykmans posits several subsequent redactions of this manuscript by Burchard including one (referred to as B** in Dykmans' edition) that includes over two hundred additions, many of them lengthy. Produced during the pontificate of Julius II, this set of amendments can be dated between late 1503 and Burchard's death in 1506. It is in Burchard's annotations that we find the first comprehensive incorporation of ambassadors into curial ceremony. They immediately pre-date Grassi's *De Oratoribus*, the first ceremonial text devoted solely to the role of diplomats. Burchard's diary, covering the period 1483–1506, also includes numerous notes on the reception of ambassadors, as do the subsequent diaries of Grassi (1506–21) and Biagio Martinelli da Cesena (1517–40). Through their work it is possible to track developments in diplomatic ritual over a period of over fifty years during which resident diplomacy

---

[7] Dykmans, 'Introduction', *L'Oeuvre de Patrizi Piccolomini*, 1*–15*.
[8] The earlier ceremonials are in Marc Dykmans (ed.) *Le Cérémonial Papal de La Fin du Moyen Âge à la Fin de la Renaissance*, 4 vols (Brussels: Institut Historique Belge de Rome, 1977–85).

changed from a sometimes-tolerated problem to an institutionalised feature of life at the Roman curia.

The masters-of-ceremonies represented themselves as jealous guardians of ceremonial propriety and tradition. As we will see, they buttressed their arguments by reference to precedent. As court officials, however, they were expected to support the pope's implementation of his own policy and programme. Julius II's ceremonialists, for example, had to make ritual fit the very different contexts of Bologna, Perugia and Ferrara, where Julius travelled on campaign.[9] Ceremony has a paradoxical character.[10] It is supposed to be fixed, indeed, the appeal to tradition is a vital means of legitimating ritual.[11] At the same time, however, ceremony changes to accommodate shifting political circumstances: the point at which it stops adapting is the point at which it can reasonably be said to be empty. In the early sixteenth century, the liturgical ceremony of the papal court had to adapt to encompass a quite new institution: the resident ambassador. It was further elaborated over the course of the sixteenth century, as a comparison of seventeenth-century Roman ceremonies with those outlined here demonstrates.[12] However, even in elaborated form, ceremonial practice had to remain malleable. As Barbara

[9] DeSilva, 'Ritual negotiations', pp. 95–7, and for a wider discussion of the ceremonialists' role in constructing papal identity, see Chapter 4, 'Paris de' Grassi and the construction of Popes Julius II and Leo X's ritual identities', pp. 208–80.

[10] A useful introduction to papal ritual is Peter Burke, *The Historical Anthropology of Early Modern Italy: Essays on Perception and Communication* (Cambridge: Cambridge University Press, 1987), pp. 168–82. On diplomatic ceremonial and the order of precedence in general, see William Roosen, 'Early modern diplomatic ceremonial: a systems approach', *Journal of Modern History* 52 (1980), 452–76. In relation to Rome in particular, see Maria Antonietta Visceglia, 'Il Cerimoniale come Linguaggio Politico', in Visceglia and Catherine Brice (eds), *Cérémonial et Rituel à Rome (XVIe–XIXe siècle)* (Rome: École Française de Rome, 1997), pp. 117–76: this offers a useful discussion on conflicts relating to precedence, albeit focusing on the later sixteenth and seventeenth centuries, with extensive bibliography. For case-studies from the later sixteenth century, see Michael J. Levin, 'A new world order: the Spanish campaign for precedence in early modern Europe', *Journal of Early Modern History* 6 (2002), 233–64 and Toby Osborne, 'The surrogate war between the Savoys and the Medici: sovereignty and precedence in early modern Italy', *The International History Review* 29 (2007): 1–21.

[11] I discuss the relationship between tradition and ritual in liturgical ceremony in 'The altar of Saint Maurice'. See also Catherine Bell, *Ritual: Perspectives and Dimensions* (New York and Oxford: Oxford University Press, 1997).

[12] For examples of ceremony in seventeenth-century Rome, see Peter Rietbergen, *Power and Religion in Baroque Rome: Barberini Cultural Policies* (Leiden: Brill, 2006), especially Chapter 4, 'Prince Eckembergh comes to dinner, or: power through culinary ceremony', pp. 181–217; Peter Gillgren and Mårten Snickare, *Performativity and Performance in Baroque Rome* (Farnham: Ashgate, 2012), especially the essays by Peter Burke, 'Varieties of performance in seventeenth-century Italy', pp. 15–23 and Martin Olin, 'Diplomatic performances and the applied arts in seventeenth-century Europe', pp. 25–45.

Stollberg-Rilinger has argued, 'ambiguity and indistinctiveness' are precisely the factors that make symbolic communication powerful.[13] Andrew Brown and Graeme Small, in their discussion of Burgundian ceremonial, argue that 'ceremonies work because meaning is not fixed'. For ceremonies to fulfil their function of reconciling participants with conflicting interests, there had to be sufficient ambiguity in their symbolism to allow those people to engage – in a way they could not collectively participate in a written treaty, for example.[14] In short, even while asserting its immutability and referring to tradition, ceremony had to allow space for innovation.

The references to ambassadors in the earliest Patrizi text are few. They had roles on only a handful of occasions in the liturgical calendar. Ambassadors were given responsibility for guarding one of the four entrances to the conclave.[15] At the coronation of a new pope they, along with noblemen, might carry the *baldacchino* (canopy) and, when not so engaged, took their place in the processions.[16] Patrizi described places for ambassadors at a papal banquet, noted that they may attend the arrival of an emperor at the gates of Rome for his coronation 'at their pleasure', and that they may also be present for an Imperial entry procession.[17] He detailed the places where ambassadors should stand or sit on a variety of formal occasions, including the public consistory, general council meetings and certain processions.[18] It is clear that all these were events that envoys were expected to attend. During the public consistory, they stood to the right of the pope between the step to his throne and the wall.[19] Patrizi included a short discussion of the reception of ambassadors or envoys.[20] Later in this chapter, I will discuss how and why visiting ambassadors tried to circumvent the conventions of diplomatic entries, but for now I will focus on the prescriptions. The day prior to their arrival in Rome, they were required to give notice of their entry. If they were coming to pledge obedience, or were on important business pertaining to the public good, they would be welcomed by the households of cardinals and prelates. If they were arriving on their prince's private business, they would be received only by private (personal)

---

[13] Barbara Stollberg-Rilinger, 'The impact of communication theory on the analysis of the early modern statebuilding processes', pp. 313–18, in Wim Blockmans, André Holenstein and Jon Mathieu (eds), *Empowering Interactions: Political Cultures and the Emergence of the State in Europe 1300–1900* (Farnham: Ashgate, 2009), p. 315.

[14] Andrew Brown and Graeme Small, *Court and Civic Society in the Burgundian Low Countries c. 1420–1530* (Manchester: Manchester University Press, 2007).

[15] Patrizi, *L'Oeuvre*, p. 30.   [16] Patrizi, *L'Oeuvre*, pp. 66, 78–79.

[17] Patrizi, *L'Oeuvre*, pp. 88, 96–97.

[18] Patrizi, *L'Oeuvre*, p. 215; pp. 182, 184–5, 192, 196, 202–3.

[19] Patrizi, *L'Oeuvre*, p. 166.   [20] Patrizi, *L'Oeuvre*, pp. 204–10.

friends. Patrizi commented that during the pontificate of Sixtus IV, 'fawning' and inappropriate efforts to please have seen these ceremonies conducted in a rather relaxed way. 'It would be good if matters were returned to the appropriate dignity,' he observed. It is a useful reminder that these treatises refer to ideals and not, necessarily, practice, but it is the change in what was prescribed that we are concerned with here. Patrizi's text continued with an account of the processional order for the entry and the conduct of the public consistory.

Burchard's edition of Patrizi, which can be dated between 1503 and 1506, elaborated significantly on the detail of the reception ceremony, doubling the length of the section. It was one of the most heavily emended parts of Patrizi's text. He added a note excluding religious orders and subjects of the Church from sending ambassadors, an issue discussed further below. Most of his amendments, however, concerned material aspects of ambassadors' reception, and suggested a concern to impose rules, set standards (not only for ambassadors but also for his colleagues) and convey a sense of papal majesty. He added, for example, a discussion of appropriate clothing for entry and gave precise guidance on the doffing of hats. He included notes on the adornment of the rooms for ambassadors' reception in the papal palace: wall-hangings were to be put up and carpets placed on the floor for those who would sit at the pope's feet. If it was winter, a fire should be lit in the room where ambassadors would wait for their audience. Burchard's text, here, conveys the importance of magnificence in the reception of ambassadors in a manner that Patrizi's does not. As we will see in Chapter 6, where the space of the court is considered in more detail, magnificence was an important virtue in the diplomatic context. Burchard's discussion here is significant in terms of the changing model of papal government and the gradual development of a more courtly style. Some of Burchard's annotations to this section re-visit material from other sections of the ceremonial.[21] Nonetheless, it is worth observing that Burchard found it useful to collect together information on ambassadors into a single section of his amended text.

By the time Paride Grassi held the office of master-of-ceremonies, the presence of diplomats at Rome had expanded to such an extent as to justify the compilation of an entire handbook devoted to their ceremonial role. Born around 1460 in Bologna, Paride followed his uncle in pursuing a curial career and took up his role in the ceremonial office under Julius II.[22] His *De Oratoribus Romanae Curiae* was written principally

---

[21] For example, the chapter dealing with the public consistory: Patrizi, *L'Oeuvre*, p. 209.

[22] Marc Dykmans, 'Paris de Grassi', *Ephemerides Liturgicae* 96 (1982), 407–482.

between 1505 and 1509, but worked on up until at least 1516, while its author was papal master-of-ceremonies.[23] It runs to 160 folios (and over 200 in some copies): three copies survive in the Vatican Library but have been almost entirely neglected in studies of diplomacy. We can safely assume that this text was referred to well beyond the immediate years of its composition. Grassi's successor Biagio Martinelli responded to a query from the Pope about a 1529 dispute over precedence 'according to our ceremonies and the annotations of my predecessors'; when a Hungarian ambassador tried to assert his precedence over the English, Martinelli was sent by the Pope to show him the decisions of earlier ceremonialists on the matter.[24] Grassi's text takes the form of a working handbook for the ceremonial office. It adds a vast quantity of detail to the Patrizi text, even as amended by Burchard. Its focus is resolutely practical, a reflection of the master-of-ceremonies' role. (An example of ceremonialists struggling to balance prescription and practicality may be found in Burchard's diary entry from 1493, when the senior cardinals lobbied for the Corpus Christi Day procession to take a different route, for fear the rain and mud would ruin their vestments.[25]) Grassi's handbook is a recognition that as the number of diplomats in Rome had expanded, so had the number of problems that might arise. Many of his chapters deal with the practicalities of specific cases that had simply not been addressed in earlier texts, such as the presence of ambassadors from Christian Africa and from non-Christian states.[26] The former were accorded a ceremonial welcome: the latter were not, in general, but in at least one case, political exigencies forced an exception to the rule. Grassi details an occasion in 1489 when Sixtus IV welcomed first Djem, half-brother and rival of Sultan Bayezid II to Rome (Sixtus had cut a deal with Bayezid to hold Djem hostage), then held a secret consistory for an audience with the Sultan's ambassador. The account of the ceremonies for the ambassador's arrival suggests he was accorded a similar welcome to Imperial envoys of the period.[27]

---

[23] A description of the manuscripts is in Dykmans, 'Paris de Grassi II', 400–3.

[24] 'Respondi secundum cerimonias nostras, et annotationes predecessorum meorum'. BAV, MS Vat. Lat. 12276, fol. 92r. In the Hungarian case: 'ostendi plures decisiones ceremoniarum et predecessorum meorum in officio per quae dabatur precedentia Angliae'; *ibid.*, fol. 87r.

[25] Burchard, *Liber Notarum*, Vol. I, p. 439; see also Dykmans, *L'Oeuvre*, 212*.

[26] On ambassadors from Christian Africa, see Lowe, '"Representing" Africa', especially pp. 119–20 for a consideration of Grassi's prescriptions.

[27] BAV, Vat. Lat. 12270, fols. 70v–78r. The envoy was welcomed a mile away from the gates (fol. 75r), an honour accorded only to the highest-ranking ambassadors. See the discussion of entries in Chapter 6.

The problem-solving tone of Grassi's handbook is best expressed in a section detailing advice to be given to a new ambassador by the master-of-ceremonies. Burchard had already highlighted that the ceremonialists should advise the ambassador not to forget his credentials, and to arrive in good time so as not to keep the pope waiting.[28] Grassi amplified these notes into an exhaustive briefing, which makes apparent the extent to which the ceremonial office was involved in stage-managing diplomatic entries, audiences and appearances. Grassi extended to eight to ten days the period between entry and public consistory, facilitating a degree of preparation that shorter notice precluded.[29] He listed a string of tasks for envoys to complete prior to their audience. They should send a copy of their oration to the papal secretary in advance so that the pope could prepare his response and the secretary make any necessary corrections.[30] They should ensure others' servants are available to take care of their horses when their own servants are invited to kiss the pope's foot. They should ensure that the papal officials are advised of the internal order of precedence of the embassy. Actors and jesters should not be brought to Consistory, though trumpeters may be, provided they leave their instruments outside. Swords should not be worn. Credentials in the vernacular should be sent in advance for translation into Latin, and the ceremonialists should listen to a run-through of the proposed oration, the better to advise on its style and on the tone of voice suited to the room (though not on the art of oratory). This detailed explanation, running to nine folios, was supplemented in the earliest MS copy by a checklist of headings that appears to function as a 'to-do' list for diplomats. The handbook is, in short, testimony to the high degree of organisation that lay behind a successful diplomatic reception. Certain of its prescriptions are undoubtedly the product of a ceremonial office jealous of its own role. Grassi was known for his bluntness with members of the curia whose comportment fell short of expectations. He reproved Cardinal Bainbridge, for example, when the cardinal failed to finish an acceptance speech for the Golden Rose, though other

---

[28] Patrizi, *L'Oeuvre*, p. 207.

[29] Patrizi, *L'Oeuvre*, p. 207, after the section on entry and not going out in public until received by the pope then goes on: 'Die deinde statuta parabitur consistorium publicum in aula convenienti oratoribus, ut alias diximus. Et in sero precedent intimetur cardinalibus, prelatis et officialibus curie. Hora consueta domini cardinals veniunt ad palatium, et summus pontifex, paratus in pluviali et mitra pretiosis, exit ad publicum consistorium. Interim oratores ipsi veniunt ad palatium associate ab amicis, et aliqui cardinals amici solent mittere familias suas ad eos deducendos ad palatium. Nam tales cardinals preveniunt aliquantulum alios, et statim mittunt familias.' BAV, Vat. Lat. 12270 fol. 39r.

[30] For an example of such a discussion, see *Dispacci*, p. 19.

observers at the ceremony recorded no problems.[31] Nonetheless, his handbook illustrates both the expectations and the vast expansion of formal diplomatic involvement in curia ceremony.

Beyond the general sense of stricter attention to detail conveyed by Grassi's handbook, it documents a series of shifts in the conduct of ceremony that have important implications for broader trends in diplomacy, particularly in relation to the selection of diplomatic personnel. The liturgical ceremony of the papal court was constructed in such a way that the Christian princes could display their status on the Roman stage. If a prince happened to be present in person, he could, and would, take part himself: his ambassador would be redundant.[32] In his absence, though, these ceremonial duties fell to his ambassador, who became responsible for conveying his prince's status and honour by means of his comportment, appearance and challenges to others. The most elaborate ceremony was reserved for special ambassadors who came to pledge the allegiance of their prince or republic to the Pope; however within the liturgical calendar, there were a number of occasions when the diplomatic corps at Rome played a collective role, for example on the Feast of the Purification, during the Easter celebrations and at the Feast of Saints Peter and Paul. Roles might be undertaken by either special or resident ambassadors. Often a high-ranking special envoy would take part in ceremony, but the diaries of the masters-of-ceremony show that in the absence of any such figure, a lay resident was an entirely acceptable participant. Indeed, his familiarity with the ceremonial choreography probably made him a safer option.

One set of changes that can be tracked over time relates to rank. The question of the rank order of ambassadors – and its relationship to the order of precedence – shifts across the three ceremonial texts. In his discussion of the public consistory, Patrizi categorises ambassadors according to the rank of their master: those of emperors and kings, on the one hand, and those of other princes and republics on the other.[33] The former are to be received in the *Aula Magna* or royal hall, adjacent to the Sistine Chapel. One name for this room, *Sala Regia*, derived from its function as the location for pledges of obedience to the popes by kings and emperors.[34] The latter are received in the third hall, or ducal hall

[31] Chambers, *Cardinal Bainbridge*, p. 31.   [32] Behrens, 'Origins', p. 647, fn. 3.
[33] Patrizi, *L'Oeuvre*, pp. 164–5.
[34] Anna Maria de Strobel and Fabrizio Mancinelli, 'La Sala Regia e la Sala Ducale', pp. 73–9 in Pietrangeli, *Il Palazzo Apostolico Vaticano* (Florence: Cardini, 1992), p. 73, citing BAV, Vat. Lat. 7031, fol. 280.

(*Sala Ducale*).[35] These distinctions formed a basis for later, more detailed, orders of precedence that would add a hierarchy of princes within each rank. There is a similar hint at ordering by rank in Pius II's observation that ambassadors and nobles were 'marshalled according to their rank' to carry the baldacchino for the St Andrew's head ceremony.[36]

In order to explain how the rank order worked, some detail of the papal mass is necessary. There were three regular ceremonial duties carried out by laymen at mass, and in the absence of higher-ranking noblemen, these fell to the ambassadors of foreign princes and to the Senator Urbis, Rome's most senior lay government official. The three duties were carrying the papal baldacchinoor canopy, carrying the pope's train, and bringing water for the pope to wash his hands during mass.[37] There were eight occasions during the year on which the Pope would go to mass underneath the baldacchino: on Christmas Day, on the Feast of the Purification, on Palm Sunday, on the fifth and sixth days of Holy Week; on Easter Sunday, on the Feast of Corpus Christi and on the Feast of Saints Peter and Paul.[38] Eight people were required to carry the papal canopy, so any one ambassador would have a reasonable chance of doing so during his residency, although if any princes or minor lords were present, they too could undertake this task, if they wished.[39] The earlier texts of Patrizi and Pius II suggest that there was some rotation of bearers in the course of processions: Patrizi specified that in the Corpus Christi procession, higher-ranking noblemen or lay orators should carry the baldacchino at the start and finish, while lower-ranking ones could take their turn in the middle section.[40] On the visit of Pius II to Florence in 1459, the bearers of the papal litter were rotated, enabling a number of 'distinguished citizens' to take part.[41] Grassi, however, firmly separated 'minor noblemen, knights and sons of barons' from 'major noblemen and relatives of the pope' in the processional order.[42]

The second duty at mass allocated to a lay ambassador (in the absence of any duke or prince who wished to carry it out) was to carry the pope's

[35] In Patrizi, *L'Oeuvre*, the 'third hall or ducal hall' – because the *Sala Ducale* had originally been divided into two parts, the second and third halls. De Strobel and Mancinelli, 'La Sala Regia', p. 73.
[36] Pius, *Commentarii* Vol. II, pp. 1532–3 (*Secret Memoirs*, p. 243).
[37] Luciano Orsini, *La Sacrestia Papale: Suppellettili e Paramenti Liturgici* (Milan: Edizioni San Paolo, 2000); Wharton Marriott, *Vestiarium Christianum* (London: Rivingtons, 1868).
[38] BAV, MS Vat. Lat. 12270, fols. 193r–193v.
[39] For the number, see BAV, MS Vat. Lat. 12270, fol. 193v.
[40] Patrizi, *L'Oeuvre*, pp. 428–9.
[41] Pius, *I Commentarii* Vol. I, pp. 348–9 (*Secret Memoirs*, p. 99).
[42] BAV, MS Vat. Lat. 12270, fol. 31v.

cauda or train. There were fewer occasions on which an ambassador might aspire to this role, partly because it was required only when the pope went to mass on foot rather than in a litter, and partly because it involved only one individual. Patrizi stated that the train should be carried by 'some great nobleman or lay orator', and did not specify how this individual would be selected.[43] Grassi, however, declared that this duty fell to the highest-ranking (*dignior*) ambassador present,[44] and the evidence from his successor's diary is that this rule was generally observed. The third task carried out by the ranking laymen in the papal chapel was to bring water for the pope to wash his hands. This happened on four occasions during mass, which gave even the ambassadors of smaller states, a fair chance of getting in at fourth place at some point during their stay at Rome. The first ceremonial washing took place before the pope put on his vestments (*capiat paramenta*), the second before the offertory, the third after the offertory and the fourth after the purification. The water would be brought by the four most senior laymen in the papal chapel, including a king or even the Emperor, should they be present. In the performance of these duties, visiting princes or their representatives symbolically demonstrated their allegiance to the Vicar of Christ on earth. Just as at other royal courts, the performance of intimate bodily service functioned as a mark of favour.[45]

According to Burchard, the selection of laymen for this role was at the discretion of the pope.[46] (It is likely that this was also the situation in relation to carrying the train.) By Grassi's time, however, and subsequently, the rules of precedence had been applied, and the senior laymen served in reverse order: the representative of the lowest-ranking prince or republic would bring the first bowl of water.[47] On Easter Sunday 1532, the water for the pope's hands was brought by the Venetian ambassador, the English ambassador, the Senator Urbis and the Imperial ambassador, in that order.[48] In an environment where it was usual for only one or two ambassadors to be attending any given feast, papal discretion might well have been adequate as a basis on which to choose participants. Grassi's rules point to a more tightly-ordered, hierarchical court culture.

[43] 'Cauda Vero Pluvialis Detur fFerenda Alicui Magno Nobili vel Oratori Laico.' Patrizi, *L'Oeuvre*, p. 260.

[44] BAV, MS Vat. Lat. 12270, fols. 92v–93r.

[45] Starkey, 'Representation through intimacy'.

[46] Patrizi, *L'Oeuvre*, p. 298: 'Quibus dictis cerimoniarius interrogans pontificem de quatuor ex nobilioribus aut oratoribus laicis quos vult sibi aquam pro lavandis minibus ministrare.'

[47] BAV, MS Vat. Lat. 12270 fol. 95r. Queller, *Office of Ambassador*, p. 201, does not acknowledge that this changed.

[48] BAV, MS Vat. Lat. 12276, fols. 172v–173r.

Moreover, by the time he was writing the presence of multiple long-term embassies in Rome was commonplace, and it is plausible that for reasons of practicality alone, some rules were necessary. A formal order enabled the popes to avoid constant requests for favour. This was particularly significant in the context of wartime when the envoys of hostile powers were present at mass. The stricter codification of ceremony did not imply, however, that there was no scope at all for flexibility, as will be shown below.

A second significant development apparent in the texts is the shift towards enforcement of the rule that excluded clerics holding the title of ambassador from the ceremonial roles discussed above. They took their place in a separate clerical order of precedence.[49] The distinction between laymen and clerics was already apparent in the work of Patrizi, but evidence from Burchard's diary suggests that during the 1480s and 1490s, it was sometimes ignored. On 24 May 1487, Ascension Day, the English ambassador John Weston, prior of the Order of St John of Jerusalem, was allowed to carry the train of the papal cope, although (Burchard noted) this duty was customarily reserved to laymen.[50] In 1489, bishops were permitted to carry the baldacchino, but only because there was a shortage of suitable lay personnel.[51] On Palm Sunday 1493, Burchard inadvertently omitted to summon a layman to carry the papal train and had to allow a protonotary, de Sermoneta, to do so instead.[52] By the 1520s, however, the evidence from Martinelli's diary is that exceptions were no longer made. While clerics were still sent to Rome as ambassadors, they were almost entirely excluded from ceremonial roles. As Chapter 4 will show, this stricter application of the ceremonial conventions had important implications for the selection of ambassadors to Rome.

b.   Re-thinking the order of precedence

The point of an order of precedence is precisely *to order*, to establish in symbolic form, a hierarchy of power with the aim of resolving or settling disputes. It cannot be a coincidence that the one section of his treatise in which Grassi most clearly demonstrated his lack of certainty about protocol concerned precisely the sphere in which power relations were

---

[49] For example, in the procession entering Consistory. See BAV, MS Vat. Lat. 12270, fol. 58v.
[50] Burchard, *Liber Notarum*, Vol. I, p. 201.   [51] Burchard, *Liber Notarum*, Vol. I, p. 262.
[52] Burchard, *Liber Notarum*, Vol. I, pp. 412–13.

most sharply symbolically contested.[53] He included in his *De Oratoribus* two different versions of the *Ordo Regum* (Order of Kings), with the note above the second 'alibi legitur' – 'elsewhere, one reads'.[54] The main list begins with the Emperor, then the king of the Romans, king of France, king of Spain, king of Aragon, king of Portugal and king of England (who is 'in discord' – *discors* – with the preceding three). The second, marginal list, headed 'alibi legitur' gives the king of the Romans, king of France, king of Castile and León, king of England, king of Aragon, king of Sicily and Jerusalem, king of Hungary and king of Portugal. The orders came, wrote Grassi, from Patrizi's book and from the records of the Camera and Cancelleria Apostolica.[55] No order of precedence is given in the surviving manuscripts of Patrizi's ceremonial identified by Dykmans. They distinguish only between ranks of princes in general (though Patrizi does note that the Imperial ambassador precedes the Senator Urbis, representative of the citizens of Rome).[56] But the order had evidently existed in Patrizi's time because Burchard referred back to decisions that had been made in the pontificate of Pius II (for example, during a 1487 dispute between Scotland and Hungary).[57]

Contests over the order of precedence arose regularly, as dynastic marriages and accidents of inheritance changed the dynamics of European politics and as rulers were raised to the rank of duke (or later grandduke). The union of the crowns of Castile and Aragon created a Spanish monarchy; the kings of England continued to assert their right to the crown of France; following the split of the Holy Roman Empire in the mid-sixteenth century, the Spanish launched a campaign for precedence over France; the newly-elevated dukes of Mantua and Florence fought for an appropriate place in the hierarchy.[58] The order of precedence was

---

[53] For another instance in which ceremonialists could not agree on correct protocol, this one concerning the 1505 creation of a cardinal, see DeSilva, 'Ritual negotiations', p. 152.

[54] BAV, MS Vat. Lat. 12270, fols. 98r–99r.

[55] BAV, MS Vat. Lat. 12270, fol. 98r. The order of kings in the main text is given as: Emperor, king of the Romans, France, Spain, Aragon, Portugal, England (in dispute with the previous three), Sicily (contending with the King of Portugal), Scotland, Hungary (in dispute with one another), Navarre, Cyprus, Bohemia, Poland, Dacia (Romania), Majorca, Sardinia, Cyprus [sic], Norway, Sweden, Armenia, Ireland, Bosnia. The order of dukes is given as: Brittany, Burgundy, Bavaria, Count Palatine, Saxony, Marquess of Brandenburg, Austria, Savoy, Milan, Venice, Bavaria, Francia (an ancient title pertaining to the kingdom of the Franks), Lorraine, Battonya (in Hungary), Orléans, Genoa, Ferrara. Grassi notes that the dukes of Bavaria, Francia, Lorraine, Battonya and Orléans do not pledge obedience to the pope because they are subjects of the Emperor. Note here that Venice and Genoa were treated as duchies although their Doges were elected.

[56] Patrizi, *L'Oeuvre*, p. 182.   [57] Burchard, *Liber Notarum*, Vol. I, p. 180.

[58] Levin, 'A New World Order'.

the symbolic terrain on which these disputes played out.[59] Grassi advised new ambassadors at Rome to be prepared for such contests, which, he said, were frequently seen between the French and the English (because the king of England claimed the crown of France).[60] In May 1504, pledging obedience to Pope Julius II, the English ambassador pronounced his monarch 'Henricus, Dei gratia, Anglie et Francie Rex et dux Hibernie etc.' to which his French counterpart insisted on responding.[61] In December 1509, Christopher Bainbridge, archbishop of York and ambassador for the king of England, took a place in front of his French counterpart, Étienne Poncher, archbishop of Embrun, and had to be shooed back to his proper seat by Grassi.[62]

In order to appreciate the full significance of these interactions, it is important to bear in mind that envoys were understood to embody their princes. By sitting, or standing in the place allotted to another prince's ambassador, they might symbolically proclaim their superiority, or even stake a claim to his territory. Ambassadors were expected to assert their prince's position in the order of precedence and to guard against attempts by other diplomats to usurp that place for their own masters. Questions of precedence frequently aroused contention, particularly if an ambassador believed his prince's honour had been slighted, and given the importance of honour in the conduct of international relations during this period, it should be no surprise that there are many such cases that might be cited. In 1459, at the Congress of Mantua, Pius II had to rule that 'a back seat should imply no loss and a front seat no increase of honour or privilege'. That failed to resolve a heated dispute between the Venetians and Savoyards and later, Pius records that the princes and ambassadors of Italy were seated by district.[63] Even in 1526, by which time matters were more firmly regulated, Clement VII still had to arbitrate on occasion. This incident was described by the Mantuan ambassador Francesco Gonzaga:

It being Christmas day in the chapel, the Scottish ambassador went to sit in the ambassadors' place; Portugal having carried the pope's train then returned to sit down, but Scotland didn't want to give up his place, saying that there, where he was, was his place, and that Portugal should sit beneath him if he wanted to sit down; Portugal refused to do it saying that his king preceded Scotland; they went on arguing for a bit until finally the master of ceremonies was called, who went to the pope to find out who should take precedence; His Holiness said that Portugal

---

[59] Visceglia, 'Cerimoniale', p. 126.   [60] BAV, MS Vat. Lat. 12270, fol. 47r.
[61] Burchard, *Liber Notarum*, Vol. II, p. 451.
[62] Grassi, BL Add. MS 8441, fol. 328v, cited in Chambers, *Cardinal Bainbridge*, pp. 26–7.
[63] Pius, *I Commentarii*, pp. 448–51, 570–3, 576–7 (*Secret Memoirs*, pp. 117, 131, 133).

should be first; on seeing that Scotland got up and left the mass, saying he didn't intend to put his king in that position, and Portugal remained in his place.[64]

The ambassadors of Scotland and Portugal were well-mannered by comparison to their counterparts of three decades earlier. On 28 May 1490, Pope Innocent VIII learned that the Neapolitan ambassador was planning to come to mass armed in order to settle his dispute over precedence with the Scots. He called together his advisers in an effort to avoid a showdown at Pentecost, when he himself would preside. Such was the animosity among the diplomats in Rome – the week before had seen contention between not only Scotland and Naples but also Venice, Milan, Florence and several envoys from the Imperial princes – that the only practicable solution was for every diplomat involved to absent himself from mass.[65] Resolving conflicts over precedence was a delicate business, because the ambassador's duty to promote his prince's honour made it difficult to back down in the face of a rival. For every diplomat in Rome to absent himself from mass was an extreme solution, but there were other possible compromises. In 1485, for example, during a dispute between the ambassadors of Milan and Savoy, Innocent had ruled that they should take turns to attend.[66] England and Spain adopted the same strategy in 1487.[67] Twenty-four years later, the Anglo-Spanish dispute was still going on: in 1511, Kings Ferdinand of Aragon and Henry VIII of England, then in alliance, negotiated over how best to avoid open contention at the Lateran Council. They considered alternating their ambassadors' attendance, or that the English might accredit the Spanish envoy. Eventually, they took advantage of the separation of lay and clerical envoys in papal ceremony, and England was represented by Cardinal Bainbridge, who would sit among his fellow cardinals, and another long-standing English resident in Rome, Silvestro Gigli, also a cleric: neither would have to compete for position with a Spanish lay

---

[64] 'Essendo il di de Natale in capella lo Ambassatore di Scotia a seder al loco dove stanno li oratori et havendo portato Portugal la coda al Papa et dappoi ritornato per sedere Scotia non li volse cedere dicendo che li dove stava era il loco suo et che si dovesse mettere di sotto lui sel volea sedere Portugallo recusando di farlo dicendo che'l suo Re precedea Scotia steteron per un pezzo in contentione finalmente fu chiamato il Maestro de Ceremonie qual ando al Papa et intender da S. Santita che dovea precedere la qual fece declaratione che Portugallo havesse ad essere primo vedendo Scozia cosi se levo et partitosi da la missa dicendo che non intendea di far questo caricho al suo Re et Portugallo resto al loco suo.' ASMn, Archivio Gonzaga 873, c. 3r.
[65] Burchard, *Liber Notarum*, Vol. I, p. 309.
[66] Burchard, *Liber Notarum*, Vol. I, pp. 109–10.
[67] Burchard, *Liber Notarum*, Vol. I, p. 199.

diplomat.[68] The following year, Henry took up Ferdinand's second proposed compromise, mandating the Spanish ambassador to add his name to the adherents of the Holy League.[69]

As the order of precedence became more explicitly codified, and scope for the exercise of papal discretion narrowed, participants in ceremony sought new methods to challenge it. Just as there was scope for dissimulation in the world of negotiation where, as Chapter 2 showed, ambassadors periodically stepped into their private persona, so there was scope for the manipulation of ceremonial rules. For example, the ambassador's *personal* status could be used to trump the rules of precedence. Roosen suggests that this came into play only in rare cases and ought to be set aside in the interests of establishing the general rules of ceremonial.[70] In Rome, however, high-ranking visitors were common enough, and the pressure to subvert the rules and gain symbolic status was such, that the matter merits consideration. The cases that follow illustrate how popes might, through the exercise of discretion, hint symbolically at favour for a particular power without committing to that favour in speech or text.

In 1492, ducal status should have trumped the order of precedence, but it was in turn trumped by nepotism. Present for mass were an ambassador of Venice, a duke representing Naples, a lay French orator who (according to Burchard) was a relative of the Pope and Don Federico, second son of the king of Naples. Burchard noted that the duke should have gone third, but the pope had given his relative priority.[71] In 1503, debate ensued about the order in which a mixed embassy from the duke of Ferrara, including a protonotary and laymen, should greet the Pope. The matter was complicated by the fact that the protonotary was the duke's son. Despite the protests of ambassadors from Spain, France and Portugal, that laymen preceded not only protonotaries but bishops too, Burchard allowed the protonotary to go first.[72] This symbol of favour to the duke of Ferrara was evidently a priority for the new pope Julius II, who was in the business of building military alliances. Sophisticated manipulation of the rules is apparent in the diplomatic service of John Stewart, second duke of Albany. In June 1520, the Duke came to pledge obedience at the court of Pope Leo X as the ambassador of King

[68] British Library, Additional MS, 28,572, fol. 101 (*L&P*, Vol. I, pp. 501–2), discussed in Fletcher, 'Performing Henry'.
[69] Sanuto, *I Diarii*, XIV, cols. 224–5. 'A dì 17 si farà la 3a sessione et si publicherà l'intrar di la liga che à fato il serenissimo re de Ingaltera, qual, per sue letere di 26 april, à mandato in ampla forma a l'orator yspano sotoscrivi a la liga per suo nome, et si farà fuogi e feste.' (*L&P*, Vol. I, p. 557).
[70] Roosen, 'Diplomatic ceremonial', p. 462.
[71] Burchard, *Liber Notarum*, Vol. I, p. 387.   [72] Burchard, *Liber Notarum*, Vol. II, p. 422.

James V of Scotland. However, the fact that he was both a duke and the infant king's regent complicated the rules of precedence. It would have been inappropriate to put him in the lowly position normally allocated to the king of Scotland's ambassador, given that he was in effect, the heir to that kingdom, so he was allowed to sit with the cardinal-deacons at mass rather than with the other ambassadors, although this concession was made also (according to the master-of-ceremonies Biagio Martinelli) 'by the grace of the Pope, because they are related'.[73] Some of the scope for papal discretion in Burchard's early discussion of ablutions, in which the choice of participants was left to the will of the pontiff, had evidently survived.

Ten years later, in 1530, Albany was appointed French ambassador to the Holy See, and this posed new problems.[74] The king of France came third in the standard order of precedence, after the Holy Roman Emperor and the king of the Romans. However, dukes outranked ambassadors. When Clement VII called in Martinelli to discuss the appropriate placing for the duke in the papal chapel, the ceremonialists enquired whether the Pope wanted Albany to be considered as a duke or as the French ambassador.[75] The conclusion was that he should be treated as a duke (and a relative of the pope's besides), however it was agreed that nothing should be said about the fact that previously he had been elevated to sit with the cardinal-deacons, presumably in the hope that no one would remember.[76] There was scope for different degrees of symbolic favour, depending on circumstances. In November 1530, the duke was responsible for carrying the papal train and at Christmas 1531, the order in which the ambassadors brought water for washing the pope's hands was (by reverse precedence) Venice, England, Imperial, duke of Albany.[77] However, he did not always choose to assert his precedence. At the Candlemas celebrations of 1532, the task of carrying the papal train fell to the lower-ranking English ambassador, while Albany took responsibility for the ablutions. The most plausible explanation for this is that while Albany liked to pull rank over the Holy Roman Emperor, he was happy to cede precedence to England, thus indicating his commitment to the Anglo-French alliance.[78] There were surely more reasons for Albany's appointment as ambassador than out-scoring the Imperialists in the order of precedence, not least his family

---

[73] 'ex gratia Papae quia eius affinis.' BAV, MS Vat. Lat. 12276, fols. 32r–32v. The Duke's cousin and sister-in-law Madeleine de la Tour d'Auvergne was married to Lorenzo II de' Medici. See his entry in the *Oxford Dictionary of National Biography*.

[74] I discuss envoys who served more than one prince in Chapter 4.

[75] BAV, MS Vat. Lat. 12276, fol. 151r. [76] *Ibid.*, fol. 151v.

[77] *Ibid.*, fols. 151v–152v. [78] BAV, MS Vat. Lat. 12276, fol. 153r.

ties to the Medici Pope Clement. Nonetheless, it must have been a satisfying side-effect for the French to be 'top nation' in the ceremonial *teatrum mundi*, especially in the context of the later 1520s and early 1530s, when the country had suffered serious reversals in the Italian wars. While cases like those of Albany and the Ferrara princeling may not have been common, they make the point that the personal status of an envoy was not irrelevant.

By the 1520s, even the interviews which the Pope might hold on matters of importance with ambassadors were expected to be conducted in conformity with the order of precedence. When a pope wished to ignore the rules, as Clement VII did in order to consult with two Imperial ambassadors, Miguel Mai and Andrea Borgo, about the duke of Savoy's demand for 200,000 ducats to defend himself from the Lutheran 'furore', *before* meeting the duke of Albany (who should have preceded them), he did so only at the risk of 'scandal'. The Ferrarese diplomat Antonio Romeo explained that Clement saw them 'first and separately from the others to avoid the scandals which could arise over precedence between them and the duke of Albany'.[79] It is not clear whether the French ever discovered that transgression of protocol. Quick-witted ambassadors could, however, use the threat of 'scandal' to assert their right to a papal audience. In early 1529, having been obliged to wait several weeks for an audience due to Clement's illness, the English diplomats Sir Francis Bryan and Pietro Vanni discovered that the Imperial ambassador had been allowed to see the Pope and used that fact as leverage to gain a hearing themselves. 'So as not to demonstrate partiality, His Holiness gave them audience,' wrote their Venetian counterpart Gasparo Contarini.[80] Whatever the realities of the Pope's current political alliances, and however much the court might be aware of them, appearances and protocol were all-important. Particularly in the context of wartime, a careful observance of precedence enabled Clement to avoid conflict, returning to the original function of ordering in its sense of resolving or settling matters.

---

[79] 'Dal Signor Andrea da Borgo ho inteso che esso & il Signor Mayo hoggi sono stati chiamati da N. S. & che hanno detto il parere suo prima che fussero chiamati li altri oratori in quel che diro di sotto & che lo dissero prima & appartatamente da li altri per evitare li scandali che potessero nascere per le precedentie fra essi & il Duca dalbania.' ASMo, Archivio Estense, Ambasciatori, Italia, Roma, b. 32, c. 214iii/11. Antonio Romeo to Duke of Ferrara. The letter is undated but an archive note suggests 15 August 1530.

[80] 'Li do Oratori di Anglia doppo che sepeno l'orator Cesareo esser sta admesso ad far riverentia et basar li piedi del Pont. hanno anchor loro tentato lo istesso, talmente che per non dimonstrar partialita, Sua Sant. alli 6 li dete audientia.' Biblioteca Nazionale Marciana, Codices Italiani VII, 1043 (=7616) Lettere di Gasparo Contarini (1528–1529) (hereafter G. Contarini), fol. 172v.

c.   Contextualising Grassi's handbook

A consequence of the ever-stricter regulation of diplomacy was institu-tionalised manipulation of the rules and an accommodation to pretence. The idea that Renaissance diplomats engaged in both simulation and dissimulation is bordering on the commonplace.[81] Extracts from two sixteenth-century texts on the ambassador (discussed above, Chapter 2) illustrate contemporary thinking. Machiavelli advised Raffaello Girolami:

> And if, to be sure, sometimes you need to conceal a fact with words, do it in such a way that it does not become known, or, if it does become known, that you have a quick and ready defense.[82]

Étienne Dolet wrote of the ambassador:

> If he has some business to transact with the people of Venice or the Pope at Rome or other princes of Italy, inasmuch as they are past masters of pretense and dissimulation, he should likewise pretend and dissimulate, and should let his speech be greatly at variance with his thoughts.[83]

Both Machiavelli and Dolet allowed for the possibility that the diplomat might simulate (that is, actively feign or pretend), as well as dissimulate (withdraw into silence permitting a false impression to stand).[84] The idea of the courtier as dissimulator is, of course, standard fare, immortalised in the *Libro del Cortegiano* of Baldassarre Castiglione, himself a former diplomat.[85] It should be no surprise that as the papal court became more 'courtly', the behaviour of its courtiers accommodated to these new realities. However, the literature on diplomacy has not fully acknow-ledged the extent to which dissimulation and its fellow, simulation, were institutionalised. For example, in his notes of advice to be given to new ambassadors by the master of ceremonies, Paride Grassi wrote:

> Before they have their first audience with the pope, in the public Consistory, they should under no circumstances leave the house, even if they are invited by a prince, duke, cardinal or whosoever, nor allow any person at all to visit them publicly, not even the pope himself, *unless in private, or in disguise, or secretly at night, if need be.*[86]

---

[81] J. R. Woodhouse, 'Honourable dissimulation: some Italian advice for the Renaissance diplomat', *Proceedings of the British Academy* 84 (1994), 25–50.

[82] Machiavelli, 'Advice', pp. 116–17.   [83] Dolet, 'De Officio Legati', p. 88.

[84] Snyder, *Dissimulation*, especially pp. 110–12.

[85] *Ibid.*, pp. 74–5. Cesare Vasoli, 'Il Cortegiano, il Diplomatico, il Principe: Intellettuali e Potere nell'Italia del Cinquecento', in Adriano Prosperi (ed.), *La Corte e il "Cortegiano"*, 2 vols (Rome: Bulzoni, 1980), Vol. II, pp. 173–93 (p. 192). Woodhouse also discusses *The Courtier* as a manual for diplomacy in 'Honourable dissimulation', pp. 28–30.

[86] 'Primum antequam audientiam in Consistorio publico a Papa habuerint nequaquam extra domum etiama Principe Duce Cardinali vel quoquam alio invitati exeant, nec penitus aliquem quicumque ille sit publice visitent nec ipsumdenique Pontificem nisi

This was a substantial shift from Patrizi, who had simply written that ambassadors should not go out in public before they had visited the pope.[87] While on the one hand trying to impose the formalities, Grassi acknowledged that provided things *appeared* to proceed in line, the rules could be broken. Both in the symbolic world of the court at Rome, and in its practical functions, pretence and the performance of fictions were part of day-to-day life. Even while the masters-of-ceremonies tried to maintain protocol, they also accommodated a certain amount of *trompe l'oeil*.

Notable here is Grassi's implicit acknowledgement that ambassadors might be conscious participants in a fiction. This is not (or not only) performance as an analytic category of the modern historian, but performance as discussed in Renaissance Rome and an example of the 'performative self' of the Renaissance individual. One of several forms of identity conceptualised by John Jeffries Martin in his study of the 'self' in this period, the 'performative self' was not necessarily engaged in deception: performance, whether in street theatre or ritual, was also 'a means through which men and women were able to forge a sense of community or belonging'.[88] One case in which this is apparent is in the staging of entries. In May 1486, for example, two ambassadors from the king of Poland, who had in fact arrived in Rome four days earlier 'without pomp' and had stayed 'secretly' in the city until the appointed hour for their entry, left the city, 'more secretly still', riding out to the Spinelli vineyard at Monte Mario and thence to the church of San Lazzaro to begin their entry.[89] It was acceptable, in practice, to feign a formal entry. Indeed, it was not even particularly deceitful, because what mattered was the spectacle, the proper performance of the entry that established them ritually as part of the ambassadorial community at the papal court. Yet while simulation done well might be the order of the day in Rome, done badly it was worse than none at all. When, in 1504, twelve Genoese ambassadors entered Rome, Burchard noted that in fact they had already

---

privato vel transformato habitu, vel nocte clam ac secrete si opus erit.' BAV, MS Vat. Lat. 12270, fol. 39v. My italics.

[87] 'Neque Prius Exibut in Publicum quam Visitaverint Summum Pontificem'. Patrizi, *L'Oeuvre*, p. 207.

[88] Martin, *Myths of Renaissance Individualism*, p. 36.

[89] Burchard, *Liber Notarum*, Vol. I, p. 153. 'Feria quarta, xvii maii, hora xx vel circa, intrarunt Urbem venerabilis d. Joannes [...] et quidam miles laicus, oratores illustrissimi Cazimiri Polonie regis pro obedientia SS. D. N. prestanda, cum equis de suis circa xxx a pluribus curialibus polonis associati. Hi venerunt Romam die sabbati proximi preteriti, in sero, sine pompa et hospitio recepti sunt in domo Bufalorum, ubi manserunt secrete usque in ohdiernum diem, quo, circa horam xviii, equitarunt per viam transtyberinam secretius cum suis et amicis ad domum de Spinellis extra portam Viridarii, ubi expectarunt horam convenientem pro introitu suo; qua adveniente, equitarunt usque ad ecclesiam sancti Lazari leprosorum.'

been in Rome for eight days, or thereabouts, '*secrete*' but '*omnibus scientibus*' – with everyone knowing about it. The papal household did not go out of the city gates to meet them, as they should have done, past the Spinelli church, but welcomed them instead inside the gates.[90] One breach of protocol, the lack of thorough secrecy, deserved another, the inferior welcome.

Much recent analysis of early modern ceremony has focused on its symbolic function, employing the concepts of performance and performativity to explore its uses and meaning. In speaking of diplomatic performances, however, we need to disentangle the two ways in which we might talk of diplomats 'performing'. On the one hand, diplomats performed in the way that any participant in ceremony performs: by engaging in particular symbolic rituals. On the other, diplomats were also performers in a more literal sense. While other participants in papal ceremony were there on their own account (cardinals, for example), ambassadors were there as representatives. In his ceremonial activity, the ambassador symbolically communicated the policy and person of his prince. Ambassadors were actors both in the simple sense of doing things, and in the theatrical sense of playing the part of another. They are not the only participants in ceremony who might be regarded as having multiple identities: one thinks, for example, of cardinal-protectors. However, even cardinal-protectors did not stand in for an individual in the way that ambassadors of princes did. Unpicking this particularity of ambassadorial performances is, I think, relevant to a comprehensive understanding of both early modern ceremonial and the figure of the diplomat.

The development of a relatively firm order of precedence in Rome demonstrates both the shifting nature of papal government and the growing formalisation of diplomatic practice. In the later fifteenth and early sixteenth century, ambassadors were few enough in number that the system could function on a relatively ad-hoc basis. After 1494, in the context of war and as the numbers of envoys grew, clearer rules became necessary, but as the regulations became stricter, ambassadors found ways to circumvent them. Historians of diplomacy are accustomed to the idea of simulation and dissimulation in speech, or in text, but these

---

[90] Burchard, *Liber Notarum*, Vol. II, p. 455. 'Post prandium, post horam xxii, per portam Viridarii intraverunt Urbem xii oratores Januenses, laici omnes [...] recepti a familiis pape et cardinalium, more solito. Fuerant in Urbe ad octo dies vel circa secrete, omnibus scientibus, et hodie exierunt usque ad domum olim Petri Caranza, iuxta viridarium pape: inde exierunt, precedentibus lxx mulis cum salmis etc. et circiter lxxx equis [...] familia pape non exivit portam Urbis, sed intra et iuxta porta accepit eos, episcopo Britonoriensi pro omnibus loquente.'

cases highlight the presence of the former in the world of spectacle and ceremony too. While the masters-of-ceremonies permitted some degree of adaptation and pretence in the staging of this spectacle, there were limits to their tolerance. As stage managers of the theatre of the world, they were tasked with ensuring an honourable performance. Their ceremonial texts demonstrate how the papal court adapted to the increasing use of resident diplomacy in a context where the curia itself was shifting towards a more elaborate, formalised courtly style. Details of rank became important; scope for papal discretion was reduced. But as the rules became firmer, the actors found ways around them. Through secrecy and simulation they appeared to conform. The ambiguity of ceremonial symbolism permitted hints at favour. So did the ambiguity of the diplomat's persona: his two selves might be used to a prince's advantage. His personal status could be deployed to manoeuvre around the rules of precedence. To achieve a more spectacular arrival in Rome, he could enter the city first as a 'private' individual and return in his official guise a few days later. In subsequent chapters, I explore the ways these two *personae* were deployed in the realms of hospitality, travel and gift-giving.

4   The personnel of diplomacy

Writers on the office of ambassador were wont to provide exhaustive lists of the desired characteristics of the diplomat. Étienne Dolet wrote that he should be of middle age, a man of ability and worth (nobility, though not necessary, would be a bonus). He should be 'suitable to his office in figure, face and stature'. He should 'possess such ability as a speaker as to be able to turn, lead, draw, and compel the minds of those with whom he may be dealing.'[1] Against the backdrop of the shifting political context outlined in Chapter 1, the conceptualisations of the ambassador discussed in Chapter 2 and the ceremonial considerations assessed in Chapter 3, this chapter reflects on trends in the type of men employed as envoys to the court of Rome. Their variety is illustrated in the memoirs of Pope Pius II. A French embassy to Rome in 1462 included two cardinals, two bishops and 'a number of abbots and most exalted nobles headed by Pierre, Count of Chaumont, whose character and years gave him authority. There were also among the envoys certain doctors and secretaries of the king. It was a brilliant embassy befitting a sovereign, with a great number of horsemen and a long line of attendants.'[2] Special embassies were as splendid as could be afforded: they functioned to convey the wealth and status of the prince or republic they represented. Their size meant that they could combine all manner of expertise: a sociable nobleman could drop into appropriate court circles; doctors of law could draft treaties; bishops could testify to the strength of their national church. In selecting a resident ambassador, often the sole representative of his prince, choices had to be made. I argue here that the most significant shift in those choices came with the outbreak of war in 1494.

The chapter deals first with ambassadors themselves, tracking the transition from early unofficial envoys through formalised residence and into the period of the Italian wars. Agents and secretaries, below

[1] Dolet, 'De Officio Legati', pp. 82–5.
[2] Pius, *Commentarii* Vol. II, pp. 1462–3 (*Secret Memoirs*, p. 227).

the rank of ambassador, also had important roles to play, and the chapter's second section considers diplomatic staff below the rank of ambassador and the functioning of the diplomatic household. Finally, it assesses the sometimes elusive role of women: princesses, mistresses, diplomatic wives and courtesans. For the most part women were excluded from official roles in diplomacy, and particularly so at the ecclesiastical court of Rome. Nonetheless, their presence and contribution to diplomatic work may sometimes be discerned.

a.   Personnel choices

Étienne Dolet, who served as secretary to the French ambassador to Venice in 1528–9, struggled to make up his mind whether clerics or laymen made better ambassadors. In his treatise on the office of ambassador, Dolet wrote:

> Up to the present time, however, it has been the prevalent practice among kings and other princes to employ men of ecclesiastical rank on embassies, I suppose either because of their reputation for letters and learning, or because they think that in view of their holy character they will be in less danger of personal injury.[3]

He went on to say that the clerical or secular status of a proposed ambassador made 'no difference': now that the nobility took the study of letters seriously, the need to send clerics because of their superior learning was a thing of the past. He did, however, concede that 'perhaps' it would be more appropriate to send a secular ambassador to a secular court, and an ecclesiastical ambassador to an ecclesiastical one.[4]

Dolet's uncertainty on this theme is not surprising, given the changing patterns of diplomatic personnel. Broadly speaking, with the outbreak of war in Italy, there was a move away from the employment of clerics as diplomats towards the employment of laymen. While Burchard did not identify the status of every ambassador he mentioned in his diary, his records indicate a shift towards lay representation after the French invasion. Clerics outnumber laymen in his records of ambassadors to Rome for seven of the nine years before 1494 but for none of the ten years afterward. However, the patterns are complex. Different states tended towards different models of representation. In practice, suitable candidates (loyal, competent, capable speakers of Italian and not needed for other roles) were often few. As Chapter 3 showed, the rules of ceremony at Rome gave an impetus to the employment of laymen too, and as the regulations were more tightly enforced, the imperative of such a choice

---

[3] Dolet, 'De Officio Legati', p. 83.   [4] Dolet, 'De Officio Legati', pp. 83–4.

increased. Giry-Deloison has noted that in England and France, wartime gave an impetus to the employment of military men, and this influenced appointments to Italy too.[5] Yet caution is necessary: trends in diplomatic representation are difficult to track. There are many variables: the exigencies of war or peace; the availability of personnel; the priorities of a new prince; the perceived priorities of a new pope. It is, however, possible to make some observations about developments over the period 1450–1530. In this section, I discuss in turn the practice of the Italian and ultramontane powers before 1494, the employment of Italians in foreign diplomatic service, and the rise of the 'soldier-diplomat' or 'courtier-diplomat' in the early years of the sixteenth century.

i.   *The Italian states pre-1494: lawyers and humanists*

Anello Arcamone, resident ambassador in Rome for King Ferrante of Naples from 1473 to 1486, was typical of the men sent as envoys to Rome by the Italian princely states. Trained in law and from a prominent local family, he had spent time in royal administration and had served as an envoy to Venice before his posting to Rome. His replacement, Antonio d'Alessandro, was likewise a lawyer and had been a royal councillor.[6] Both Anello and Antonio were laymen, and this was a significant difference between the practice of the Italian states and that of other European powers. Of the five men who served as resident agents in Rome for Milan between 1450 and 1500, two (Nicodemo Tranchedini and Agostino Rossi) were certainly laymen; two others were lawyers (Ottone del Carretto and Jacopo Calcaterra) and no mention is made of their clerical status. The only identifiable cleric in Milanese service at Rome was Stefano Taverna, resident from 1489 to 1498, who became bishop of Parma in 1497,[7] though the Milanese also engaged the services of curia officials to assist their resident agents.[8] Guglielmo Rocca, Ferrante d'Aragona's ambassador to Rome in the 1460s, was a churchman, but as Dover points out in his study of ambassadors to Rome during the papacy of Paul II (1464–71), 'very few' were clerics.[9] Many of these

---

[5] Charles Giry-Deloison, 'Le Personnel Diplomatique au Début du XVIe Ssiècle. L'exemple des Relations Franco-Anglaises de l'Avènement de Henry VII au Camp du Drap d'Or (1485–1520)', *Journal des Savants* (July–December 1987), 205–53.

[6] Dover, 'Royal diplomacy', pp. 70, 75.

[7] Lydia Cerioni, *La Diplomazia Sforzesca nella Seconda Metà del Quattrocento e i Suoi Cifrari Segreti*, 2 vols (Rome: Il centro di ricerca editore, 1970), Vol. I, biographies on pp. 152, 158, 217, 242 and the listing of envoys on pp. 105–9.

[8] Leverotti, *Diplomazia e Governo*, p. 78.

[9] Dover, 'Royal diplomacy', p. 93 and 'Saper la mente', p. 24.

Italian lay ambassadors had legal training or a humanist background. Agostino Rossi, for example, was a doctor of both laws (that is, canon and civil law). In 1465, he replaced another jurist, Ottone del Carretto, as resident diplomat in Rome. Rossi had worked with del Carretto at the papal court before, and was thus both practised in curia protocol and acquainted with curia personnel.[10] Such experience was an important consideration. When in 1457, the secret council of Milan sought to send one Corradino Giorgi to the court of France, the duke intervened, requesting them to send someone else, because Giorgi 'was not very expert in French affairs'.[11] Knowledge of the court to which one was posted was a valued asset. The detailed advice that Paride Grassi recommended should be given to ambassadors in advance of their first public audience suggests that many new arrivals were poorly prepared for the occasion.[12] Those diplomats who had experience of and access to Roman noble circles must have had a considerable advantage over newcomers.

Many ambassadors had enjoyed a humanist education. An intellectual method, rather than an ideology, humanism's emphasis on rhetoric, good Latin writing and oratory gave potential diplomats skills that states valued.[13] In turn, diplomatic employment gave some humanists an income that sustained their philological activities. Niccolò Perotti (1429–80), a humanist scholar in the service of Cardinal Bessarion, combined work translating Greek texts for Nicholas V with diplomatic missions to Naples, Mantua, Germany and Venice. He wrote a life of his patron and a commentary on the Latin language.[14] Yet, it is important to beware simple cause-and-effect models here. As Beverley has noted for Venice, men who were heavily engaged in diplomacy often had a humanist education, but this correlation does not mean there was a causal relationship. Both the diplomatic role and the education may have been a product of their membership of a 'high political echelon'.[15] Nor should humanist and diplomatic cultures be elided. Senatore makes the point that humanists who might write to one another in their best classicizing Latin style adopted a quite different register when they corresponded in their capacity of chancellery official or ambassador.[16] Moreover, while

---

[10] Leverotti, *Diplomazia e Governo*, p. 73.
[11] 'Non Era Molto Esperto nelle Cose di Francia', Leverotti, *Diplomazia e Governo*, p. 82, fn 197.
[12] BAV, MS Vat. Lat. 12270, fols. 39r–47v.
[13] D'Amico, *Renaissance Humanism*, pp. 35, 45.
[14] D'Amico, *Renaissance Humanism*, p. 13.
[15] Beverley, 'Venetian ambassadors', pp. 160–1.
[16] Senatore, *Uno Mundo de Carta*, p. 169.

humanist education was valued, it was not an essential qualification for envoys. The detailed analyses of Milanese diplomatic personnel by Cerioni, Leverotti and Margaroli suggest that a far wider variety of factors than humanistic education were relevant in selection for diplomatic roles. The *famigli cavalcanti* (literally, 'riding servants') who served in Francesco Sforza's diplomatic service between 1450 and 1466 included men with experience in military affairs and tax-collecting; some were appointed for their family conections (Sforza's regime-building is apparent here); they were in general, close to the new duke. Indeed, their title, *famigli*, indicated their privileged relationship with him: they were men of proven fidelity.[17] As such, they could be trusted to embody their prince.

Venice was exceptional in sending high-ranking citizens to reside abroad, but Beverley has argued that as a result Venetian resident embassies tended to be relatively short-term. Individual patricians preferred to avoid long absences from domestic politics, and in turn, the system helped to limit the development of overly close and potentially disloyal relationships at the host court.[18] Genoa sent twelve of its leading citizens on embassy to Rome in 1504, all laymen, but this was a short-term special embassy.[19] Even among the Italian powers, while it is possible to identify certain common traits among the group of diplomats in Rome, the choice of ambassador was contingent on the particular circumstances of the prince or republic sending him. Italian princes, moreover, arguably had less need for ambassadors to personify them at the papal court. They could and did come to Rome, which their ultramontane counterparts did rarely. They could despatch high-ranking special envoys to convey their messages in a matter of days, which the northern rulers could not.

While by no means ubiquitous it is clear that the posting of laymen to Rome was an Italian practice first, only later adopted by the ultramontane powers. The diary of papal master-of-ceremonies Johannes Burchard for May–June 1492 identifies five powers with lay orators in Rome: Venice, Milan, Florence, Siena and Poland. Spain and England were represented by bishops, and Poland's double embassy included a bishop as well as his lay counterpart.[20] The Italian states arguably had more dealings with the papacy as temporal power than did the rest of Europe, and it is likely that the 'dual loyalty' of clerics was felt particularly sharply on the Italian peninsula, where the papacy was more assertive

[17] Leverotti, *Diplomazia e Governo*, pp. 18–19.
[18] Beverley, 'Venetian ambassadors', pp. 218–26.
[19] Burchard, *Liber Notarum*, Vol. II, pp. 434–5.
[20] Burchard, *Liber Notarum*, Vol. I, pp. 346, 364, 370.

about interfering with appointments to benefices.[21] Elsewhere in Europe, the popes generally respected the right of local rulers to select bishops. In Venice, however, they did not, and the Republic responded by banning churchmen posted to Rome from accepting gifts of benefices, a point discussed further in Chapter 7.

ii.   The ultramontane powers pre-1494: a clerical tradition

The practice of the ultramontane powers was markedly different. They typically entrusted their curia business to a resident churchman, preferably a bishop, who might well hold other offices in the structures of the curia to supplement the income from his benefice. John Shirwood, who acted as English orator to Rome in the 1470s and 1480s, was a protonotary and held the office of treasurer of the English pilgrim hospital in Rome.[22] That, of course, also gave him reason to stay in Rome beyond the six-month limit, still an issue at the time of his embassy. The English crown also used the bishopric of Worcester as a reward for its Italian diplomatic agents at the papal court. It was held from 1497 to 1521 by members of the Gigli family of Lucca, first Giovanni Gigli and then Silvestro; Girolamo Ghinucci, who took over the post in 1522, was appointed ambassador to Rome in 1525.[23] Among the clerics in the Imperial service was Philibert Naturelli, ambassador for the king of the Romans, resident in Rome between 1497 and 1501.[24] One cleric in the French service was Claude de Seyssel, employed by Louis XII of France as his ambassador to Rome in 1513–15. An illegitimate son of the governor of Piedmont, Claude went into the church and studied canon and civil law at Pavia and Turin. He was a councillor to the duke of Savoy before entering Louis' service, where his legal experience proved useful when Louis decided to divorce his wife Jeanne. He was a conclavist with Cardinal Georges d'Amboise in 1503 when Amboise was *papabile*, and went on embassy to England. In 1509, he became bishop of Marseilles; having participated in a number of other diplomatic missions, he went on embassy to Rome in 1513 following the election of Leo X, and stayed

---

[21] Fletcher, *Our Man in Rome*, pp. 22–3, 41, 49, 72.   [22] Behrens, 'Origins', p. 645.

[23] See Bell, *Handlist*, according to which Silvestro Gigli was an ambassador 1512–1521 (when he died). His uncle, Giovanni Gigli, had been appointed bishop of Worcester in 1497, a post which he held for only a year until his death, but had clearly had a diplomatic role earlier. Ghinucci became Auditor of the Camera in 1514: see Mandell Creighton, 'The Italian bishops of Worcester', in *Historical Essays and Reviews* (London: Longmans, Green, 1911), pp. 202–34 and his *DBI* entry. He was nuncio to England in 1518 and appointed bishop of Worcester on 26 September 1522 after Giulio de' Medici ceded the position.

[24] Burchard, Vol. I, p. 414; Vol. II, p. 270.

until his master's death in January 1515.[25] Though there was a bias towards clerical representation, there were some significant differences in embassy practice among the ultramontane powers. The French embassy secretary, not a fully-accredited ambassador, seems to have had similar duties to some English accredited residents. One such secretary was Nicolas Raince, who was born in Paris but perhaps to an Italian family (the name Raince is a French spelling of the Italian Renzo or Ranzo). He was an apostolic protonotary, in holy orders, and was in Rome from late 1523 but fell from favour in the late 1530s.[26]

There are several possible explanations for the differences between Italian and non-Italian practice in ambassadorial appointments. While Italian rulers could often find laymen with legal training and familiarity with the curia, perhaps through family or commercial networks, in northern Europe, the only people likely to have curia experience were men who had previously spent time in Rome as a curia official, or who had studied at one of the Italian universities. By and large these men were clerics. It may also be that the different patterns of appointment were a product of the differing university systems. Italian universities had more lay professors, while their northern counterparts were more often staffed by clergy.[27] The make-up of educated elites differed from place to place. Local priorities may also explain the choices: for an ultramontane power whose interest in Rome largely concerned church matters, an ecclesiastical appointment may well have made sense. For an Italian power concerned too with the potential for war or peace on the peninsula, the diplomatic role was more varied. Once the ultramontane princes began to take an interest in the Italian wars, their personnel choices changed too.

iii.   Italian expertise

Though the cases of Ghinucci and Raince demonstrate that curia clerics did not disappear from the scene, as the Italian wars continued, the European powers made increasing use of lay Italian representatives in Rome. In 1505, the French sent Michele Rizzio, a Neapolitan lawyer, as part of a special embassy to Rome.[28] This trend continued into the 1520s. Andrea Borgo or Burgo (1467–1533), for example, was a member

---

[25] Émile Picot, *Les Français Italianisants aux XVIe Siècle*, 2 vols (Paris: Honoré Champion, 1906–7), Vol. I, pp. 1–25.

[26] Picot, Vol. I, pp. 79–94.

[27] Paul F. Grendler, *The Universities of the Italian Renaissance* (Baltimore and London: Johns Hopkins University Press, 2002), pp. 4–5.

[28] Burchard, *Liber Notarum*, Vol. II, pp. 477–8.

of a Cremonese merchant family. Initially in the service of Ludovico Sforza, duke of Milan, he joined the Imperial diplomatic service around 1500 and was active into the 1530s.[29] Alberto Pio da Carpi (1475–1531) was for much of his life engaged in a contest with his cousin for control of the family lordship of Carpi, in which he enlisted the support of first the Holy Roman Emperor and subsequently the French. He was employed on diplomatic missions to Pope Leo X by the Emperor and to Pope Clement VII by the king of France during his respective alliances. Such changes of employer were not exceptional.[30] Giovanni Giacchino da Passano, who also served the French, was the son of Niccolò Passano, who had been a lieutenant-general in the service of Pope Sixtus IV. He had been a commander of the papal galleys, and was a commander of infantry at the 1515 siege of Alessandria.[31] It seems likely that the role of resident envoy for a foreign power was perceived by curia careerists as simply another office in Rome to which they might aspire, perhaps all the more so given the notably cosmopolitan nature of the papal court.[32]

The general consensus of the literature on the Renaissance ambassador is that ethnic or national origin was not a decisive factor in the employment of any particular diplomat. Elite individuals could move between different sovereigns' military or diplomatic service, choosing or rejecting ties of allegiance.[33] There were long precedents both inside and outside Italy. The Genoese knight Niccolò Fieschi arrived in England on embassy in 1336 and returned to his home city as an ambassador for the English king Edward III, also travelling on the king's behalf to Pope Benedict XII at Avignon.[34] In the 1470s, Antonio da Trezzo switched from the role of Milanese ambassador in Naples to Neapolitan ambassador in Milan; his Bolognese contemporary Giovanni Battista

[29] *ad vocem.*

[30] Christine Isom-Verhaaren, 'Shifting identities: foreign state servants in France and the Ottoman empire', *Journal of Early Modern History* 8 (2004), 109–34 (p. 132).

[31] Passano and Pio: Corrado Argegni, *Condottieri, Capitani, Tribuni*, Enciclopedia biografica e bibliografica "italiana" Serie XIX, 3 vols (Milan: Istituto Editoriale Italiano Bernardo Carlo Tosi, 1937), Vol. II, pp. 410 and 436. Pio: Minnich, '"Protestatio" of Alberto Pio'.

[32] On the growing competition from foreigners for papal offices faced by the Roman nobility, see Anna Modigliani, '"Li Nobili Huomini di Roma". Comportamenti economici e scelte professionali', in Gensini (ed.), *Roma Capitale*, pp. 345–72 (p. 370).

[33] For some case-studies, see Rita Mazzei, 'Quasi un Paradigma: "Lodovicus Montius Mutinensis" fra Italia e Polonia a Metà del Cinquecento', *Rivista Storica Italiana* 115 (2003), 5–36 and 'La Carriera di un Lucchese Segretario del re di Polonia a Metà del Cinquecento', *Archivio Storico Italiano* 164 (2006), 419–56. Also Esther Hildebrant, 'Christopher Mont, Anglo-German Diplomat', *Sixteenth Century Journal* 15 (1984), 281–92 (p. 292), and Behrens, 'Office'.

[34] Pierre Chaplais, *English Diplomatic Practice in the Middle Ages* (London: Hambledon and London, 2002), pp. 172–4. Frey and Frey, *Diplomatic Immunity*, p. 75.

Bentivolgio served first Federico da Montefeltro, duke of Urbino and subsequently, Ferrante d'Aragona, king of Naples.[35] European rulers perceived distinct advantages in employing 'foreign state servants'.[36] When Gregorio Casali was first sent on a diplomatic mission to Rome by the English, in 1525, the English ambassador to Rome, John Clerk, bishop of Bath, wrote that Casali:

> In the declaration [*of*] the kynges highnes good mynd towardes the affayres of [. . .] Italye, and other his highnes is ryche qwalytes, is t[*he*] better belevyd, nott by cause he spekythe in them more fervently than I doo, butt by cause he is off ther own nation heir, and therfor hathe the mor creditt.[37]

This 'credit' of foreign state servants, deriving from personal connections to curia patrons and the Roman nobility, complemented more practical assets like social networks and linguistic abilities. Behrens, for example, emphasises the ability of Tommaso Spinelli, an English diplomat in the Low Countries, to gather news through the networks of his Florentine mercantile family, and his wide range of social contacts.[38] Hildebrandt points to the Anglo-German diplomat Christopher Mont's social circle, as well as his linguistic capacities, knowledge of the English court and education, and Mazzei to humanistic education, prior experience of diplomacy and personal networks.[39] Isom-Verhaaren concludes that what rulers appreciated were 'skills and connections'.[40] All of these things could, of course, be acquired over time by a resident ambassador of whatever national origin, particularly if he had earlier experience in the country, perhaps through a role as secretary or through university education. Nonetheless, it would be difficult for such a person to replicate the full structural advantages that the foreign state servants enjoyed. That is not to say there were no suspicions: English cardinal and ambassador Christopher Bainbridge manoeuvred against an Italian diplomat in the English service, Silvestro Gigli, claiming that Gigli's secretary had overheard his master saying 'Latt thies barbarous people of France and Englond every oon kill odre what shuld we care therefore, soo we have their money to maike merye withal here.'[41] Yet such concerns do not appear to have been decisive.

The appreciation by the major European powers of the Italian roots of the developing diplomatic system was undoubtedly an important

---

[35] Dover, 'Royal diplomacy', pp. 90–1.
[36] I borrow this term from Isom-Verhaaren, 'Shifting identities'.
[37] BL, Cotton MSS, Vit. B, Vol. VII, fol. 67–67v (*L&P*, Vol. IV, p. 1131).
[38] Behrens, 'Office', pp. 167–8, 171, 173.
[39] Hildebrant, 'Christopher Mont', p. 285. Mazzei, 'Carriera di un Lucchese', p. 420.
[40] Isom-Verhaaren, 'Shifting identities', p. 132.
[41] Cited in Chambers, *Cardinal Bainbridge*, p. 59.

consideration in their decision to engage Italian expertise directly.[42] An interesting take on contemporary opinion about Italians can be found in a letter from Gregorio Casali to Montmorency about the employment of Italian mercenary captains, in which he wrote that:

> Should the Most Christian King want to make war in Italy, he must employ Italian captains, because in truth you French lords are too valorous [*troppo valenthuomini*] to have to deal with Spaniards, who fight only with cunning and fraud.[43]

The image of Italian captains presented here – experienced in dealing with subterfuge and deceit – is surely one that extends to the sphere of diplomacy too. However, there were also more subtle considerations in the choice of ambassador, and contemporaries cited very particular reasons for the employment of foreigners in diplomatic roles that related rather less to the strictly practical issues and rather more to the possibilities that these men provided in terms of their ability to dissimulate and their freedom of manoeuvre. In late 1527, during the imprisonment of Pope Clement VII in the Castel Sant'Angelo, Cardinal Wolsey sought to use England's Italian-born representatives in Rome to get a message to the Pope.[44] He instructed one, Gregorio Casali, to disguise himself and pretend to be a messenger from the duke of Ferrara or some other prince.[45] The scheme was 'feasible', as Wolsey put it, precisely because Casali was a foreign freelance diplomat.[46]

A similar tactic was employed to enable discussions between England and France during the imprisonment of Francis I, after the Battle of Pavia in 1525. While England remained in alliance with the Holy Roman Empire, the dowager Queen of France, Louise of Savoy, sent Giovanni Gioacchino da Passano, an Italian agent without full ambassadorial status, to England to begin negotiations about an Anglo-French alliance. According to Mattingly, this enabled Wolsey 'to assure the Spanish

---

[42] Behrens, 'Origins', p. 653. Maria Franca Mellano, *Rappresentanti Italiani della Corona Inglese a Roma ai Primi del Cinquecento* (Rome: Istituto di Studi Romani, 1970), p. 22. Mattingly, *Renaissance Diplomacy*, p. 149.

[43] 'Volendo la Maes. Chris. far guerra in Italia era necessario ch'ella si servisse di capi italiani, perchè in vero voi signori francesi sete troppo valenthuomini ad havere a fare co Spagniuoli, i quali combattono solamente con astutia et fraude.' Giuseppe Molini (ed.), *Documenti di Storia Italiana*, 2 vols (Florence: Tipografia all'Insegna di Dante, 1836–37), Vol. II, p. 213.

[44] *St P*, Vol. I, pp. 270, 272 (*L&P*, Vol. IV, p. 3400).

[45] Gilbert Burnet, *History of the Reformation of the Church of England*, ed.Nicholas Pocock, 7 vols (Oxford: Clarendon Press, 1865), Vol. IV, pp. 22 (*L&P*, Vol. IV, p. 3641).

[46] For further details of this case, see Catherine Fletcher, 'War, diplomacy and social mobility: the Casali family in the service of Henry VIII', *Journal of Early Modern History* 14 (2010), 569–70.

ambassador that this Genoese banker was merely the queen dowager's personal man of business'.[47] Mattingly does not discuss the relevance of Passano's national origin, but the pretence (whether or not the Spaniards entirely believed it) was surely made more convincing by the fact that he was not a Frenchman. The foreign-born ambassadors were not only able to pretend that they were acting on behalf of other princes, or in a private business capacity, but could also give the impression that they were acting for themselves, beyond any mission with which they might have been entrusted by their employer. While envoys of any national origin could switch between official and unofficial personae, foreign state servants were peculiarly able to walk the stage in masks.

The practice of employing foreigners in diplomacy has some parallels with developments in the military sphere, where over the course of the fifteenth century, *condottieri* became more likely to be employed on longer contracts, and many developed a close identification with the prince or republic they served. Are there insights to be gained through a comparison of the two roles? In comparison to their fourteenth-century predecessors, fifteenth-century *condottieri* were, Michael Mallett has argued, 'relatively faithful, increasingly aristocratic, and highly professional'.[48] Frigo has suggested that this period saw a rapprochement between the identities of mercenary captain and 'cavalier' in which greater emphasis was placed on service to the prince.[49] To this extent, there seem to be some commonalities in ways that the roles of mercenary captain and diplomat were understood. The traditional account, in contrast, has tended to counterpose them: Hale, for example, has argued that the aristocracy gradually moved away from military careers into new administrative and court-based occupations, one of which was diplomacy.[50] It seems plausible that there might have been some overlap between the mentalities of military and diplomatic service. The structures, however, were notably different. While military mercenaries were engaged on contract (the *condotta*), the diplomat's relationship to his master rested on ties of allegiance that had no

---

[47] Mattingly, *Renaissance Diplomacy*, pp. 166–7.
[48] Michael Mallett, *Mercenaries and Their Masters: Warfare in Renaissance Italy* (London: Military Book Society, 1974), pp. 83, 257. On the post-1494 period, see Mallett's 'I Condottieri nelle Guerre d'Italia', in Mario del Treppo (ed.), *Condottieri e Uomini d'Arme nell'Italia del Rinascimento* (Naples: Liguori, 2001), pp. 347–60.
[49] Daniela Frigo, 'Principe e Capitano, Pace e Guerra: Figure del 'Politico' tra Cinque e Seicento', in Marcello Fantoni (ed.), *Il "Perfetto Capitano": Immagini e Realtà (secoli XV–XVII)* (Rome: Bulzoni, 2001), pp. 273–304 (pp. 279–80).
[50] J. R. Hale, *War and Society in Renaissance Europe 1450–1620* (Leicester: Leicester University Press, 1985), p. 97.

such legal basis. I discuss some family networks and their engagement in diplomacy in Chapter 5.

iv.   The diplomacy of war

As Chapter 3 showed, clerics were specifically excluded from parts of the ceremonial world of Rome. This must have been an incentive for princes serious about their image at Rome to ensure that they had at least one accredited lay ambassador at the papal court available to carry out these ceremonial roles. Clerics were not invariably the best choice for missions to the pope, although when diplomatic negotiations involved questions of law or theology their expertise was valuable. In fact, developments at the papal court reflect a broader European trend of appointing lay resident ambassadors with military experience in times of war. A number of the Italians discussed above are of this type, and, as I have discussed elsewhere, Henry VIII made a switch towards it in the 1520s.[51] Moreover, 'courtier-diplomats', sometimes of high rank, sometimes favourites of the ruler, would be perceived as close to their prince and able to speak his mind. The dispatch of a trusted favourite as ambassador could underline a monarch's seriousness: Sir Francis Bryan played such a role in Rome for Henry VIII in 1529.[52] As the case of the duke of Albany showed, the French used similar tactics; the Holy Roman Empire also sent high-ranking noblemen to Rome, notably the duke of Sessa (active in the 1520s). In terms of rank, the personnel of the Roman diplomatic corps can generally be characterised as noble or patrician, but it was not usual for very senior members of the aristocracy to reside as ambassadors in Rome. The dukes of Sessa and Albany were on short-term missions. More significant was the shift towards the employment of 'soldier-diplomats',[53] men with expertise in diplomacy that would serve them well in the new context.

Indeed, a look at the resident ambassadors in Rome of the 1520s suggests a military background was an asset. The Imperial ambassador was Miguel Mai, a 'gentleman of Barcelona' who had studied law and humanities and, according to the Venetian ambassador Gasparo

---

[51] Fletcher, 'War, diplomacy and social mobility', pp. 559–78 and 'Performing Henry'.

[52] Fletcher, *Our Man in Rome*, p. 57. This was also the case at other courts: on high-ranking ambassadors sent by Imperial princes to the Emperor, see Stollberg-Rilinger, 'Le Rituel', p. 23.

[53] The phrase 'soldier diplomat' is used in David Potter, 'Foreign policy', in Diarmaid MacCulloch (ed.), *The Reign of Henry VIII: Politics, Policy and Piety* (Basingstoke: Macmillan, 1995), pp. 101–33 (p. 104).

Contarini, had been a *rettore* at the University of Padua.[54] He had had
some naval experience and was subsequently an official at the Imperial
court before being appointed ambassador.[55] Giovanni Gioacchino da
Passano and Gregorio Casali, discussed above, had military back-
grounds too. The duke of Ferrara employed Conte Roberto Boschetti,
a former *condottiere* in the service of Pope Leo X, as his representative in
Rome during the papacy of Leo's cousin Clement VII.[56] During his
embassy he was involved in military discussions between the papacy and
Venice.[57] This was a period of dramatic change in warfare: indeed,
Michael Mallett labelled it a 'transformation'. Characterised by rising
troop numbers, longer-term service and the increasing significance of
gunpowder, between 1495 and 1525, the Italian wars saw a shift from
'an approximately equal division between cavalry and infantry, to an
infantry predominance of 6:1'.[58] Finding ambassadors sufficiently
familiar with these trends to provide reliable assessments of the contending armies was of central importance. In the course of his residence, the French embassy secretary Nicolas Raince welcomed at least
sixteen different ambassadors to Rome. Among them were Alberto Pio,
ambassador from 1525 to 1538; Guillaume du Bellay, at the end of
1526; François de La Tour d'Auvergne, Vicomte de Turenne, from
April 1528 to 1529; Giovanni Gioacchino da Passano, in 1528; John
Stuart, duke of Albany, November 1530 to May 1531; and Jean du
Bellay, February 1534 to 1535. Of the fourteen whose status can be
securely identified, exactly half were laymen and half were clerics.
There is a strong correlation between the lay/clerical appointments
and the periods of war and peace: the laymen served overwhelmingly
before the Ladies' Peace of 1529; the clerics served after it.[59] The later
period is beyond the scope of this study, but the French case suggests
that the 1530s saw a shift away from lay diplomacy. There is, of course,
a very likely reason for this trend: the need for a response to religious
reform.

---

[54] G. Contarini, fol. 166r. Contarini had also studied at Padua, from 1501 to 1509. E. G.
Gleason, *Gasparo Contarini: Venice, Rome and Reform* (Berkeley and Los Angeles:
University of California Press, 1993), p. 8. The post of rector was elected by students;
some rectors taught at the university. Grendler, *Universities*, pp. 27, 42, 158.

[55] See his entry (under Miquel May) in the *Diccionari Biogràfic* (Barcelona: Alberti, 1969).
For a discussion of his 1529–32 mission to Rome, see Levin, *Agents of Empire*, pp. 45–53.

[56] Argegni, *Condottieri*, Vol. I, p. 106.

[57] Lambeth Palace Library, MS 4434, fols. 26v–27r.

[58] Michael Mallett, 'The transformation of war, 1494–1530', in Shaw (ed.), *Italy and the
European Powers*, pp. 3–21 (p. 5).

[59] Picot, *Les Français*, Vol. I, pp. 82–3.

b.   Agents, secretaries and servants

The work of the ambassador was underpinned by the efforts of many others: secretaries, agents and servants. Sebastiano del Piombo's portrait of Ferry Carondelet, Margaret of Austria's ambassador to Rome, shows him alongside two men presumed to be his secretaries, one of whom is taking down a letter while the other hovers in the background. Given the quantity of correspondence ambassadors dealt with, secretarial support was vital. Letters of several pages had to be written (and often ciphered) each day, and others had to be copied for forwarding. In a treatise on the proper management of a prelate's court in Rome, Francesco Priscianese noted that the secretary needed to understand ciphering well, be diligent in ensuring that no paperwork was lost and everything was registered. He should note the day, month and hour of receipt, and other particulars, keeping the letters ordered in files or bundles.[60] More important still is Priscianese's assessment of the secretary's general comportment:

The honour of lords is largely concentrated in the hands of secretaries, and this is sometimes their ruin. It is impossible to say how important it is to have in that office a worthy man, principally secret (as the name suggests), loyal, diligent and expeditious; a beautiful, graceful and eloquent writer, and as concise as possible; and prudent.[61]

Note the reference to prudence here: this is a virtue not only relevant to ambassadors but to their secretaries too. Their roles went well beyond writing letters. In 1529, Baptista Sambuelo, a member of the English embassy staff, was sent to negotiate with the Genoese admiral Andrea Doria about the provision of galleys.[62] During his visit, he extracted from Doria's men, the news that Doria was considering abandoning the French service and joining the Imperialists, important information which his master immediately passed onto the French.[63] Other staff may have given an intellectual gloss to the embassy as well as performing more practical tasks. Richard Herde, who accompanied Stephen Gardiner and Edward Fox to Orvieto in 1528 was, they wrote, 'a young man, being

---

[60] Francesco Priscianese, *Del Governo della Corte d'un Signore in Roma* (Città di Castello: S. Lapi Editore, 1883), p. 69. The preface to this treatise is dated 1543.

[61] *Ibid.*, p. 68. 'Onde l'onor de' Signori in gran parte è posto nelle mani de' Segretari, e qualche volta le rovine loro. Perchè non si potrebbe dire di quanta importanza sia lo avere in così fatto ufficio un uomo degno, segreto principalmente (come ne ammonisce il nome), leale, diligente ed espedito, bello scrittore ed eloquente e leggiadro e breve quanto si può, e prudente.'

[62] Pocock, *Records*, Vol. I, pp. 170–1 (*L&P*, Vol. IV, p. 4379). TNA, SP 1/48 fols. 191r–192r (*L&P*, Vol. IV, p. 4401).

[63] Molini, *Documenti*, Vol. II, p. 36.

himself singularly well learned in physic, in the Greek and Latin tongues, as any we know'; a Mantuan observer noted his abilities in philosophy too.[64] In Florence, provisions of 1498 and 1529 established a formalised role for such young men, who might act as deputies to the chief ambassador on a particular mission, participating under his authority in negotiations; they might also spy on him to ensure he did not exceed his mandate.[65]

Writers of this period expressed considerable anxiety about the role of servants. Dolet commented that 'an ambassador, of all men, ought to employ none but faithful and close-mouthed servants. For what involves more risk than the disclosure of your aims through disloyal servants, bribed by the enemy of your prince, or the frustration of your efforts by their drunken garrulity?'[66] Castiglionchio noted that 'knavish' men would ensure they knew precisely who those they were lobbying employed 'as managers of property, as servants, as valets', presumably to no good end.[67] In a testament to the loyalty of French embassy secretary Nicolas Raince, François de Billon noted that he had turned down 'not fifty, not two thousand, but five thousand ducats' offered by an Imperial lord in return for copies of French state papers.[68] Less principled, so it was claimed, was a secretary to the English resident Silvestro Gigli, who was spotted leaving the house of the French ambassador on a 'dirke nyght', and taking a 'secret bake layne' home rather than the more obvious route.[69]

The size of ambassadors' households varied, but about twelve servants was a typical number. In 1485, Genoese orators arriving in Rome were accompanied by eleven servants each.[70] Two English special envoys to Rome brought twelve servants on their journey in 1529, but then joined the household of the resident, which was already staffed.[71] In the 1526 Roman census, the Florentine ambassador's household had eleven members; the Milanese ambassador's five; the Portuguese ambassador's seventy. The English orator, who lived in his own family house in Rome,

[64] Pocock, *Records*, Vol. II, p. 88 (*L&P*, Vol. IV, p. 4090). ASMn, Archivio Gonzaga 877, c. 28v.
[65] Giuseppe Vedovato, 'I Giovani nelle Ambascerie della Repubblica Fiorentina', Estratto Dagli *Scritti in Onore di Niccolò Rodolico* (Florence, 1944), especially pp. 32–5.
[66] Dolet, 'De Officio Legati', p. 86.   [67] Lapo, *De Curiae Commodis*, p. 163.
[68] François de Billon, *Le Fort Inexpugnable de l'Honneur du Sexe Femenin, Construit par Françoys de Billon, Secretaire* (Paris: Jean d'Allyer, 1555), p. 246, cited in Picot, Vol. I, pp. 86–7.
[69] Chambers, *Cardinal Bainbridge*, pp. 58–9.
[70] Burchard, *Liber Notarum*, Vol. I, p. 112.
[71] See the report of Lope de Soria to the Emperor, 10 January 1529. *CSP Sp*, Vol. III. ii , p. 612.

had a household of fifteen members.[72] Caution must be exercised in relation to the accuracy of the census, especially given the highly uncertain political situation that prevailed when it was drawn up in the second half of November 1526.[73] However, by comparison to cardinals' households, which averaged around 150 persons, ambassadors' households were relatively small.[74] As Heal has argued in relation to England, however, a smaller household need not preclude adherence to 'the ethos of generosity that was a part of the honour community'.[75] Furthermore, during the visits of special ambassadors the resident's household size must have expanded significantly.

Just as it is hard to disentangle the ambassador's personal or familial activities from his activities in office, so it is hard to disentangle the activities of his household. The members of the ambassador's *familia*, their status and conduct were a vital consideration for contemporaries in assessing the diplomat's work, and the treatises provide a wealth of comment on this subject. In doing so, they reflect concerns that were the subject of an extensive literature in this period emphasizing the parallel between the household and the polity in terms of good order and government.[76] One of the most interesting treatises in this regard is that of Étienne Dolet, who stated bluntly in his first paragraph that even before the question of prudent conduct, the household should be the ambassador's priority:

Every ambassador who is desirous of rendering due aid, whether it be to a king, or some lesser prince, or to some independent people, and who hopes for praise and honor from the discharge of his office, should guide his course in such a manner as to give special consideration to two matters: first to the condition of his own household, and then to the employment of prudence at the court to which he has been sent.[77]

It is striking that the household comes first. The conduct of servants was a problem that taxed Renaissance writers on the household in general,

---

[72] *Descriptio Urbis: The Roman Census of 1527*, ed. Egmont Lee (Rome: Bulzoni, 1985), p. 92.

[73] Lee, in his introduction to the census, raises a series of concerns about its accuracy, including the omission of several well-known long-term residents of Rome; duplicate entries for particular households citing different numbers of people resident; and a lack of congruence with other contemporary sources. *Descriptio Urbis*, pp. 21–4.

[74] Gigliola Fragnito, 'Cardinals' courts in sixteenth-century Rome', *Journal of Modern History* 65 (1993), 26–56 (p. 26).

[75] Felicity Heal, *Hospitality in Early Modern England* (Oxford: Clarendon Press, 1990), p. 47.

[76] Dennis Romano, *Housecraft and Statecraft: Domestic Service in Renaissance Venice, 1400–1600* (Baltimore and London: Johns Hopkins University Press, 1996), pp. 1–4. Daniela Frigo, *Il Padre di Famiglia: Governo della Casa e Governo Civile nella Tradizione dell' "Economica" tra Cinque e Seicento* (Roma: Bulzoni, 1985), pp. 17–48.

[77] Dolet, 'De Officio Legati', p. 82.

and those who wrote on the subject of the ambassador's servants were no exception. Ermolao Barbaro, whose uncle Francesco had written a treatise on household management, cited a 'common proverb', which he said was known not only in Italy but abroad: 'Let no-one make accords without surety of the continence of the ambassadors, their retinue and household.'[78] Dolet said that ensuring an orderly household was essential for the ambassador, commenting that he would be judged by their conduct of its members and stressing the importance of their discretion and sobriety.[79] That the state of the ambassador's household was of concern to writers on the subject should not be surprising given the way that contemporaries would have understood these precepts. As Romano has argued, they regarded effective household management as a metaphor for effective government.[80] For an ambassador, as the personification of his prince's dignity, the good government of his own household was symbolic of the good government of his prince's realm. Behrens' categorisation of household management as one of the many issues on which Dolet's treatise is 'strictly utilitarian' misses this point entirely.[81] Dolet did, obviously, have some practical considerations in mind. For example, his reference to sobriety echoes the comment in Erasmus' 'Convivium religiosum', in which one character comments: 'It's not safe for priests or servants of kings to be fond of wine, because wine commonly brings to the tip of man's tongue whatever he was hiding in his heart.'[82] However, for all the potential problems that drunken servants posed, Dolet's injunction also concerned the importance for the diplomat of establishing himself as a responsible *paterfamilias*. His house and household had to embody his own and his prince's virtues.

c. Women and diplomacy

The question of women's involvement in diplomacy at Rome poses a methodological problem. With the exception of royal women and those whose dynastic marriages were a matter of political concern, only rarely

---

[78] 'Nunquam Sine Vase Continentiae Legatorum et Comites et Familia Respondeant.' Barbaro, 'De Officio Legati', p. 166. On Francesco's treatise and Ermolao's response, see Romano, *Housecraft and Statecraft*, pp. 10–13; Margaret L. King, 'Caldiera and the Barbaros on marriage and the family: humanist reflections of Venetian realities', *Journal of Medieval and Renaissance Studies* 6 (1976), 19–50.
[79] Dolet, 'De Officio Legati', pp. 85–6.   [80] Romano, *Housecraft and Statecraft*, p. 23.
[81] Behrens, 'Treatises', pp. 625–6.
[82] 'Admonet Non Esse Tutum Sacerdotibus aut Regum Famulis Indulgere Vino.' Desiderii Erasmi Roterodami, 'Convivium Religiosum', in *Opera Omnia*, Series 1, Vol. 3 (Amsterdam: North-Holland Publishing Company, 1972), pp. 231–66 (p. 248). Translation from Desiderius Erasmus, *Collected Works of Erasmus* (Toronto: University of Toronto Press, 1974–), Vol. 39, p. 189.

do ambassadors refer directly to women in their correspondence. It is quite possible that their anonymous highly-placed informants were wives, daughters and mistresses, but we simply do not know. Nor was the role of women a matter that concerned the authors of the treatises. It is at the bottom and top of the social scale that we can be most certain about women's involvement in diplomacy. Maidservants and housekeepers like Julie de la Fontana and Stephanea, English embassy staff in the 1530s,[83] carried out the domestic tasks that sustained the embassy's work. It is in these poorly-documented household roles that women probably made the most sustained contribution to the work of an embassy. Far more prominent in the sources, though still rare, are the cases of high-ranking women pursuing diplomatic projects at the curia. Carlotta, queen of Cyprus, came to Rome in 1461 to beg assistance in opposing her illegitimate brother, who had usurped her throne with Egyptian backing. She had a public ceremonial reception and was then accorded a private audience for discussion. She and her retinue were accommodated in the papal palace, an honour certainly not allowed to every royal visitor, and in the course of their ten-day visit, had a further four or five audiences.[84] They visited the principal churches of Rome, an activity undertaken by special ambassadors on other occasions, notably by a Venetian embassy in 1522.[85] In 1459, during Pius' visit to Mantua, he was greeted by Bianca Maria Visconti, duchess of Milan, and her daughter Ippolita Sforza. While there is no record of an oration at Carlotta's reception, during Bianca's audience in Mantua, the fourteen-year-old Ippolita 'delivered a speech before the Pope in such elegant Latin that all present were lost in wonder and admiration'.[86] Judith Bryce plausibly suggests that the numerous copies of Ippolita's oration surviving in European libraries are testament to the rarity of such an event.[87] Another atypical Renaissance woman was Isabella d'Este, who made two extended visits to Rome, one in 1514–15 and another in 1525–7. The latter trip was at least in part motivated by a desire to lobby for the promotion of her son Ercole Gonzaga to the cardinalate, an aim achieved in 1527 when the besieged Pope Clement VII found himself in need of Gonzaga funds. Isabella liaised with the ambassadors of her Este relatives as well as those of her husband's family. She promoted a

[83] Archivio Casali di Monticelli, cassetta I, no. 15, fol. 2.
[84] Pius, *Commentarii* Vol. II, pp. 1386–97 (*Secret Memoirs*, p. 211).
[85] Albèri, Eugenio (ed.), *Relazioni Degli Ambasciatori Veneti al Senato*, 15 vols (Florence: Società editrice fiorentina, 1839–63), ser. 2, Vol. III, pp. 77–120.
[86] Pius, *Commentarii* Vol. I, pp. 420–1 (*Secret Memoirs*, p. 111).
[87] Judith Bryce, "'Fa Finire Uno Bello Studio et Dice Volere Studiare,'" Ippolita Sforza and her books', *Bibliothèque d'Humanisme et Renaissance*, 64 (2002), pp. 55–69 (p. 60).

marriage between her son Federico and a daughter of the king of Poland, though the plans came to naught. She pursued her interests in art collection and patronage. During the Sack of May 1527, the ambassadors of Ferrara, Urbino and Venice found sanctuary in her house.[88] As the wife of the marquis of Mantua (and following her husband's death in 1519, the mother of a new marquis) and the sister of the duke of Ferrara, both of whom held territory of strategic importance, her influence was significant and she was able to leverage it to good end for her relatives.[89] It is, however, hard to find parallels for her activities in Rome.

The papal court was, officially, an all-male business, but as the popes became more dynastically-minded, their female relatives adopted a more prominent role. Pope Alexander VI's decision to leave his daughter Lucrezia Borgia in charge of the papal court while on a tour of fortresses in Genazzano, Marino and Rocca di Papa is perhaps the most extreme and notorious example of such activity, but it was hardly commonplace behaviour.[90] The thirteen-year-old Lucrezia had been married in the Vatican in 1493, in a ceremony attended by her father's mistress Giulia Farnese and dozens of Roman women.[91] Members of her household mingled in diplomatic circles, for example, accompanying the ambassadors of the king and queen of Navarre as they processed to their house in 1500.[92] Felice della Rovere, illegitimate daughter of Alexander's successor Julius II, kept a lower profile but is known to have invited the wife of an English ambassador to dinner and certainly moved in high social circles.[93] During the Medici papacies the popes' female relatives also had prominent roles at court.[94] In this most secular period of papal rule, women relatives of the popes came closest to the types of role accorded to royal women at courts elsewhere in Europe: as informal, and sometimes formal, facilitators of political business.[95] In doing so, however, they

---

[88] Alessandro Luzio, 'Isabella d'Este e il Sacco di Roma', *Archivio Storico Lombardo* 10 (1908), 5–107.

[89] Sarah Cockram, *Isabella d'Este and Francesco Gonzaga: Power-Sharing at the Italian Renaissance Court* (Aldershot: Ashgate, 2013).

[90] Mallett, *The Borgias*, p. 162.   [91] Burchard, *Liber Notarum*, Vol. I, pp. 443–7.

[92] Burchard, *Liber Notarum*, Vol. II, p. 199.

[93] Caroline P. Murphy, *The Pope's Daughter* (London: Faber & Faber, 2006), p. 286. S. Feci, 'Manetti, Latino Giovenale', *Dizionario Biografico degli Italiani* (Roma: Enciclopedia Italiana, 1960–).

[94] Natalie Tomas, *The Medici Women: Gender and Power in Renaissance Florence* (Aldershot: Ashgate, 2005), pp. 124–63 and 'All in the family: The Medici women and Pope Clement VII', in Gouwens and Reiss (eds), *Pontificate of Clement VII*, pp. 41–53.

[95] The degree to which women's roles changed over time remains to be established: it is evident that some women exercised significant power in Rome during the following century. Olimpia Maidalchini Pamphili, sister-in-law of Pope Innocent X, is a case in point. See Stefano Tabacci, 'Olimpia Maidalchini', in *Dizionario Biografico degli*

attracted criticism. When Leo X's three sisters, Lucrezia, Maddalena and Contessina moved to Rome to join the new pope, along with his sister-in-law Alfonsina and her daughter Clarice, Leo's opponents branded them ambitious and greedy, implying that this female presence in the traditionally male domain of the papal court was disruptive.[96]

The few women rulers in Europe sent their own embassies to Rome. Anne of Brittany, queen of France, sent envoys in 1499 to pledge obedience in her name. Debate ensued as to whether a queen could pledge obedience without a king, although formally, the embassy came on behalf of Brittany, which Anne ruled in her own right. Only once it was established that they came with the permission of the king of France were they granted a formal audience.[97] When women did take central roles in diplomacy it was overwhelmingly as regents for their husbands, nephews and sons. As a consequence, there were almost no women involved in the diplomacy of the Italian republics. In 1529, Louise of Savoy and Margaret of Austria negotiated the Treaty of Cambrai, known as the 'Ladies' Peace', on behalf of Louise's son Francis I and Margaret's nephew Charles V. Both women were experienced in diplomacy. Margaret had been involved in discussions over the League of Cambrai in 1503, alongside Cardinal Georges d'Amboise, archbishop of Rouen. As regent of the Netherlands during Charles' minority and again after his election as Emperor, she was well accustomed to dealing with ambassadors. Louise had been regent of France during her son's two Italian campaigns, and likewise had extensive knowledge of diplomatic affairs.[98]

Some ambassadors were married, but references to wives in diplomatic correspondence are scarce. Gregorio Casali, English ambassador to Rome, married Livia Pallavicino in 1530, just over half-way through his residence. Yet she is referred to in none of his hundreds of surviving official letters, and her existence is detectable only through family records, a couple of gossipy letters from acquaintances, and in passing, in an account of an English embassy to Bologna written by a herald, Thomas Wall, who noted that on her arrival there as a new bride 'there was at supper great feasting and many Ladyes and gentylwome[n]'.[99] Livia came to Rome later the same year, and after that time, presumably,

Italiani at www.treccani.it/enciclopedia/olimpia-maidalchini_%28Dizionario-Biografico%29/[accessed 24 June 2014].

[96] Tomas, *Medici Women*, pp. 124–5.   [97] Burchard, *Liber Notarum*, Vol. II, p. 128.

[98] J. G. Russell, 'Women diplomats: the Ladies' Peace of 1529', in *Diplomats at Work: Three Renaissance Studies* (Stroud: Sutton, 1992), pp. 94–152.

[99] Fletcher, *Our Man in Rome*. Thomas Wall, *The Voyage of Sir Nicholas Carewe to the Emperor Charles V in the Year 1529*, ed. R. J. Knecht (Cambridge: Cambridge University Press, 1959), p. 83.

had an important role in the running of the household, but the extent to which she acted as a diplomatic hostess is not known. Given her family connections (her uncle Latino Giovenale Manetti was secretary to Cardinal Alessandro Farnese, the future Pope Paul III), she may well have been involved in social activities with members of the curia.[100]

Yet despite the lack of detail, there is no doubt that contemporaries perceived the ambassador's relationship with his wife – and indeed other women – to be significant.[101] An insight into their understandings can be gleaned from the case of one servant with whom Casali and his wife had trouble: Giovanni Bernardino de' Ferrari, a young man who worked as a secretary first for Casali and subsequently for Benedetto Accolti, the cardinal of Ravenna.[102] Giovanni Bernardino gave evidence against Accolti during the latter's trial in 1535 for corruption and abuse of power. The cardinal obviously had an axe to grind against his former servant, but nonetheless his comments are interesting. Ermolao Barbaro had warned that 'contumelia et impudicitia' – insults and lewdness – must not be countenanced in the ambassador's household, cautioning that such conduct would provoke discord and scandal.[103] Giovanni Bernardino, on the cardinal's account, was guilty of both offences. First, Accolti wrote (in an *aide-memoire* either for himself or his lawyer) that Gregorio Casali had once had Giovanni Bernardino slung into the local prison, Corte Savella, for casting doubt on the legitimacy of Casali's son.[104] This was an excellent example of firm action to uphold the values Barbaro advocated. For a member of the household to make such an allegation was a serious slur on Casali's personal honour, implying as it did a failure to manage both his wife and his servants effectively. Furthermore, in his role as ambassador, such disorder also reflected badly on the honour of the prince he represented.

From insults, we move on to lewdness: Cardinal Accolti's second accusation was that Giovanni Bernardino 'Never held any office more important there in [Casali's] household than being a *ruffiano*'.[105] That

---

[100] S. Feci, 'Manetti, Latino Giovenale', *Dizionario Biografico degli Italiani*.

[101] There is better evidence for the seventeenth century, by which time the role of the ambassador's wife was more established. See Helen Jacobsen, *Luxury and Power: The Material World of the Stuart Diplomat, 1660–1714* (Oxford: Oxford University Press, 2012), pp. 54–60.

[102] Archivio di Stato di Roma (hereafter ASR), Tribunale del Governatore di Roma, Processi 3; 2 II; 3 May 1535 and *L&P*, Vol. VII, p. 144.

[103] Barbaro, 'De Officio Legati', p. 166–7.

[104] Archivio di Stato di Firenze (hereafter ASF), Fondo Accolti, 9, no. 15, fol. 1. There is more detail of this incident in *Our Man in Rome*, p. 153.

[105] 'Nè Fece Mai Offitio Più Importante á li di Suoi che d'Esser Ruffiano.' ASF, Fondo Accolti, 9, no. 15, fol. 1.

could imply that he was a flatterer or hanger-on, but the overall tone of the document suggests that the more plausible translation is 'pimp'. Were there many *ruffiani* hanging around the households of diplomats in order to arrange their fellows' liaisons with the local courtesans? It is hard to say, although the record in the 1517 census of a German courtesan, 'Madona Paula', who rented a nearby house from Casali's mother Antonina, would suggest that such services were easily accessible. There is ample evidence for the role of courtesans in the social life of Roman elites: this was, after all, a court where respectable gentlemen far outnumbered respectable ladies.[106] Lapo Da Castiglionchio noted not only the 'courtesans of more honourable status', but also 'common prostitution and harlotry' and men who 'zealously seek out beautiful servant boys to serve the meals, as well as catamites and men whose hair is done a little too finely.'[107] Imperia, a prominent Roman courtesan in the early years of the sixteenth century, numbered among her clients, a Spanish envoy, Enriques de Toledo,[108] and it was said that the English diplomat Sir Francis Bryan slept with a courtesan to gain intelligence while on a special embassy to Rome in the 1520s.[109] Whether or not true, that tale confirms that pillow talk was regarded as a potential source of information for diplomats. The treatises warn against such behaviour on moral grounds,[110] though, of course, for every diplomat gaining secret intelligence from a lover, there was someone whose information was leaked – a utilitarian reason to avoid such encounters.

At the turn of the sixteenth century, there were two significant shifts in the personnel of diplomacy at the court of Rome: to lay diplomacy and to the employment of freelance Italian agents as accredited ambassadors. The outbreak of war underlay both these changes. There were, however, other reasons for the extension of lay diplomacy. As Chapter 3 showed, only lay diplomats were allowed to embody their princes in Rome's ceremonial world. As the curia became more of a court, there was ever more reason for the men dispatched there to appear more courtier-like. This understanding of the ambassador as personification of his prince extended to his 'private' conduct too: in his management of wife and *familia*, he was expected to exercise good governance.

---

[106] *Habitatores in Urbe: The Population of Renaissance Rome*, ed. Egmont Lee (Rome: La Sapienza, 2006), p. 98. Georgina Masson, *Courtesans of the Italian Renaissance* (London: Secker & Warburg, 1975). Tessa Storey, *Carnal Commerce in Counter-Reformation Rome* (Cambridge: Cambridge University Press, 2008), especially pp. 57–66.

[107] Lapo, *De Curiae Commodis*, pp. 181, 187.   [108] Masson, *Courtesans*, p. 38.

[109] Susan Brigden, '"The shadow that you know": Sir Francis Bryan and Sir Thomas Wyatt at court and in embassy', *Historical Journal* 39 (1996), 1–31 (p. 6).

[110] Dolet, 'De Officio Legati', p. 17; Barbaro, 'De Officio Legati', p. 166.

5 Information and communication

A diplomatic letter typically began its life as a draft in a letter-book. A secretary would make a fair copy for dispatch to the principal; other copies might be produced for members of the ambassador's wider network. The envoy would hope no member of his household was spying on his correspondence. All or part of the letter might be ciphered, in an effort to protect its contents from prying eyes. It would be folded, sealed and addressed. Often, it would be added to a packet containing other letters to the same destination, including correspondence from representatives of other (allied) powers and copies of letters received from elsewhere. It might be sent immediately, or it might have to wait for a suitable courier to be available. During inclement weather, there could be long delays. *En route* to its destination, the packet might be intercepted, copied or stolen; it might be damaged by rain. On its arrival its contents might be deciphered, translated, filtered and summarised by a secretary before reaching their intended recipient. Copies might be made for further distribution. Finally, they would be filed. The chancellery of the ambassador's home court would keep folders of letters sent to him and received from him, and copies of instructions and relations. At the end of his mission an envoy was expected to hand over his own files too.[1]

Perhaps because this was all so commonplace, neither Barbaro nor Dolet wrote much about the process of despatching of information. Nonetheless, this brief biography of a diplomatic letter makes apparent the complexity of the communication process. This chapter considers that process in detail, beginning with an exploration of Rome's role as 'international gossip shop', then assessing competition and co-operation in newsgathering, the post road as a political space and the role of family and commercial networks in diplomacy. Much has been written about diplomatic letters, their relationship to literature and their role in the

---

[1] Senatore, *"Uno Mundo de Carta"*, p. 86.

circulation of ideas in early modern Europe.[2] This chapter is not so much about their contents or rhetoric: these are inevitably specific to circumstances. Rather, it explores the networks and structures that facilitated the acquisition of information and its communication.

a.   Rome as international 'gossip shop'

The diaries of Marin Sanuto are testament to the quantity of correspondence that originated in Rome in this period: more than any other city, Italian or European, Rome was the source of news received and noted down by the Venetian senator.[3] Lapo Da Castiglionchio's 1438 description emphasised the centrality of information to city life:

> Really, almost every day some sort of newly arrived legations are present. Every day some news is conveyed by letters, messengers and rumours, and no day or even hour in the whole year goes by in which something is not suggested. Nothing that is done in the whole world is not known directly in the curia. Nor can it happen otherwise where there is this throng, this multitude of men who are informed about matters in their homeland by the letters and messengers of their servants.[4]

Lapo's comments give a sense of the problems of reliability (rumours), of the range of sources for news (the whole world) and of the role of servants in the provision of news. Moreover, he emphasises the importance of news *received* in Rome as well as news *despatched* from Rome.

Rome offered numerous opportunities to the diplomat seeking information. Some were official and organised, others less so. He would have private audiences with the pope or formal meetings with others in the curia and report on those directly. He might attend semi-formal meetings with the pope and cardinals, such as the lunch that typically followed a papal mass. He might engage in informal discussion, for example with colleagues before or after mass in the Sistine Chapel. Once collected, news was appraised and distributed. A fine image of the process is presented in a letter from Gregorio Casali and Girolamo Ghinucci, dated 7 February 1526 and written just as news of the Treaty of Madrid was becoming public:

> As to the peace, or concord, between the Emperor and the king of France, there are the following indications: first, letters of January 28, from Lyons, say that it was publicly talked of there, and that Momorensi [Montmorency] was daily expected with the terms and conditions of peace. Letters of Jan. 29 say that he

---

[2] De Vivo, *Information and Communication*; Robyn Adams and Rosanna Cox (eds), *Diplomacy and Early Modern Culture* (Basingstoke: Palgrave, 2011).
[3] Sanuto, *I Diarii.*   [4] Lapo, *De Curiae Commodis*, p. 175.

had arrived, and had brought the conclusion or concord of peace and the terms. It is said that the duke of Savoy wrote that he had letters from his agents at the Imperial court, who wrote that peace had been made; however, he did not give details. The duke of Suessa, the Imperial ambassador, says he has letters from Genoa, signifying that letters had come from Barcelona which announce that peace or concord has been made... The duke of Ferrara wrote to the Imperial ambassador here that he has letters from his agent in France announcing that peace has been made.[5]

Casali and Ghinucci were in a somewhat difficult position, for no-one in Rome appeared to know the details of the treaty for sure, but the letter illustrates the process of marshalling evidence and points too to the ambassador's role in appraising its reliability. Here, second-hand letters from France and Barcelona together make a convincing case, while the names of three dukes are invoked to add authority. As Machiavelli wrote in his advice to Raffaello Girolami:

Since some of the things you pick up may be true and some false but probable, you need to weigh them in your judgment.[6]

Galeazzo Maria Sforza, duke of Milan, instructed his envoy in Bologna to seek to understand well and in depth (literally 'to fish diligently to the seabed'). He should not give credence too easily, or everyone would make a fool of him.[7] Lorenzo da Pesaro, writing to the previous duke, Francesco Sforza, was no-one's fool, least of all Paul II's, of whom he observed, 'His Holiness speaks very well, but his words differ from the facts.'[8] Ambassadors were careful to explain the sources of their news, thus giving an account of how they had come to their judgements. Ludovico Gonzaga's ambassador in Milan, Vincenzo della Scalona, did so in a letter of 1459: 'I have seen letters from Florence dated 26th of the previous written by a merchant, who says that according to letters of the 24th from Rome it is understood that a certain Signor of Rocagulielma, ten miles from Gaieta, has come to terms with the Duke of Lorena.'[9] Though he does not say so explicitly, a reader could infer from the chain of communication that these reports might not be entirely reliable. A 1509 report from Venetian ambassadors *en route* to Rome shows the

---

[5] BL, Cotton MSS, Vit. B, vol. VIII, fol. 14r (*L&P*, Vol. IV, 1957). Translation adapted from *L&P*.

[6] Machiavelli, 'Advice', p. 118.

[7] 'volere bene intendere et pescare diligentemente al fondo... non essere troppo facele al credere... lì tu sei ozellato da omni homo...' Leverotti, *Diplomazia e Governo*, pp. 80–81 citing *Carteggi Diplomatici fra Milano Sforzesca e la Bologna*, ed. E. Sestan (Rome: Istituto Storico Italiano per l'Età Moderna e Contemporanea, 1985), Vol. II, p. 303.

[8] Cited in Dover, 'Saper la Mente', p. 16.

[9] *Carteggi Diplomatici*, Vol. I, p. 466 (letter no. 350).

type of language used to convey an impression of greater reliability: 'We have understood from a person worthy of trust that the aforesaid Most Reverend Legate has had letters this morning from Rome, informing him that His Holiness the Pope has gout with a touch of fever, but that this illness is judged more likely fiction than truth.'[10] While the phrase 'worthy of trust' suggests that the ambassadors endorsed the news that the letters arrived, the subsequent 'it is judged' gives a more neutral tone to their assessment of the illness's veracity. A step up again from the anonymous trusty source was someone like Pietro Cavallucchio, who carried out military assessments for Gregorio Casali in 1529. Casali emphasised to Wolsey that Cavallucchio was 'a close friend and very expert in military matters'.[11] Moreover, the type of information he provided was a commodity that could be exchanged with others, as this letter from the Ferrarese ambassador Antonio Romeo to the duke of Ferrara describes:

> The French ambassador has letters from Barletta, and I have also seen from others that things at Puglia are going better every day for the French, and I have seen other reports written from there that conclude that... Monopoli will finally ruin the Imperialists... And the Cavalier Casali tells me that a servant of his brother's who has just come from Puglia, says that the aforesaid Imperialists have retreated from Monopoli.[12]

Once again we see the confluence of a variety of sources and personal connections employed to emphasise the report's reliability. This news from Puglia also found its way to Mantua via the English ambassador in Venice (another brother of Casali), who passed it on to his Mantuan counterpart,[13] a further indication of the extent of dissemination. Gathering information was not sufficient: it had to be reliable. Personal and particularly family connections could be important in guaranteeing that. The provision of useful news would, diplomats hoped, lead to the receipt of similar information in return.

In order to appear well-informed, it was important to report everything possibly relevant. Ambassadors could not afford to appear behind with

---

[10] *Dispacci*, p. 14, 'Habiamo inteso da persona digna di fede che'l prefato reverendissimo legato ha hauto questa matima [sic] letere da Roma, che li significa che la Sanctità del Pontefice era cum le gotte cum uno pocho de febre, ma che'l tal male se judicava piui [sic] tosto ficto che vero, perchè el mal ha Sua Sanctità era un sdegno grandissimo conceputo contra i ambassatori françesi, che li era sta facto intender tractavano di atosicarlo.' The legate in question was Cardinal Gonzaga, legate to Ancona.

[11] The National Archives, SP 1/53, fols. 232r–232v, (*L&P*, Vol. IV, 5479). For other missions of Cavallucchio, see Fletcher, *Our Man in Rome*, pp. 3, 77, 97.

[12] ASMo, Archivio Estense, Ambasciatori, Italia, Roma, b. 32, c. 214ii/41, 19 June 1529.

[13] ASMn, AG 1463, unnumbered letter of 4 October 1529.

the news. Though he must have guessed she would receive the news from elsewhere, on 23 August 1458, Bartolomeo Bonatti, the Mantuan resident in Milan, wrote to Barbara of Brandenburg that news had arrived of the election of Enea Silvio Piccolomini as Pope.[14] The following year, Vincenzo della Scalona, also a Mantuan resident in Milan, wrote to Ludovico Gonzaga with news about Pope Pius II's planned departure from Rome for Mantua and his itinerary. This he had obtained from a priest who had travelled from the city.[15] In another letter he prefaced further comment on papal affairs with the observation that 'although it is certain that Your Excellency will have all the news of the Pope from Bartolomeo or by other means, I will however write what we have here.'[16] The letter was as much a demonstration of della Scalona's superior sources as it was information of practical use.

While a detailed consideration of chancellery practices is outside the scope of this study, it is worth noting that the fact that a letter was written did not guarantee that it was written by the ambassador himself nor indeed that it was read by his principal. Drafts were often prepared by secretaries. In a treatise on the proper management of a prelate's court in Rome, written in the 1540s, Francesco Priscianese observed that it was vital for a secretary to be familiar with his lord's mind, his comings and goings and his humours in order to satisfy him fully. He added: 'It is necessary to be very alert and adroit in this, and when writing to transform into him.'[17] The idea that a secretary should effectively become his master is testimony to the importance of this role; moreover, this comment shows that the concept of the representative at times personifying his master resonated beyond the figure of the ambassador. In the act of writing, at least, the secretary had a *persona mixta* too. He also had a key role at the home court. In England, for example, Henry VIII's Latin

---

[14] *Carteggio degli Oratori Mantovani Alla Corte Sforzesca (1450–1500)*, ed. Isabella Lazzarini (Rome: Ministero per i beni e le attività culturali, 1999), Vol. I, no. 58, p. 165.

[15] *Carteggio*, Vol. I, no. 106, p. 215.

[16] Vincenzo della Scalona to Ludovico Gonzaga, 4 February 1459, Milan. Letter no. 127, Vol. I, p. 237: 'Del papa benché sia certo la vostra excellentia haverà el tuto da Bartholomeo o per altra via, tamen scriverò quello se ne ha qui. Dal dì de la partita da Roma, erano partite le sue zornate per modo che in xii zorni se doveva trovare in Perosa, ove se stima che sua sanctità sia giunta et lì ha a dimorare xv zorni, exinde trasferirsi a Fiorenza ove sarà circa 'l fine de questo o principio de la'tro mese; da Fiorenza in qua per ancor non si sente la deliberazione de sua sanctità.'

[17] Priscianese, *Del Governo della Corte*, p. 69. 'Ma con tutto ciò, se egli non avesse bene la mente del suo Signore, e non sapesse i modi e gli andar suoi, e conoscesse (come si dice) gli umori, impossibil cosa sarebbe il potergli sodisfare a pieno. Bisogna adunque che in questo sia molto avvertito e destro, e scrivendo si trasformi in lui, togliendo di suo solamente l'artificio delle sentenze e delle parole; e così potrà adempiere il suo desiderio.'

secretary Pietro Vanni (an Italian by birth) summarised and sometimes translated reports from Rome for Cardinal Wolsey.[18] The envoys of Italian states were expected to write daily reports, and it is hard to imagine that every one was read by the prince. Nonetheless, princes insisted. In 1476, Galeazzo Maria Sforza commanded his resident ambassador in Bologna to write every day on pain of death![19] The records of the Mantuan envoys to Rome suggest they did likewise, as did Gasparo Contarini, Venetian ambassador, during his 1528–9 mission. Things were different for the ultramontane powers. Reliable couriers did not leave Rome that frequently, and the postal service was at times seriously inadequate. While on occasion we find sequences of letters that appear to have been written almost daily,[20] it was impossible to maintain such a routine in the longer term. By June 1528, as serious negotiations got underway about ending Henry VIII's marriage to Catherine of Aragon, the English did not even have a functioning weekly post service to and from Rome.[21] To compensate, envoys often shared couriers, though this had its own hazards. In May 1529, papal officials shared messengers with the English when sending letters to Cardinal Salviati, the papal legate in France.[22] However, it was subsequently discovered that the English ambassadors had opened the pope's letters to Salviati, and sent them to Venice for deciphering. Clearly their Venetian contact was not wholly reliable, for copies made their way back from Venice to Salviati and the English had to apologise.[23] In 1454, Mantuan and Milanese orators in Rome sent letters together to the Milanese court, which were initially received by Vincenzo della Scalona, Mantuan orator in Milan.[24] The practice of courier-sharing might seem unusual, even risky, but it arguably offered a level of protection to the courier. Carrying the letters of one power alone, he was vulnerable to attack; less clearly identified with any one particular nation, perhaps he was better respected. As Allen points out, though, courier-sharing only worked when there was 'a modicum of political stability'.[25]

[18] For example, *L&P*, Vol. IV, 2779, 2780, 2782, 2852 and 2853.
[19] 'Te Imponemo et Comandamo Expressamente Sotto Pena de la Testa Che Omne dì ne Scrive.' Leverotti, pp. 80–1, citing *Carteggi*, Vol. II, p. 303.
[20] For example, the run of letters from Casali alone, or Casali and John Russell, dated 23, 24, 26 and 27 February 1526. *L&P*, Vol. IV, 2910, 2912, 2918 and 2921.
[21] *St P*, Vol. VII, p.84 (*L&P*, Vol. IV, 4390).
[22] *Lettere di Principi*, ed. Girolamo Ruscelli, 3 vols (Venice: Ziletti, 1581), Vol. II, 161v (*L&P*, Vol. IV, 5528). *Lettere di Principi*, Vol. II, p. 167v (*L&P*, Vol. IV, 5546).
[23] BL, Cotton MSS, Vit. B vol. XI, fol. 185r (*L&P*, Vol. IV, 5725).
[24] *Carteggio degli Oratori Mantovani*, Vol. I, no. 12, p. 87.
[25] E. John B. Allen, *Post and Courier Service in the Diplomacy of Early Modern Europe* (The Hague: Martinus Nijhoff, 1972), p. 26.

As diplomatic structures became more firmly established, so did Europe's national postal systems. Under Louis XI (r. 1461–83), foreign couriers passing through France were obliged to stick to set post routes. Local postmasters would inspect passports and supply horses to the agents of friendly princes.[26] More peripheral powers followed in regulating their post: Spain established the position of master-of-posts in 1505 and England by 1512.[27] Couriers travelling on particularly secret matters might decide to avoid the official routes, as an English messenger did in July 1529,[28] but this was risky. The most confidential information was only ever conveyed orally. Although letters (or parts thereof) might be encrypted, the ciphers in regular use were based on letter-substitution plus a few code-names. They were easily broken and served only to protect letters from casual viewers, not determined opponents.[29]

b.   Competition and co-operation in newsgathering

The practice of courier-sharing is one example of the ways that diplomats in Rome collaborated in order to acquire and communicate news. The context for these information-sharing practices was the collective of ambassadors that had formed in Rome. Popes would often consult with ambassadors together. Pius II did so in 1463, when he summoned the Italian envoys to a joint meeting to ask their support for his planned crusade.[30] Following the death of Alexander VI in August 1503, amid fears that the city might be invaded during the *sede vacante*, the cardinals called in the ambassadors of France, Spain, Venice and the Holy Roman Empire in an effort to ensure the security of the forthcoming conclave.[31] Envoys also initiated such audiences. In 1513, the English ambassador, Cardinal Bainbridge, went together with his Imperial and Spanish counterparts to Pope Leo X to protest the re-instatement of two 'schismatic' cardinals, Sanseverino and Carvajal, who had been deprived of their benefices.[32] Diplomats talked among themselves too. In 1509, the Venetian ambassadors approached Bainbridge to lobby for his support in their ongoing conflict with the papacy.[33] A letter of 1468 describes a

[26] Allen, *Post and Courier Service*, pp. 3–4.   [27] Allen, *Post and Courier Service*, pp. 9, 13.
[28] *L&P*, Vol. IV, 5780.
[29] David Kahn, *The Codebreakers: The Story of Secret Writing* (New York: Scribner, 1996), pp. 109, 125, 150; James Westfall Thompson and Saul K. Padover, *Secret Diplomacy: Espionage and Cryptography 1500–1815* (New York: Frederick Ungar, 1963), p. 256; Mattingly, *Renaissance Diplomacy*, p. 238.
[30] Pius, *Commentarii*, Vol. II, pp. 2402–3 (*Secret Memoirs*, p. 341).
[31] Burchard, *Liber Notarum*, Vol. II, p. 360.
[32] Chambers, *Cardinal Bainbridge*, pp. 46–7.   [33] *Dispacci*, pp. 175–9.

meeting of the ambassadors of Milan, Florence and Naples at the house of the latter to exchange news.[34] In 1534, Melchior Lang wrote to the duke of Milan recommending that he write to Giorgio Andreasio, his resident ambassador in Rome and ask Andreasio to approach the other residents in the city to establish their masters' views on aspects of the conflict between Milan and the French.[35]

The existence of a group of resident diplomats at the papal court representing all the major polities enabled the Pope to use one ambassador to put pressure on another. Clement VII did so when the Venetians refused to return the towns of Ravenna and Cervia, which they had occupied during Clement's 1527 imprisonment. In 1528, the Venetian ambassador Gasparo Contarini was called in to see the Pope, and on his arrival, found the ambassadors of France, England and Milan along with Cardinals Farnese and Ridolfi.[36] The presence of the allies was intended to encourage the Venetians to settle, although the latter had some success in undermining this effort. Although the Mantuan ambassador was not at the meeting, he heard enough about it to write a detailed letter corroborating Contarini's account.[37] While allies' ambassadors would work together more frequently, there are also examples of diplomatic encounters between the ambassadors of hostile powers within the ambit of the court. The formalities of court life provided a useful space for such discussions. Contarini's correspondence offers one example: on 6 December 1528, he found himself in the chapel next to the Imperial ambassador Musetola, and asked him whether he had any letters from Naples. In turn, Musetola asked Contarini to bring to the Signoria's attention, the case of a commander of the Order of St James named Beneto who had been captured by Venetian galleys, offering to return the favour should a similar case arise, 'as can happen in wartime'.[38] At the time, the Venetians and the Holy Roman Empire were on opposing sides, and the evidence of Contarini's letter book is that he did not frequently see the Imperial ambassadors individually. The fate of Beneto is not known, but the letter demonstrates that Rome offered such channels of communication.

Information-gathering went on at a range of social levels. In his treatise on diplomacy, Étienne Dolet recommended that the ambassador should

[34] Dover, '"Saper la Mente"', p. 21.
[35] Paolo Oldrini, 'Debolezza Politica e Ingerenze Curiali al Tramonto della Dinastia Sforzesca: Il Carteggio con Roma al Tempo di Francesco II Sforza (1530–1535)', in Chittolini (ed.), *Gli Sforza*, pp. 291–340 (p. 318).
[36] G. Contarini, fol. 7v. 7 June 1528.
[37] ASMn, Archivio Gonzaga 877, c. 285r. 8 June 1528.
[38] G. Contarini, fols. 125v, 127v–128r.

have amongst his servants a man 'who will wander about the city, joining in conversations and courting familiarity with a large number of persons, to gather every breath of rumor, so that some conjecture can be drawn from them concerning the purposes of those with whom the ambassador is dealing.'[39] This engagement with street politics was complemented by more elite sociability. Ambassadors could take advantage of social circles that brought them together with cardinals and local nobility. The Mantuan ambassador, Francesco Gonzaga, describes how during a visit to Rome in 1526, Isabella d'Este Gonzaga and five other ladies attended a dinner hosted by Franceschino Cibo; the five gentlemen invited (presumably in the hope that they might support Isabella's campaign to have her son promoted to the cardinalate) were the respective diplomatic representatives of the Holy Roman Emperor, the kings of France and England, the duke of Ferrara and the marquis of Mantua.[40] The multiple functions of diplomatic sociability are considered in Chapter 6 but there is no doubt that it could be a means of keeping up with gossip.

This collective discussion – both formal and informal – provided the context for practices of information-sharing. Envoys worked together, swapped notes and lobbied each other. It was common for ambassadors to visit one another in order to exchange information and news. For example, in January 1528, the duke of Ferrara's agent at Rome, Roberto Boschetti, wrote:

I often go and visit the Cavalier Casali, who is at home with a bit of a cold; yesterday a courier arrived from his king; today I was there to find out whether he had anything pertinent to Your Excellency; he replied no, and that the dispatch was only to congratulate the Pope on his liberty and to exhort him to declare himself, etc.[41]

This was a little disingenuous on Casali's part, for Cardinal Wolsey's letter accompanying the dispatch was in no way only concerned with the offer of polite congratulations but also referred to the need to make progress on the matter of Henry VIII's marriage.[42] However, the incident makes the important point that exchanges between members of the diplomatic corps could be as much about the dissemination of half-truths and *disinformation* as about the provision of *information*. Indeed, when ambassadors were engaged in secret negotiations, they went to considerable lengths to conceal their activities. Under interrogation about his master's corrupt dealings with the English ambassadors to

---

[39] Dolet, 'De Officio Legati', p. 86.   [40] Luzio, 'Isabella d'Este', p. 367.
[41] ASMo, Archivio Estense, Ambasciatori, Italia, Roma, b. 32, c. 212i/11.
[42] *St P*, Vol. VII, p. 42 (*L&P*, Vol. IV, 3770).

Rome, the cardinal of Ravenna's former secretary explained that he used to see them 'going secretly into the cardinal of Ravenna's house, by the back door, just the two of them'.[43] In short, the resident ambassadors formed a network: representatives of friendly powers would see each other regularly, at home or at court. They acted collectively and co-operated in order to achieve their aims, whether in gathering information, communicating it or negotiating with the pope. As the one centre to which all European powers sent representatives, Rome offered a unique space for the daily discussion of international issues, where hostile powers might communicate unofficially, and where the representatives of allies might plan.

c.   The post route as political space

The distance embodied by the long post routes across Europe has traditionally been regarded as a problem in early modern politics. Fernand Braudel called such distance 'the first enemy', commenting that '[s]tatesmen and ambassadors, whom we usually imagine with weighty matters on their minds, are often preoccupied by the arrival or delays of the mail'.[44] Pius II worried that envoys from Mesopotamia and Persia might not be genuine. 'In matters carried on from a distance,' he wrote, 'there is abundant opportunity for deception and the truth can seldom be discovered.'[45] Slow communication was not the only difficulty facing sixteenth-century diplomats: they also had to contend with the threat of kidnapping or attack, the adversities of war and weather, with broken limbs and with over-zealous local officials. In 1456, the Milanese ambassador to Rome, Giacomo Calcaterra, drowned in the Tiber on his journey back to Rome from Castro Giubileo, where he had fled to avoid the plague.[46] Much trouble ensued as the Milanese authorities attempted to ensure that his confidential papers were gathered together. Letters were dispatched to Calcaterra's relative (*nipote*), Leone da Treviso, requesting that he gather together the writings so no misfortune should come to them (literally, *che non vadano in sinistro*).[47] The 'difficulty of the road'

---

[43] ASR, Tribunale del Governatore di Roma, Processi 3; 2 II; 3 May 1535. For the background to these dealings, see Chapter 7.

[44] Fernand Braudel, *The Mediterranean and the Mediterranean World in the Age of Philip II*, trans. Siân Reynolds (London: Fontana, 1975) pp. 355–6.

[45] Pius, *Commentarii*, Vol. I, pp. 906–7 (*Secret Memoirs*, p. 177).

[46] Senatore, *Uno Mundo de Carta*, p. 157.

[47] le scripture lassate per messer Jacomo volemo che tu debbi recogliere et servare, et che ne avisi come le haveray in ordine perché te avisaremo quello ne haveray ad fare; recomanda molto bene che non vadano in sinistro'. ASM SPE, Roma, 44, c. 91, cited in Senatore, *Uno mundo de carta*, p. 157.

could also be cited as an excuse: Christopher Bainbridge used it as a reason not to travel personally with a Venetian envoy to see Pope Julius II at Civitavecchia, sending a more junior diplomat, Christopher Fisher, instead.[48] However, the post road was not simply an obstacle course to be negotiated. Rather, it was an important space for all sorts of political encounters, from the friendly to the decidedly hostile.

The post route from Paris to Rome, to take one example, went first via Lyons, then east to Chambéry and across the Alps to Susa and Turin, although the coast road to Genoa was also an option. A series of post-houses along the way provided facilities for refreshment. A variety of routes were available through northern Italy: conditions of weather and war were determinants in which was taken. Envoys might travel via Alessandria, or via Milan. Some went by sea from Genoa to Lucca and rejoined the post road at Florence. The route through Italy passed through numerous polities: territories of the dukes of Savoy and Ferrara, of the popes, of the Florentine and Sienese republics, before heading into papal territory and on to Viterbo and Rome.[49] In wartime, if the Cenis Pass in Piedmont was held by hostile troops, travellers had to choose from the other available options: the Septimer, the Splügen, the St Bernard, the St Gothard or the Brenner.[50] The Brenner Pass took couriers from Italy to Vienna: from Rome the route led past Bologna, Mantua, Trent, through the Alps then to Innsbruck and Salzburg.[51] Visitors (and dispatches) from Spain arrived by sea from Barcelona or Valencia. An impression of the travel times involved can be gleaned from the calculation that in good circumstances, professional couriers did the journey from Rome to London in just over two weeks.[52] An ambassador

---

[48] 'Luoi Non Puo Venir a Civita per Esser el Camin Longo et Tropo Sinestro' AS Venice, Arch. Proprio, Roma, iii, fol. 77, cited in Chambers, *Cardinal Bainbridge*, p. 30.

[49] My accounts of the route are derived from Wall, *Voyage*, the letters of Richard Croke, and those of Sir Francis Bryan and Pietro Vanni, calendared in *L&P*. These have been cross-referenced with George Henry Freeling (ed.), *Informacõn for Pylgrymes unto the Holy Londe* (London, 1824 [1498]). Biblioteca Braidense Milano, ms AG.XI.42, Vignatense, *Itinerario Militare*, cc. 160–160v. *Elenco delle Poste tra Parigi, Milano e Roma, nel 1513 circa*, cit. in Clemente Fedele and Mario Gallenga, *Per Servizio di Nostro Signore: Strade, Corrieri e Poste dei Papi dal Medioevo al 1870* (= *Quaderni di Storia Postale* 10, 1998), pp. 212–13. Nicole Le Huen, *Le Grant Voyage de Jherusalem* (Paris, 1517), fol. 197v.

[50] G. Dickinson, *Du Bellay in Rome* (Leiden: Brill, 1960), pp. 11–40, especially p. 13.

[51] Allen, *Post and Courier Service*, p. 65.

[52] This was the approximate speed of the English couriers Alexander and Taddeo who carried messages between London and Rome during the final period of serious negotiations with Clement VII about Henry VIII's marriage between April and June 1529 prior to the advocation of the case to Rome, derived from an analysis of their known arrival and departure dates. *L&P*, Vol. IV, 5530, *L&P*, Vol. V, pp. 311–12, *St P*, Vol. VII, p. 168.

riding post tended to take somewhat longer. In 1529, the English ambassador Stephen Gardiner took 24 days to get from Dover to Rome;[53] later
that year, Sir Nicholas Carew and Richard Sampson, travelling in more
ceremonial style to the coronation of the Holy Roman Emperor Charles
V, proceeded at a leisurely pace. They were at Calais on 12 October
1529, but did not arrive in Bologna until 2 December: a total of 52 days
on the road.[54]

The herald Thomas Wall's account of Carew and Sampson's voyage
provides rich detail of how 'on the road' diplomacy might work. On their
way, they met Francis I, the king of France, and his mother, Louise of
Savoy. It was standard practice, during this period of Anglo-French
alliance, for English diplomats *en route* to Italy to pay such a visit.[55] They
dined with the English ambassador in Paris, who would have been able to
update them on the political situation there. Further along their route,
they met an ambassador from the pope to the French king, a papal
nuncio travelling to England and another English ambassador who was
returning from Italy. At Lyons, Carew and Sampson dined with a Florentine merchant. They met the duke of Savoy in Turin and the city
governor in Piacenza. Theirs was a journey full of opportunities for
discussion and diplomacy.[56] As we will see in Chapter 7, they also
received presents *en route*, gift exchange being a symbolic means of
political expression.

Much explicit political activity went on along the post route too.
Giovanni Caimo, envoy of Francesco Sforza to Pope Calixtus II, met
Enea Silvio Piccolomini, (the future Pope Pius II) at Viterbo prior to
Caimo's arrival in Rome. They discussed Milanese–papal affairs.[57] In
May 1528, Gasparo Contarini, *en route* to Viterbo, met Eleonora Gonzaga della Rovere, duchess of Urbino.[58] Her husband, Francesco Maria
della Rovere, was the mercenary captain-general of the Venetian army,
and the meeting gave Contarini an opportunity to pass on word of the
Venetians' 'high satisfaction' with the duke's service. Sometimes, discussions on the road were a matter of news-gathering. Another member of
the Contarini family, Francesco, travelling from Venice to the Imperial

---

[53] Gardiner left Dover on 22 January 1529 and arrived at Rome on 15 February. *L&P*, Vol.
IV, 5195, 5294. Bonner left Bologna on 8 January 1533 and arrived in London on the
24th or 25th. *L&P*, Vol. VI, 101. *CSP Ven*, Vol. IV, 847.
[54] Wall, *Voyage*.
[55] For other examples, see *St P*, Vol. VII, pp. 54–5 (*L&P*, Vol. IV, 3954) and BL, Cotton
MSS, Vit. B, vol. x, fol. 189 (*L&P*, Vol. IV, 5042).
[56] Wall, *Voyage*, pp. 50, 55–58.
[57] Pius, *Commentarii*, Vol. I, pp. 194–5 (*Secret Memoirs*, pp. 73–4).
[58] G. Contarini, fol. 2r.

court at Vienna in 1534, wrote home with reports from merchants he had met in Villach about the latest developments in the struggle for the Hungarian throne.[59] In short, the type of news-gathering activity that was expected of an ambassador in his day-to-day work did not stop simply because he was travelling. On the contrary, he would exploit the opportunities to acquire information that his journey provided.

The presence of so many interested parties along the post road made it a prime spot for spying. Though their mission was meant to be discreet, news that the English diplomats Stephen Gardiner and Edward Fox had been spotted at Lyons quickly made its way to Venice, thanks to the intelligence networks of a Milanese cardinal.[60] The structures of the post route were such that secrecy was virtually impossible. As Gardiner and Fox lamented, post-horses could only be obtained after travellers had presented themselves to the local captain and 'shewed what they be'.[61] Another English ambassador, William Knight, travelling to Rome in 1527, discovered that one of his fellow travellers, a friar from Calabria, 'in veari dede was a Spagniarde and a spye'.[62] Even supposedly friendly travelling companions might spy on each other. Vicenzo Casali, a cousin of the English ambassador Gregorio, was tasked with keeping a watchful eye on his companion Francesco Campano, one of the pope's chamberlains, as the pair journeyed to London.[63]

The problems that one diplomat faced on the road were often created by and to the benefit of another. In an effort to delay the start of negotiations between Charles V and Clement VII, in May 1528, the ambassadors of England, France, Venice and Urbino conspired to kidnap an Imperial agent, Sigismondo di Ferrara. Sigismondo had a papal safe-conduct but, although widely used, safe-conducts were accorded limited respect in times of war.[64] After an abortive attempt to kidnap Sigismondo in the territories of the duke of Urbino (thereby avoiding an infringement of the papal safe-conduct) the English ambassador succeeded in imprisoning Sigismondo in the Braccian fortress of

---

[59] Biblioteca Nazionale Marciana, Codices Italiani VII 802 (= 8219) (hereafter F. Contarini), fol. 20v.
[60] Sanuto XLVII cols. 77–78 (*CSP Ven*, Vol. IV, 251).
[61] Pocock, *Records*, Vol. I, p. 87 (*L&P*, Vol. IV, 4007).
[62] *St P*, Vol. VII, p. 16 (*L&P*, Vol. IV, 3638).   [63] *L&P*, Vol. IV, 5073, 5037.
[64] Bibliothèque Nationale de France, MS Français 3040, fol. 58r; ASMn, Archivio Gonzaga 877, c. 272r; Molini, *Documenti*, Vol. II, p. 39. G. Contarini, fols. 17r–17v. ASMn, Archivio Gonzaga 877, c. 350r. For a more detailed account of these events, see *Our Man in Rome*, pp. 35–8. E. R. Adair, *The Exterritoriality of Ambassadors in the Sixteenth and Seventeenth Centuries* (London: Longmans, Green, 1929), pp. 125–6, Frey and Frey, *Diplomatic Immunity*, pp. 134–6 and Allen, *Post and Courier Service*, pp. 22–4.

the Orsini family and intercepting some useful information.[65] There were no serious political consequences, beyond what the Mantuan ambassador called 'a good ticking-off' from the Pope, for the English and French.[66] This was by no means an exceptional incident. In 1503, the train of a French ambassador on his way to Rome was set upon by bandits. His goods were stolen and a member of his entourage gravely wounded.[67] In 1527, the English agent Thomas Wyatt was kidnapped by Imperial troops.[68] The Abbot of Farfa, Napoleone Orsini, who had imprisoned Sigismondo at Bracciano, went on in August 1529, to kidnap the Spanish Cardinal Quiñones, a papal legate, on the road out of Rome. He successfully held him to ransom for 2,700 ducats.[69] A report of the same month, from a Mantuan ambassador, Giacomo Malatesta, describes another of Gregorio Casali's enterprises: this time dispatching one Pietro Cavallucchio with both cavalry and infantry, to the border area between Brescia and Verona in order to intercept some documents relating to Henry VIII's divorce.[70] As we saw in Chapter 4, Cavallucchio was 'very expert in military matters',[71] and these cases remind us that an ability to manage military operations could be an important asset to an ambassador. Far from being restricted to fixed locations like the audience chamber, the work of information-gathering continued along the hundreds of miles of the post routes. While this distance undoubtedly posed many problems for travellers, it also provided opportunities for the exchange of information, the hindrance of opponents and the maintenance of political relationships. While the time required for travel and communication was, of course, an important factor in the ways that diplomacy was conducted, the post road should not be regarded merely as a gap between the diplomat and his master but rather as a space for early modern politics.

d.   Diplomatic networks

Besides exploiting the social circles of Rome to obtain news from their fellow envoys, diplomats drew on family and commercial networks to gather information and expedite diplomatic business. In a mutually beneficial relationship the employing prince would gain access to his

[65] Molini, *Documenti*, Vol. II, p. 42. G. Contarini, fol. 22r.
[66] ASMn, Archivio Gonzaga 877, c. 358r.   [67] Burchard, *Liber Notarum*, Vol. II, p. 217.
[68] Susan Brigden and Jonathan Woolfson, 'Thomas Wyatt in Italy', *Renaissance Quarterly* 58 (2005), 464–511.
[69] G. Contarini, fols. 287r–288v.
[70] ASMn, Archivio Gonzaga 1463, unnumbered letter of 2 August 1529.
[71] TNA, SP 1/53, fols. 232r–232v (*L&P*, Vol. IV, 5479).

envoy's personal networks, while the envoy's family and friends gained valuable contacts with potential patrons in the European courts.[72] The choice in 1450 of Vincenzo Amidani as an envoy to Rome by Francesco Sforza, then about to enter Milan, was likely influenced by the fact that Vincenzo's brother, Niccolò Amidani, bishop of Piacenza, was present at the court of Rome as a vice-chamberlain.[73] These networks were a Europe-wide phenomenon and are a diplomatic variant of the *consorterie* that sustained numerous Italian family enterprises.[74] In the early fifteenth century, members of the Scolari family based in Buda acted as formal and informal diplomatic intermediaries between their home state of Florence and Hungary, serving as Hungarian ambassadors to the Signoria in 1410 and 1424.[75] In the early sixteenth century, Tommaso Spinelli, member of another Florentine merchant family, acted as an English agent and then ambassador in the Low Countries; his relative Leonardo was a chamberlain (*cubicularius*) to Pope Leo X and went on a diplomatic mission to England for the pope.[76] Another such merchant family was the Gigli family of Lucca, discussed in Chapter 4. Two Gigli clerics served as English orators in Rome, but their contacts with England arose initially from the family's presence as mercery merchants in London.[77] Some arrangements were more formal than others. Neither Pierfrancesco Bardi nor Giovanni Cavalcanti was a Florentine or papal ambassador, but their company house in London functioned as an informal diplomatic outpost for the Medici family.[78] These fifteenth-century networks often rested on trade connections, but as diplomacy became more professional, princely and formalised in the sixteenth

---

[72] For a series of case-studies, which I touch on only briefly here, see the special issue of the *Journal of Early Modern History* 14 (2010), Catherine Fletcher and Jennifer M. DeSilva (eds), on Italian ambassadorial networks in early modern Europe.

[73] Margaroli, *Diplomazia e Stati Rinascimentali*, pp. 70–1.

[74] For an example, see Carol M. Richardson, 'Francesco Todeschini Piccolomini (1439–1503), Sant'Eustachio and the Consorteria Piccolomini', in Mary Hollingsworth and Carol M. Richardson (eds), *The Possessions of a Cardinal: Politics, Piety and Art, 1450–1700* (University Park: Pennsylvania State University Press, 2009), pp. 46–60.

[75] Katalin Prajda, 'The Florentine Scolari family at the court of Sigismund of Luxemburg in Buda', *Journal of Early Modern History* 14 (2010), 513–33.

[76] Behrens, 'Office', p. 167. Robert Babcock, *The Spinelli Family: Florence in the Renaissance 1430–1535: Guide to an Exhibition at the Beinecke Library* (New Haven: Beinecke Rare Book and Manuscript Library, 1989).

[77] Cecil H. Clough, 'Three Gigli of Lucca in England during the fifteenth and early sixteenth centuries: diversification in a family of mercery merchants', *The Ricardian* 13 (2003), 121–47.

[78] Cinzia M. Sicca, 'Consumption and trade of art between Italy and England in the first half of the sixteenth century: the London house of the Bardi and Cavalcanti company'. *Renaissance Studies* 16 (2002), 163–201.

century, we begin to find networks whose service was more exclusively political and military in nature.

In the 1520s, the Gigli were superseded by the Casali family of Bologna, members of which served as papal nuncios to England, English ambassadors to Rome, Venice and Hungary and Hungarian ambassador to Rome as well as taking roles in military service and the government of Bologna.[79] Though they maintained some of the mercantile and landholding interests that had helped the family establish itself in fifteenth-century Bologna, the careers of this generation lay firmly in foreign service. Agamemnon Grassi, Bolognese orator to Rome, was a brother of Paride Grassi, papal master-of-ceremonies; a third Grassi brother, Achilles, became a cardinal.[80] Giacomo Malatesta, Mantuan ambassador to Venice, asked his brother to substitute for him temporarily in August 1526; his counterpart in Rome, Francesco Gonzaga, brought his son Girolamo into the family business.[81] On the death of his father Mariano, Agostino Chigi took over his role as Sienese ambassador to Rome.[82] Contemporaries understood and accepted the service of a relative as a substitute: the blood tie was sufficient guarantee. Similar family *consorterie* were to be found elsewhere in Europe. Jean de Dinteville, one of Holbein's *Ambassadors*, had two brothers in diplomatic service: François de Dinteville, bishop of Auxerre, went as French ambassador to Rome in 1530, while Louis de Dinteville, a Knight Hospitaller, went as an ambassador of the Order of the Knights of St John of Jerusalem to the Emperor Charles V's coronation in 1529–30.[83] Alberto Pio da Carpi, in service first to the Holy Roman Emperor Maximilian and later to King Francis I of France, was the uncle of Rodolfo Pio da Carpi, bishop of Faenza, who became a cardinal in 1536.[84] The Du Bellay family included several diplomats: Guillaume, seigneur de Langey, was an ambassador to Venice and dedicatee of Dolet's treatise *De Officio Legati*; his brother Jean du Bellay carried out missions to Rome and went on to be a cardinal.[85] Two brothers from a Florentine merchant family in Hungary, Francesco di Jacopo and Giovanni Marsuppini, the latter, a papal *cubicularius*, served

---

[79] Fletcher, 'War, diplomacy and social mobility'.
[80] Jennifer M. DeSilva, 'Official and unofficial diplomacy between Rome and Bologna: the de' Grassi family under Pope Julius II, 1503–13', *JEMH* 14 (2010), 535–57.
[81] ASMn, AG 1460, c. 160r; AG 880 c. 291r.
[82] Agostino Chigi, *The Correspondence of Agostino Chigi (1466–1520)*, ed. Ingrid Rowland, Studi e Testi 399 (Vatican City: BAV, 2001), p. 43.
[83] Mary F. S. Hervey, *Holbein's "Ambassadors": The Picture and the Men. An Historical Study* (London: George Bell and Sons, 1900), pp. 53–5.
[84] Picot, *Les Français Italianisants*, Vol. I, p. 85n.
[85] Hervey, *Holbein's "Ambassadors"*, p. 47 and n.

as the Roman procurators of János Szapolyai, contender for the Hungarian throne, from 1517.[86]

As earlier examples showed, the citation of a family relationship or friendship was a means of establishing a source's credit. Family connections ensured a back-up, should one sibling be temporarily out of action. Moreover, these networks facilitated the provision of reliable information from trusted sources. Members of the network could benefit from independent checks on information received from their masters, while the master could benefit from the service of multiple family members. Particularly when employing a 'mercenary' diplomat, a prince got an entire family at his service. News might be had from 'a servant of my brother's', and family contacts, as Chapter 6 shows, could offer hospitality and accommodation. The family, in turn, could cultivate patrons in a series of courts. The informal network system, however, also had its dangers. One 'weak link' could compromise the interests of the whole family.[87] The cases here underscore the importance of 'privatistic' structures in diplomatic practice. Informal networks – whether along the post route or acquired through family connections – were essential to the smooth functioning of diplomacy. Kinship ties were, on the whole, a sufficient guarantee of fidelity to the principal. Coming back to the ambassador's dual persona, here we see the uses of its 'private' or 'familial' side. In the course of information-gathering, the diplomat would draw as much on personal resources and connections as on his official status. Indeed, without this informal networking, the official persona could not effectively function.

---

[86] Megan K. Williams, '"Dui fratelli... con dui principi": family and fidelity on a failed diplomatic mission', *JEMH* 14 (2010), 579–611 (p. 590).
[87] Fletcher, *Our Man in Rome*, p. 130.

6   Locating diplomacy in the city of Rome

In 1523, four Venetian ambassadors arrived outside Rome, on their way to pledge obedience to the newly elected Pope Adrian VI. Approaching the city through some beautiful meadows, they came to a *vigna* half a mile outside the city walls. In this pastoral setting, more a country retreat than a working vineyard, they were each provided with a room hung with tapestries and cloths of silk, in which to get changed for their formal entrance. They were offered 'all the most noble refreshments to be found in Rome, and precious wines of many sorts'. A couple of hours later, they and their entourage processed into the city, although so many people came out to meet them that progress was slow indeed. There were, the ambassadors proudly reported, at least two thousand horses present.[1] Such events required considerable planning. The city family that owned the *vigna* had to plan and play host. The curia *familiares* had to be organised to turn out. Most importantly, though, this case emphasises the significance of Rome's approaches, streets, gates and buildings as locations for diplomacy. Processions and splendid display – on the part of diplomats and their hosts – were a performance of power.

Street politics were enormously important in Renaissance Rome.[2] From festivals to the *possesso* of the city by a new pope, from processions between Vatican and Lateran to the polemics pinned on the statue of Pasquino, the spaces of the city were sites for political life. The street had a darker side too: there were commonly riots on the death of a pope or in cases of food shortage; the danger of flooding was perennial. This chapter discusses the spaces of Rome that diplomats inhabited. It begins with a discussion of the entry route, the first point of encounter for the visiting envoy, assessing its symbolic resonance in light of contemporary visions

---

[1] 'Tutti i Più Nobili Rinfrescamenti Che in Roma si Potessero Trovare, e Vini Preziosissimi di Molte Sorta', *Relazioni*, ser. 2, Vol. III, pp. 90–3.

[2] Carol M. Richardson, *Reclaiming Rome*, gives a rich account of the transformation of the city's fabric in the fifteenth century. Laurie Nussdorfer, 'The politics of space in early modern Rome', *Memoirs of the American Academy in Rome* 42 (1997), 161–86, is focused on the seventeenth century but gives further important context.

of the ancient city and the topography of Renaissance Rome. It considers a series of physical spaces that diplomats occupied, in the Vatican Palace, in cardinals' houses, and on the streets of Rome. It then turns to assess accommodation options and shifting trends in ambassadors' choice of housing. This is contextualised with a discussion of the importance of sociability, returning to the question of the ambassador's dual persona raised in earlier chapters.

a.   The Renaissance city

Rome was a growing city in the later fifteenth and early sixteenth century. Its population was perhaps 25–30,000 in the middle of the fifteenth century and somewhere over 50,000 by the time of the 1526–7 census, though this may be an underestimate.[3] This small population was easily enclosed within the old city walls: significant areas of the ancient city were no longer inhabited. Rome was divided into fourteen districts (*rioni*), most clustered in the bend of the River Tiber with the exception of Trastevere and Borgo, the latter, the site of the Vatican Palace. Each *rione* elected a *caporione* (head of the district) to serve for a term of three months, and the city as a whole was governed by a lay official known as the *governatore*, referred to in the liturgical texts as the Senator Urbis. As discussed in Chapter 1, this was a period that saw the popes promote a policy of renewing Rome. That meant renovating the fabric of the city as well as attending to the spiritual health of the Church. Alexander VI, Julius II and Leo X were among the popes who sponsored projects in urban planning: their new streets bore their names as the Via Alessandrina (replaced by the Via della Conciliazione), Via Giulia and Via Leonina (now Ripetta).[4] Cardinals were given new financial incentives to invest in property development (via permission to leave it to persons of their choice) and at least some of them took up the opportunity.[5]

---

[3] Gensini (ed.), *Roma Capitale* offers a comprehensive portrait of Roman society in the period between the return of the popes and the Sack. The classic account by Pio Pecchiai, *Roma nel Cinquecento* (Bologna: Licinio Cappelli, 1948), is still a valuable source. On the papal court, see Signorotto and Visceglia (eds), *Court and Politics*, and Fernández, 'The patrimony of St Peter'. There are further general accounts in P. A. Ramsey (ed.), *Rome in the Renaissance: The City and the Myth* (Binghamton: Center for Medieval and Renaissance Studies, 1982); Stinger, *The Renaissance in Rome* and Peter Partner, *Renaissance Rome 1500–1559: A Portrait of a Society* (Berkeley: University of California Press, 1976).

[4] Andrea Branchi, 'Alexander VI's plans for Rome', in Prebys (ed.), *Early Modern Rome*, pp. 548–55.

[5] For an example, see Lowe, *Church and Politics in Renaissance Italy: The Life and Career of Cardinal Francesco Soderini, 1453-1524*, , pp. 192–225.

The Palazzo Venezia and Palazzo della Cancelleria, respectively named for the Venetian origins of its Barbo patrons and the office of its owner Raffaele Riario, are two of the most prominent examples.

Papal policy did not only affect the physical fabric of the city. As Modigliani and Esposito have shown, the Roman nobility had to change in response to the changing nature of the papal court. As the curia became grander, larger and more international, the local nobility experienced greater competition from incomers for the offices they had traditionally exercised in the city. They needed to maintain a 'double strategy' of both civil and curial careers.[6] Like the cardinalate, the papal bureaucracy became more Italian over our period, a trend exacerbated by the sale of offices.[7] A son's curial career could provide a launch-pad for an immigrant family to establish itself in Rome by marrying locally.[8] Relations between the city families and the papacy were complex and sometimes tense. With the notable exceptions of Nicholas V and Paul III, most popes were outsiders. They had to balance the interests of the noble families of Rome with care.[9] Irene Fosi has shown how Julius II tried to emphasise the superiority of his court over the city's secular representatives through ceremonies such as the *possesso*.[10] Other popes tried to win over locals with entertainments including bullfights and theatre.

Ambassadors engaged with the city in a variety of ways. They might rely on the local nobility for rented accommodation, or turn to a national church or pilgrim hospital. They would have to obtain credit locally.[11] Envoys might offer financial support to a papal building project as they lobbied for favour.[12] They might take a tour of the stations of the cross, underlining their piety and, by implication, that of the state they

---

[6] Modigliani, "'Li Nobili Huomini'", p. 370; Anna Esposito, "'Li Nobili Huomini di Roma": Strategie Familiari tra Città, Curia e Municipo', in Gensini (ed.), *Roma Capitale*, pp. 373–88 (p. 374).

[7] Peter Partner, *The Pope's Men: The Papal Civil Service in the Renaissance* (Oxford: Clarendon Press, 1990), p. 12.

[8] Maria Antonietta Visceglia (ed.), *La Nobiltà Romana in Età Moderna: Profili Istituzionali e Pratiche Sociali* (Rome: Carocci, 2001), especially Benedetta Borello, 'Strategie di Insediamento in Città: i Pamphilj a Roma nel Primo Cinquecento', pp. 31–61. For further case-studies, see the essays in Gensini (ed.), *Roma Capitale*, in particular Pierre Hurtubise, 'L'Implantation d'Une Famille Florentine à Rome au Début du XVIe Ssiècle: Les Salviati', pp. 253–71, and Cesarina Casanova, *Gentilhuomini Ecclesiastici: Ceti e Mobilità Sociale nelle Legazioni Pontificie (secc. XVI–XVIII)* (Bologna: CLUEB, 1999).

[9] Christine Shaw, *Julius II: The Warrior Pope* (Oxford: Blackwell, 1993), p. 288 discusses Julius' relationship with the city.

[10] Fosi, 'Court and city', pp. 38, 41.

[11] For an example, see Fletcher, *Our Man in Rome*, p. 4.   [12] See Chapter 7.

represented.[13] Their practice as diplomats was grounded in places and spaces with symbolic meaning. To return to the metaphor of performance, the choice of backdrop could be highly significant.

b. Entries, audiences and feasts

Even before an ambassador entered Rome, he engaged symbolically with the city and its past. Approaching Rome from the north, an envoy would typically follow the road now known as the Via Trionfale into Rome. (For arrivals on other routes, the ceremonies were adapted 'proportionally', but the northern route was most common and the one detailed by Grassi in his *De Oratoribus*.[14]) This route took the ambassador over Monte Mario, located about two kilometres outside the city walls. According to myth, the Emperor Constantine, first Christian ruler of Rome, had had a vision of the Holy Cross over Monte Mario prior to his victory over Maxentius at the battle of Ponte Milvio. Probably the site of an early Christian church, an oratorio was built there for the jubilee of 1350.[15] As he caught his first glimpse of Rome from the hill top, the ambassador would have been prompted to call to mind Constantine's victory and the triumph of the first Christian emperor over the pagans, an image with much resonance for ambassadors tasked with maintaining peace and unity in Christendom, and managing the ongoing wars against the Turk.

Formal ceremonies on the northern arrival route for diplomats began a little further on, about one-and-a-half kilometres outside the city walls, at the lepers' hospital at the church of Santa Maria Magdalena extra urbem, today known as San Lazzaro dei Lebbrosi.[16] For the highest-ranking envoys, those of the Holy Roman Emperor, greetings from the papal welcoming party would start here and continue right up until the city gate, the courtiers lining the road. Under no circumstances, wrote Agostino Patrizi, should the welcome party stretch up the hill beyond the church.[17] Ambassadors would progress through the fields that later gave the name *Prati* to this quarter of Rome, past a house and vineyard owned

---

[13] *Relazioni degli Ambasciatori Veneti al Senato*, ed. Eugenio Albèri, 15 vols (Florence: Società editrice fiorentina, 1839–63), ser. 2, Vol. III, pp. 77–120.

[14] BAV, Vat. Lat. 12270, 19r–20v.

[15] Giuseppe Tomassetti, *La Campagna Romana Antica, Medioevale e Moderna*, Luisa Chiumenti and Fernando Bilancia (eds), 7 vols (Florence: Olschki, 1979) Vol. III, p. 27.

[16] BAV, Vat. Lat. 12270, 19r–20v. Christian Huelsen, *Le Chiese di Roma nel Medio Evo* (Florence: Olschki, 1927), pp. 100, 380.

[17] Patrizi, *L'Oeuvre*, p. 205. 'Si Veniunt per Portam Sancti Petri, Familie non Transeunt Domum Leprosorum, Neque Ullo Modo Ascendant Montem.'

by Falcone de' Sinibaldi and, from 1501, by Alessandro Neroni, later major-domo to Pope Leo X.[18] The Trattoria Antico Falcone, reputed to be a fifteenth-century post-house, survives on today's Via Trionfale, a curiosity amid its grand nineteenth-century neighbours. While I have found no documentation to link this building definitively to the Falcone property, both its location and name are suggestive.[19] Envoys passed the church of San Giovanni Battista alli Spinelli, which belonged to the chapter of St Peter's basilica, and then the church of San Egidio, before entering the city through the gate known as 'Porta Viridaria' or 'Porta Sancti Petri'.[20]

The route can be reconstructed (Figure 3) with the help of topographical evidence from the 1551 Bufalini map of Rome and Giambattista Nolli's own plan of 1748.[21] Hypothesising that the surviving Falcone building marks the approximate location of the earlier *vigna*, it is possible to visualise the stretches of road between Grassi's landmarks along which the welcoming party would have lined up, the most senior cardinal towards the city, the most junior farthest away. In his *Roma Triumphans* of 1459, the humanist Flavio Biondo argued that the triumphs of ancient Rome had been prepared near St Peter's.[22] In making that claim, he aimed to emphasise continuity between the papacy, recently restored to its rightful place in Rome, and the ancient empire. Although historians now agree that he was wrong about the location, the currency of such an idea does imbue the ambassadorial entry with an allusion to the Roman triumph.[23] It was, however, a limited allusion, for once within the walls, diplomats did not follow the purported ancient triumphal route

---

[18] Alessandro Ferrajoli, "Il Ruolo della Corte di Leone X", *Archivio della R. Società Romana di Storia Patria* 36 (1913), 519–84 (pp. 521–2), places this house 'Presso L'Ospedale di S. Lazaro' about half a mile from the Porta Viridaria.

[19] Ferrajoli, "Il Ruolo", p. 522, citing *Relazioni*, ser. 2, Vol. III, p. 90.

[20] Giambattista Nolli, *The 1748 Map of Rome*, ed. Jim Tice et al. at http://nolli.uoregon.edu is an interactive version of the plan. The church of Santo Giovanni Battista alli Spinelli is listed in a 1566 catalogue of the churches of Rome: Huelsen, *Chiese*, p. 143. Mariano Armellini, *Le chiese di Roma dalle loro origini sino al secolo XVI* (Rome, 1887), Vol. II, pp. 1040, 1042, 1314. Huelsen, *Chiese*, p. 164. Tomassetti, *Campagna*, Vol. III, p. 14. S. Aegidius is marked on Nolli's edition of Bufalini's 1551 map of Rome: Leonardo Bufalini and Giambattista Nolli, *Plan of Rome 1551/1748*, ed. Jim Tice et al., at http://vasi.uoregon.edu/bufalini.html.

[21] http://nolli.uoregon.edu/; http://vasi.uoregon.edu/bufalini.html.

[22] Flavio Biondo, *Roma Trionfante*, trans. Lucio Fauno (Venice: Tramezzino, 1544), 373v–374r.

[23] Mary Beard, *The Roman Triumph* (Cambridge, MA: Harvard University Press, 2007), pp. 54–5. Anthony Miller, *Roman Triumphs and Early Modern English Culture* (Basingstoke: Palgrave, 2001), pp. 42–6. Charles L. Stinger, 'Roma Triumphans: Triumphs in the thought and ceremonies of Renaissance Rome'. *Medievalia et Humanistica* 10 (1981), 189–201 (pp. 194–5).

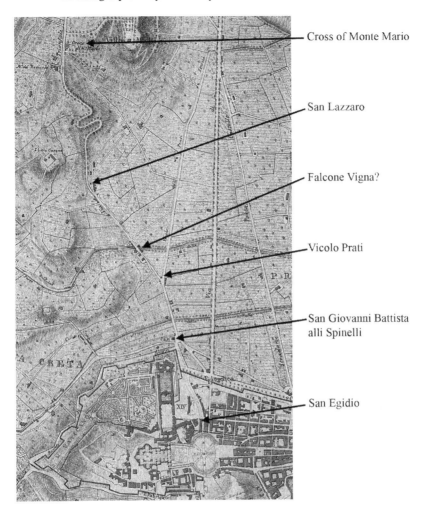

Cross of Monte Mario

San Lazzaro

Falcone Vigna?

Vicolo Prati

San Giovanni Battista
alli Spinelli

San Egidio

Figure 3: Reconstruction of the diplomatic entry route to Rome. Detail
of *Carte topografica di Roma e dintorni nel 1839* (ASC, Biblioteca
Romana, Cartella XIII, 23). Used by permission of the Archivio Storico
Capitolino, Rome.

described (or invented) by Biondo, and employed for Emperor Charles
V's 1536 entry.[24] Rather, the route of their procession through the city

[24] André Chastel, *The Sack of Rome, 1527*, trans. Beth Archer (Princeton: Princeton
University Press, 1983), pp. 209–15.

was dictated by the location of their residence, although it usually included a turn through the Campo dei Fiori.[25]

An ambassador's entry and procession through the city announced the metaphorical presence of his prince to those on the Roman streets. In 1447, Enea Silvio Piccolomini, future Pius II, entered Rome as an envoy of Federico III, king of Germany to Pope Eugenius IV. With 60 *cavalieri* in train:

> Rome was before our eyes when some papal messengers came to meet us, and obliged us to stop and not to enter without honour. Italians have great respect for ambassadors [...] We waited an hour and more. All the *curiali* were obliged to come and meet us, and a great multitude of citizens and curialists came to see us; all the prelates of ranks below cardinal welcomed us the first mile and followed us to our house, which was not far from the Campidoglio, and one after another they complimented us.[26]

The nature of the envoy's welcome was, officially at least, dictated by the rank of the prince or republic he represented. According to Grassi, only imperial ambassadors should be accompanied by the papal welcoming party all the way from San Lazzaro. Ambassadors of kings and princes were to be met at the Falcone vineyard, while those of dukes, marquesses and republics had to content themselves with an entry beginning at the junction with Vicolo Prati between the latter and the Spinelli church.[27] This correlation of distance and honour once again drew on ancient precedents.[28] Entries were a site for political contest, and while Grassi could try to regulate the location of the welcome, through magnificent display, lower-ranking powers sought to subvert the entry protocol even while complying with its formalities. Venice, treated as a duchy but still relatively low on Grassi's order of precedence, was particularly expert in this regard. When four Venetian ambassadors arrived in Rome in 1492, they brought with them two

---

[25] For numerous examples, see Burchard, *Liber Notarum*.

[26] 'avevamo già Roma davanti agli occhi, ci vennero incontro alcuni messi papali, che ci obbligarono a fermarci e non ci lasciarono entrare senza onore. Grande è il rispetto degli Italiani verso gli ambasciatori... Aspettammo un'ora e più. Tutti i curiali furono obbligati a venirci incontro; ed a vederci accorse una grande moltitudine di cittadini e di curiali; tutti I prelati di grado inferiore ai cardinali ci accolsero al primo miglio e ci seguirono sino alla nostra casa, ch'era non lontana dal Campidoglio, e tutti l'un dopo l'altro ci complimentarono... Eravamo appena scesi di cavallo quando ci si presentò Francesco, vescovo di Ferrara, tesoriere apostolico, accompagnato da molti vescovi, che ci accolsero a nome del papa; ci offri molto, ma non portò nulla.' (Paschini, 'Ambasciate', pp. 47–8).

[27] BAV, MS Vat. Lat. 12270, fols. 19v–20r.

[28] Andrew Gillett, *Envoys and Political Communication in the Late Antique West, 411–533* (Cambridge: Cambridge University Press, 2003), p. 251.

hundred horses, or thereabouts, and eighty pack-saddles.[29] Three Polish diplomats brought only about eighty horses when they arrived on 1 March 1505 to pledge obedience, though they ranked higher than the Venetians.[30] (Similar numbers were brought by three English ambassadors arriving in 1504 and a subsequent Portuguese embassy, four-strong, in 1506.[31]) In 1505, one Venetian ambassador, Domenico Pisani, aroused the indignation of the master-of-ceremonies Johannes Burchard when he was greeted on his entry by the *familiae* of pope and cardinals. Pisani was not arriving to pledge obedience, nor was he on some matter of great importance to the *respublica christiana* and welcoming him in this way, wrote Burchard, was not good practice, though he admitted that such infringements had gone on for many years.[32] A third Venetian diplomat, Domenico Venier, arriving in Rome in April 1526, contrived to be met by so many fellow orators, bishops and curial *familiares* that the total number of horses present, according to his Mantuan colleague Francesco Gonzaga, reached two thousand, perhaps an indication of scale rather than a precise number, though nonetheless striking. This was despite the fact that he was arriving to be a resident ambassador and, strictly speaking, should have had none of this welcome at all. Gonzaga credited the Venetian cardinal Francesco Pisani with arranging the ceremony so as 'to do honour to his home city'.[33] On the other hand, there might also be good political reasons for a discreet arrival. As we saw in Chapter 2, a new Imperial ambassador posted to Rome after the 1527 Sack arrived 'without pomp and without ceremony'.[34] Ambassadors often had an 'official' entrance some days after their actual arrival, but in this case the envoys seem to have eschewed all ceremony, in line with Grassi's prescription that this was acceptable in cases of urgent business.[35] English special envoys, arriving the same month formally on a mission to discuss the prospects for a European peace but in fact preoccupied by secret instructions concerning Henry VIII's divorce from Catherine of Aragon, were met simply outside the gates by a welcoming party of 'nine or ten gentlemen', friends of the English resident ambassador.[36]

---

[29] Burchard, *Liber Notarum*, Vol. I, p. 374.

[30] Burchard, *Liber Notarum*, Vol. II, p. 473. 'Habuerunt episcopus equos 36, baro 19, d. Nicolaus 12, viii salmis precedentibus in mulis, subsequentibus equis vacuis, qui salmas per vias portarunt; deinde vi vestiti ut Turci, pulcherrime ornati.'

[31] Burchard, *Liber Notarum*, Vol. II, pp. 450 and 508–9.

[32] Burchard, *Liber Notarum*, Vol. II, pp. 488–9.

[33] Archivio di Stato di Mantova, Archivio Gonzaga 871, cc. 213v–214r.

[34] Archivio di Stato di Mantova, Archivio Gonzaga 878, c. 48v.   [35] See in Chapter 2.

[36] *State Papers*, Vol. VII, p. 148.

Having entered the city, the ambassador would wait for a papal audience. These took place in the Palazzo Apostolico, transformed in the course of the later fifteenth and early sixteenth centuries as successive popes commissioned major building projects. The Sistine Chapel and the rooms now known as the Borgia Apartments and the Raphael Rooms (in the Vatican Museums) are all, largely, products of this period. As we saw in Chapter 3, ambassadors were received in the two rooms adjoining the Sistine Chapel, the Aula Regia and the Aula Ducale. From the 1530s, the Aula Regia was given a revised decorative scheme (completed only in the 1570s) that included a number of depictions of interactions between popes and kings, including a fresco of Pope Alexander III reconciling with the Emperor Frederick I Barbarossa, one recording Charlemagne's gift to the pope in 774, and a pair depicting Charles V's victory in Tunisia and Charles kissing the foot of Paul III (the latter subsequently replaced with a different image). Some of the images underlined the appropriate relationship between kings and popes: for example in the 1560s, Orazio Sommachini painted the Emperor Otto I restoring the lands of the Church to Pope Agapito II.[37] During the papacies of Julius II and Leo X, the *Sala di Costantino* (Hall of Constantine, now one of the 'Raphael Rooms') was used for banquets or 'grand semi-public audiences,' while smaller audiences might take place in the adjoining *Stanza di Eliodoro* (Room of Heliodorus).[38] Ambassadors would wait for their audience in the *Sala Vecchia degli Svizzeri* (Old Hall of the Swiss Guards). The next room in the sequence was the *Camera del Pappagallo* (Parrot Room), used as a vestry and named for a diplomatic gift from the king of Denmark that, it was claimed, could repeat the name of Pope Leo IX. In 1485, it was the site of an argument over precedence between the envoys of Milan and Savoy.[39] Though not as explicit in their references to diplomacy as the later scheme, the decorative schemes of these rooms nonetheless underlined the pope's magnificent status. For the later part of the period under discussion here, Saint Peter's Basilica was undergoing substantial restoration. The extended absence of the popes had left it in need of repair, indeed, in danger of collapse, and from Martin V onwards, more-or-less extensive schemes were devised to renew it. Major rebuilding work, however, began only in the pontificate of Julius II, and the basilica was still being outfitted in the seventeenth century.[40] The Sistine Chapel

---

[37] De Strobel and Mancinelli, 'La Sala Regia', p. 76.
[38] Arnold Nesselrath and Fabrizio Mancinelli, 'Gli appartamenti del Palazzo Apostolico Vaticano da Giulio II a Leone X', in Pietrangeli (ed.), *Il Palazzo Apostolico*, pp. 107–17.
[39] Burchard, Vol. I, p. 110.
[40] William Tronzo (ed.), *St Peter's in the Vatican* (Cambridge: Cambridge University Press, 2005).

was the principal site for liturgical ceremony involving diplomats. Popes, however, also met ambassadors in other settings. Pius II received embassies outdoors at Tivoli and in the garden, accompanied by his puppy Musetta.[41] Julius II met cardinals in the Belvedere, the rustic villa in the Vatican grounds built in imitation of its ancient counterparts and named for its beautiful views.[42] Benvenuto Cellini described the playing of motets in the Belvedere gardens while Clement VII dined there; the Venetian diplomat Gasparo Contarini referred to two mornings during the summer months at Viterbo when on his arrival at court, he found Clement in the gardens.[43] When Cardinal Sigismondo Gonzaga complained about the quality of his rented accommodation he conceded that 'at least there was a garden'.[44] Like palace interiors, gardens could convey an owner's engagement with classical culture, evoking the leisured lifestyle of an ancient elite.

Rome was a cosmopolitan city and that diversity was expressed in its institutions. In 1500, the list of 'national' hospitals in Rome included those of Saints James and Jerome, associated respectively with the Spanish and Slavs, and institutions linked to Brittany, Bohemia, Portugal, Flanders, Germans, English, French and Genoa.[45] All were still in existence by the time of the 1517 census; the 1526 census records a Polish hospital and that of Santa Brigida, associated with the Swedish, too.[46] Most visiting envoys would have found a national institution in the city, and diplomats took responsibility for facilitating the work of their national churches and hospitals and honouring saints associated with their homelands. The pilgrim hospices in Rome had long-standing semi-diplomatic functions and in the early stages of resident embassies often accommodated envoys. As discussed in Chapter 4, during the fifteenth century, English diplomatic agents had held offices at the English Hospital in the district of Regola and used it as their residence.[47] In 1485, 1490 and 1505, ambassadors of the Holy Roman Emperor, and of German dignitaries, used a property referred to by Burchard as the

---

[41] Pius, *Commentarii*, Vol. I, pp. 986–7, 2258–9 (*Secret Memoirs*, pp. 187, 315).

[42] *Dispacci*, p. 40.

[43] Benvenuto Cellini, *My Life*, trans. Julia Conaway Bondanella and Peter Bondanella (Oxford: Oxford University Press, 2002). G. Contarini, fols. 38v and 54v.

[44] D. S. Chambers, 'The enigmatic eminence of Cardinal Sigismondo Gonzaga', *Renaissance Studies* 16 (2002), 330–54 (p. 338).

[45] Burchard, Vol. II, p. 229. Lee, *Habitatores in Urbe*, CD-Rom index. Gensini (ed.), *Roma Capitale* includes essays on the Florentine, Lombard, Spanish and German 'nations' in Rome.

[46] Lee, *Habitatores in Urbe*, CD-Rom index.

[47] Cardinal Gasquet, *A History of the Venerable English College, Rome* (London: Longmans, 1920), p. 46. Behrens, 'Origins', p. 645.

'house of the Germans', located behind Campo de' Fiori, probably a house associated with the German Hospital in Rome.[48] As time went on, increasing emphasis was placed on magnificence and diplomats tended to live in properties more suited to a courtly lifestyle, yet they maintained associations with the national institutions. In 1502, the English ambassador Silvestro Gigli celebrated the feast of St Thomas of Canterbury at the English Hospital.[49] On the death of Isabella of Castile, the Spanish ambassador organised a memorial for her in the Spanish Hospital.[50] The Spanish conquest of Granada was celebrated with a mass in the national church of St James and a bullfight in the Piazza Navona.[51] National occasions were also celebrated at ambassadors' houses. To mark the signing of an Anglo-French peace treaty in 1510, Christopher Bainbridge, English ambassador to Rome, had 'a bonfire lit in front of the palace, and a long table set up with free wine for all passers-by to drink'. Embarrassed by news of the treaty, the existence of which he had been denying, Bainbridge rebuffed French calls for wider public celebrations.[52] When the English beat the Scots at Flodden in 1513, Bainbridge (for England), the English cardinal-protector Adriano Castellesi, the Spanish ambassador and the Spanish Cardinal Remolines lit bonfires outside their houses to celebrate, giving visual expression to the Anglo-Spanish alliance.[53] Such practices followed a long-standing tradition that on major feast-days or occasions of public celebration, curia dignitaries would decorate the exteriors of their houses. When the head of St Andrew was brought to Rome in 1462, the Procurator of the Knights of Rhodes put up an altar in front of his house and arranged for musicians to play as the head was brought past.[54] During the Corpus Christi procession of the same year in Viterbo (while the papal court was in residence), cardinals' houses were elaborately decorated with illustrations of the lives of saints and such like. Those from outside Italy included national styles: the French cardinals of Coutances and Lebret hung arrases, while Juan Caravajal, the Spanish Cardinal of Porto, employed embossed leather in his décor.[55]

[48] Burchard, Vol. I, p. 114 and fn, 308; Vol. II, p. 476. Lee, *Habitatores in Urbe*, finds in the 1517 census several properties connected with the German Hospital: entries pp. 1037, 1038, 1049 and 1723.

[49] Burchard, Vol. II, p. 342.   [50] Burchard, Vol. II, p. 471.

[51] Setton, *Papacy and the Levant*, Vol. II, p. 424.

[52] Chambers, *Cardinal Bainbridge*, pp. 31–3.

[53] Chambers, *Cardinal Bainbridge*, p. 53, citing Grassi, BL Add. MS 8443, 69–70.

[54] Pius, *Commentarii*, Vol. II, pp. 1538–9 (*Secret Memoirs*, p. 244).

[55] Pius, *Commentarii*, Vol. II, pp. 1598–601 (*Secret Memoirs*, pp. 256–60).

c.   Accommodating diplomats

Following the arrival of a new ambassador at Rome, it was customary for other diplomats resident in the city to visit him at his house.[56] But if the entry route to Rome was a relatively well-defined process by the beginning of the sixteenth century, the same cannot be said for the organisation of diplomats' accommodation. At this early stage of resident diplomacy, the ambassador's house was, in an important sense, his place of work. He would, of course, attend the court to which he was sent; however, there were no designated embassy buildings. Whether a resident diplomat providing general reports on the political situation, or someone sent to carry out a specific task, negotiating, say, a marriage or a peace treaty, the ambassador prepared his strategies and wrote his letters at home and, importantly, he entertained there. The style and quality of his accommodation was, therefore, important. It had to convey an appropriate impression of princely magnificence. A Venetian *relazione* of 1523, describing a special embassy to Rome, explains that the four ambassadors stayed in a complex of apartments and houses around a single courtyard:

The palace was grand and honourable; and in one part of it Dandolo lodged; at the other end Giustiniani; downstairs, next to a most beautiful garden, Pesaro; in an adjacent house, which one could reach without going downstairs, lodged Mocenigo; and in another adjacent to that Foscari: a single great and distinguished courtyard served all these houses.[57]

With their apartments as with their entry, the Venetians had done well for themselves. There was a lack of high-quality housing in Rome.[58] Competing with cardinals, diplomats were often left scrabbling around to rent or borrow the best available *palazzo* and, bearing in mind that they might have an entourage of some dozens, ample space was important.

Visiting envoys had several housing options. The first was to rent or borrow from a distinguished figure at the curia, perhaps one with

---

[56] For an example, see G. Contarini, fol. 158v.

[57] 'Era il palazzo grande e onorevole; e in una parte di esso alloggiava il Dandolo; dall'altro capo il Giustiniani; abbasso, appresso a un bellissimo giardino il Pesaro; in una casa contigua, nella quale si andava senza scendere scale, alloggiava il Mocenigo; e in un'altra contigua a quella, il Foscari: a tutte le quali case serve una sola corte grande e onorifica.' *Relazioni*, ser. 2, Vol. III, p. 94. Venice had sent four ambassadors to Rome to pay homage to the newly-elected Pope Adrian VI. It is not clear which of them wrote the document. Its editor, Tommaso Gar, suggests the most likely is Pietro Pesaro. The others were Marco Dandolo, Antonio Giustiniano and Luigi Mocenigo.

[58] Fragnito, 'Cardinals' courts', p. 39. Carol M. Richardson, 'The housing opportunities of a Renaissance cardinal', *Renaissance Studies* 17 (2003), 607–27.

associations to his home nation. In the 1480s and 1490s, the favoured residence of Venetian ambassadors was a house belonging to Pietro Romano located behind the church of Santa Maria sopra Minerva, where they stayed in 1485, 1487 and 1492.[59] Later, in 1499, this property was described as the place where the Venetian Cardinal Grimani usually lived, and it is likely that following his election in 1493, Grimani took over a property with existing Venetian associations.[60] Visiting Venetian diplomats subsequently had to look elsewhere, and in March 1495, were to be found instead in 'domum acialem Dominici Maximi,' near Campo de' Fiori on the site of the present Palazzo Massimo alle Colonne, and in 1497, at a house in the piazza of St Mark.[61] In 1517, a Venetian ambassador was renting from Giovan Andrea Nardini, in the parish of San Lorenzo in Lucina in the Campo Marzo.[62] The impression of ad hoc arrangements is compounded by the fact that Pietro Romano was now playing host to other, non-Venetian diplomats. In February 1499, he put up an embassy from Brittany, and in 1505, Portuguese envoys stayed at his house, while their Venetian counterparts occupied a house made vacant by the death of Cardinal Lodovico Podocathor, bishop of Capoccio, who had died the year before.[63] In fact, there are a number of cases where ambassadors were accommodated in the homes of more-or-less recently deceased Romans: the Ferrarese envoy in 1485, for example, stayed in the house of the late Gioacchino de Narnia, in Pelliciaria, and in 1492, an English diplomat in 1492 stayed in the house of the late Jacobo Bigneti.[64] This was obviously a convenient solution.

Just as Pietro Romano's house seems for a while to have served as a regular Venetian residence, so the English had their favoured properties. On 17 June 1496, the newly arrived English special ambassador Robert Sherborn was accompanied to the house of Giovanni Gigli, an Italian diplomatic agent of Henry VII, while in 1504, English ambassadors stayed with another Italian churchman with ties to England, Cardinal Adriano Castellesi.[65] The following year, Castellesi gifted his new palace in Piazza Scossacavalli (very near the Vatican) to King Henry for the use of English representatives in Rome.[66] This was a handy location for entertaining, for it was en route from the papal palace to the city centre. A Venetian *relazione* of 1523 records how Cardinal Cornelio, who also

[59] Burchard, Vol. I, pp. 115, 211 and 374.
[60] Burchard, Vol. II, p. 129; www2.fiu.edu/~mirandas/bios1493.htm#Grimani.
[61] Burchard, Vol. I, p. 579.   [62] *Habitatores*, 1517 census, entry 492, p. 65.
[63] Burchard, Vol. II, pp. 129, 486–88; www2.fiu.edu/~mirandas/bios1500-ii.htm#Podocator.
[64] Burchard, Vol. I, pp. 114, 370.   [65] Burchard, Vol. I, p. 614; Vol. II, p. 450.
[66] Paschini, *Tre Illustri Prelate*, pp. 63–4.

lived in the Borgo, would invite passing colleagues in for lunch.[67] Christopher Bainbridge, English ambassador from 1509 and subsequently cardinal, stayed first in the Piazza Scossacavalli palace, and after 1511, probably in the palazzo on the Via Papalis formerly occupied by Cardinal Caraffa.[68] This had previously been used as diplomatic accommodation for Caraffa's brother, who had come to Rome as Neapolitan ambassador in 1494.[69] The 'English Palace' was given to Cardinal Lorenzo Campeggio, later to become England's cardinal-protector, during his legation to England in 1519. Now known as the Palazzo Giraud-Torlonia, it survives to this day.[70]

Another option for the visiting diplomat was to take over part of a suitably large city palazzo. The Orsini family, owners of sizeable city residences in Campo de' Fiori and Montegiordano, came into their own as diplomatic hosts in the 1480s, 1490s and early 1500s.[71] Their Campo de' Fiori palazzo (now the Palazzo Pio-Righetti) is the most frequently cited residence for visiting ambassadors in Burchard's diary. There they hosted French diplomats, in February 1485 and 1505, Spanish ambassadors, in 1486, and Genoese diplomats, in 1504; in 1494, they hosted envoys from Naples at their Montegiordano complex.[72] The variety of nations permitted to lodge in Orsini property suggests that the family's long-standing association with the Guelf party (pro-Angevin, as opposed to the pro-Imperial Ghibellines) was not a definitive factor in their choice of tenants. As Shaw explains, these 'traditional associations' should not be regarded as firm allegiances.[73] The 1517 census records a number of ambassadors renting from cardinals: the Portuguese ambassador lived in Cardinal Achille Grassi's house, and the Imperial envoy Lope de Soria, in a house belonging to Cardinal Cavaglione (Giovanni Battista Pallavicino of Genoa), both in the parish of San Lorenzo in Lucina in Campo Marzio (where the Venetian ambassador also lived).[74] Cardinals' palaces were also important locations for diplomatic activity.

---

[67] *Relazioni*, ser. 2, Vol. III, p. 117.   [68] Chambers, *Cardinal Bainbridge*, pp. 112–20.

[69] Burchard, Vol. I, p. 463.

[70] W. Maziere Brady, *Anglo-Roman Papers* (London: Gardner, 1890), p. 29.

[71] On the Orsini palaces, see Kristin Adrean Triff, 'Patronage and public image in renaissance Rome: three Orsini palaces' (Ann Arbor: UMI, 2000). PhD dissertation, Brown University, 2000.

[72] Antonio De Vascho, *Il Diario della Citta' di Roma*, ed. Giuseppe Chiesa (Città di Castello, 1911), p. 519; Burchard, Vol. I, pp. 159–60; Vol. II, pp. 434, 478; Vol. I, p. 464.

[73] Christine Shaw, *The Political Role of the Orsini Family from Sixtus IV to Clement VII. Barons and Factions in the Papal States* (Rome: Istituto Storico Italiano per il Medio Evo, 2007), pp. 100, 165.

[74] For examples of ambassadors renting, see the 1517 census: *Habitatores*, pp. 65–6, entry numbers 458, 492, 519.

Indeed, in Paolo Cortesi's treatise on cardinals' conduct, *De Cardinalatu*, a 'secret door' and 'hiding places' were explicitly recommended for the cardinal's audience chamber on the basis that they would allow the observation of visitors without their knowledge and permit easy access for couriers and messengers.[75] No doubt many ambassadors would have valued such facilities too.

The census of 1526 offers a more confused picture, but that is probably a product of the chaos following the Colonna sack of Rome in that year. By that time, the Portuguese ambassador was living in the Ripa district, the Milanese ambassador in Ponte and his Florentine counterpart in the Borgo. In 1529, both the Spanish and French ambassadors were lodged in the parish of San Lorenzo in Damaso, the former in the Palazzo della Cancelleria, and the latter in what the English ambassador described as *una casetta de galli*: a little house belonging to the Galli family.[76] Once again, the locations have changed. Yet they also reflect the political alliances of the day: the Cancelleria was now occupied by Cardinal Ascanio Colonna, a stalwart Imperialist, who played host to his ally. There are too few cases to generalise, but it is possible that following the 1527 Sack, when war had reached the streets of Rome, traditional political ties became more significant in accommodation choices.

It was relatively rare for a resident ambassador in these years to live in his own family house in Rome rather than in rented property. Even cardinals struggled to find high-quality accommodation in Rome,[77] and ambassadors – who had relatively smaller households than cardinals but were nonetheless expected to project an honourable image for their prince – arguably had further difficulties.[78] The exceptions were those ambassadors (and cardinals) from Roman families, like Gregorio Casali, English ambassador to the papal court from 1525 to 1533, who was able to stay in his own substantial family house on Via Monserrato, enjoying 'halls, chambers, a kitchen, dining rooms, cellars, a garden and a stable'.[79] There he regularly hosted visiting English special envoys. Its garden would have been a particularly desirable feature: al fresco dining

[75] Kathleen Weil-Garris and John F. D'Amico, 'The Renaissance Cardinal's ideal palace: a chapter from Cortesi's *De Cardinalatu*', in Henry A. Millon (ed.), *Studies in Italian Art and Architecture 15th through 18th Centuries* (Rome: Edizioni dell'Elefante, 1980), pp. 45–123 (p. 83).

[76] Archivio di Stato di Firenze, Dieci di Balia, Responsive, 139. The Galli house may be the property belonging to Paulo Gallo, entry number 4469 in the 1526 census. *Habitatores*, p. 222.

[77] Fragnito, 'Cardinals' courts', p. 39.

[78] For the comparative sizes, see *Habitatores*, CD-Rom index.

[79] Cited in Christoph Luitpold Frommel, *Der Römische Palastbau der Hochrenaissance*, 3 vols (Tübingen: Wasmuth, 1973), Vol. 2, pp. 107, 136.

and entertainment were rather fashionable in the summer months.[80] For much of the period discussed here, therefore, diplomatic accommodation was either temporary or familial. Its status was established by the display of coats-of-arms: both those of the orators themselves and of their home state (a notable nod, there, to the two sides of the diplomat's persona: individual status and national role).[81] But there is an intriguing suggestion of a change by 1551. On Bufalini's map of that year, the residences of the ambassadors of France, Spain and Portugal are labelled not with their owners' names, but as national properties: 'Domus Oratoris Gallici', 'Domus Oratoris Hispani' and 'Domus Oratoris Lusitani'. It is, perhaps, an indicator of a shift towards a more permanent and less personal approach to diplomatic accommodation in Rome as national hospitals were supplanted first by short-term accommodation in houses owned by Roman patricians and subsequently, by identifiable embassy buildings.

d.   The uses of hospitality

The quality and space of diplomatic accommodation expressed the status and virtues of the ambassador's principal. An important source on such social virtues is the collection of five treatises (on liberality, beneficence, magnificence, conviviality and splendour) written by Giovanni Pontano, a well-known humanist whose role in the Neapolitan royal service, including as a diplomat, culminated in his 1487 appointment as first secretary to Ferrante I.[82] First published in 1498, the treatises were reprinted in the Aldine edition of Pontano's collected works in 1518–19.[83] They offer an indication of social attitudes towards these virtues that helps contextualise the activities of ambassadors; moreover, the fact of their reprinting suggests their influence spanned a longer period than Pontano's own lifetime. In his *De magnificentia*, Pontano emphasised that while magnificent hospitality was praiseworthy in 'private men', it was especially important for princes receiving guests. Moreover, in such cases, liberality alone would not suffice: splendour and magnificence were required.[84] By implication, these virtues were

---

[80] T. C. Price Zimmermann and Saul Levin, 'Fabio Vigile's *Poem of the Pheasant*: humanist conviviality in Renaissance Rome', in Ramsey (ed.), *Rome in the Renaissance*, pp. 265–78 and Michel Jeanneret, *A Feast of Words: Banquets and Table Talk in the Renaissance* (Cambridge: Polity Press, 1991), pp. 22–7.

[81] *Relazioni*, Ser. 2, Vol. III, p. 94.   [82] On his career, see Kidwell, *Pontano*.

[83] Giovanni Pontano, *I Libri delle Virtù Sociali*, ed. Francesco Tateo (Rome: Bulzoni, 1999), editor's introduction, p. 35.

[84] Pontano, *Virtù sociali*, pp. 210–11.

expected too in the prince's ambassador. As the personification of his prince at a foreign court, the ambassador needed not only to match the standards of the court to which he had been sent, but also to ensure that his hospitality was 'princely'.[85]

The importance of hospitality in sixteenth-century diplomacy is summed up in a comment from Nicholas Hawkins, English resident ambassador to the Holy Roman Emperor Charles V from 1532 to 1534,[86] about his travails at a papal-Imperial summit: 'Treuth it is, that the cnowledge of suche thing is whiche I shuld certifi the King on, for the most parte I must gett it of thother Imbassatours; and therfor must bothe invite them, and be invited.'[87] Here, Hawkins highlights the role of sociability in gathering information, but the provision of lavish hospitality would also reflect positively on the honour of the ambassador's prince. It would be wrong to impose an overly schematic distinction between the two functions: a single event might involve both of them and, besides, there was a practical value involved in promoting one's prince's virtue. The symbolic function of diplomatic hospitality is well-expressed in a letter from Sir Francis Bryan, one of Henry VIII's inner circle, who was sent as a special ambassador to Rome in early 1529.[88] Sir Francis stayed at the house of Henry's resident ambassador in Rome, Gregorio Casali, and was evidently impressed with his host's lifestyle. He wrote to Henry VIII describing:

The honnour that Your Gracys Imbassadour here does dayly to Your Grace, as by kepying a port, no oon Cardynall in Rome suche, hys house furnysshyd with gentyllmen dayly, and that of the best in Rome, and mayny tymys Cardynalles, 2 at a tyme, takyng hym at dyner or supper, wyll sytt downe with hym, and unlokyd for they fare as well as they do at whome; whych causys me to reyoyse, heryng the grett fame and honour, that dayly sprynges on Your Grace, by reson of the lyberall porte that Your Gracys servaunt dose kepe, studying dayly to incresе Your Gracys honour.[89]

Even allowing for a certain degree of enthusiastic over-statement on Bryan's part, the letter sums up rather well the belief that such conduct would reflect positively on the king. In their assessments, these English-born ambassadors must have drawn on their own notions of proper behaviour in terms of hospitality: as Felicity Heal has argued, in England, the 'appearance of an open household' was valuable for a lord's

---

[85] Paul M. Dover, 'The economic predicament of Italian Renaissance ambassadors', *Journal of Early Modern History* 12 (2008), 137–67.
[86] Bell, *Handlist.*   [87] *St P*, Vol. VII, p. 406 (*L&P*, Vol. V, 1661).
[88] On Bryan, see Brigden, '"Shadow that you know"'.
[89] *St P*, Vol. VII, p. 168 (*L&P*, Vol. IV, 5481).

reputation.[90] That liberality should be the determining virtue of the ambassador is congruent with the view that while other Renaissance social virtues, such as magnificence, lost their feudal overtones, liberality retained a stronger social sense, derived from its medieval construct as a princely virtue.[91] Furthermore, in the case of an ambassador, his liberality enhanced not only his own but also the king's honour. During Sir Francis' embassy to Rome, he regularly entertained the Cardinal of Mantua, Ercole Gonzaga, at the Casali house, writing to Henry VIII that 'twyse or thryse a weke he cummys to my loggyng to me, to supper, lyke a good felaw, without any seremony, and lykewyse hath me with hym to hys loggyng.'[92] The words 'without any ceremony' suggest a level of informality and also, perhaps, the potential for confidential discussion. However, we should be wary of concluding that such suppers were never splendid: Lucinda Byatt has noted the preference in normative texts on cardinals' conduct for small dinner parties, suggesting that these more intimate occasions were considered no less appropriate than grand banqueting.[93]

Sir Francis' reciprocal 'dining without ceremony' functioned both as a diplomatic encounter between representatives of England and Mantua and as an expression of personal friendship between two men. There is a third level of meaning: Sir Francis was lodging (and entertaining) at the Casali family house, and the Casali were clients of the Gonzaga family.[94] There is an expression of the private, familial persona of the ambassador here too. Another example of the sociable *persona mixta* is to be found in the case of the wedding of one of Gregorio Casali's sisters, in November 1525, described by the Mantuan diplomat Francesco Gonzaga:

Madama Illustrissima [Isabella d'Este] went yesterday to dinner at the house of Messer Gio. Antonio da Viterbo, father of the young woman's husband. She was handed over: it was a grand dinner, in that there were enough people, and a quite lavish meal and copious dishes: but the house not being very large, one ate in different places; there were five big tables, at one of which there were only the women without a single man: this is the Roman style; at another were the Duke of Sessa, the Portuguese ambassador, the Ferrarese ambassador, the ambassador of Urbino with prelates and other gentlemen. I was also there: the others were full

[90] Heal, *Hospitality*, p. 22.
[91] Richard A. Goldthwaite, *Wealth and the Demand for Art in Italy* (Baltimore: Johns Hopkins University Press, 1993), pp. 207–9. Pontano, *Virtù Sociali*, editor's introduction, pp. 12, 19.
[92] *St P*, Vol. VII, p. 150 (*L&P*, Vol. IV, 5213).
[93] Lucinda M. C. Byatt, 'The concept of hospitality in a cardinal's household in Renaissance Rome', *Renaissance Studies* 2 (1988), 312–20 (315).
[94] Fletcher, *Our Man in Rome*, p. 63.

of other gentlemen; there was a bit of dancing before dinner and afterwards, with tambourines, flutes and harp, at ballets according to the custom there.[95]

It is striking that even at this family event, we see the Roman diplomatic corps gathered around a single table. Such occasions must have provided an important opportunity for informal discussion of diplomatic matters and the building of social networks from which an ambassador might glean useful information, while simultaneously pursuing familial interests.

Further evidence for the importance of sociability in diplomatic practice is to be found in the herald Thomas Wall's contemporary account of the English embassy to the coronation of Charles V at Bologna in 1529–30. Wall had almost nothing to say about the content of the ambassadors' sensitive negotiations, but focused instead on ceremony, entertainment and the company the ambassadors kept, reporting repeatedly that they dined 'well accompanied', evidently a defining characteristic, to his mind, of appropriate diplomatic practice.[96] In 1523, Venetian ambassadors praised their compatriot Cardinal Cornelio in similar terms: 'he always has a house full of Roman gentlemen… He keeps a most beautiful court and treats his guests very well indeed: not a week goes by without two or three cardinals dining at his table, on two or three occasions.'[97] While this account should not be regarded as a literal description of day-to-day practice, it is evidence for the shared culture of hospitality within which ambassadors constructed their praise of individuals at the court of Rome. Within this culture, the feast was valued as a vehicle for social and political dealings.[98] Ideas about hospitality and the household drew on both Christian and classical precedents. As Heal has argued, the house 'was no mere assemblage of rooms; instead, it served to embody the qualities of its owner'.[99] Heal's research concerns early modern England, and it would be inappropriate to apply her conclusions to the Italian context indiscriminately. However, although concepts of what was appropriate in hospitality developed in rather different ways in the different European social systems, the basic idea that honour required a nobleman to be hospitable can be regarded as a constant in the period under discussion here.[100]

[95] Cited in Luzio, 'Isabella d'Este', p. 365, my translation.
[96] Wall, *Voyage*, pp. 60, 62, 65–6.   [97] *Relazioni*, ser. 2, Vol. 3, pp. 77–120.
[98] Jeanneret, *Feast of Words*, especially pp. 49–56.   [99] Heal, *Hospitality*, p. 6.
[100] On honour see Mozzarelli, 'Onore, Utile, Principe, Stato', and Mervyn James, *English Politics and the Concept of Honour (1485–1642)*, Past and Present Supplement 3 (Oxford: Past and Present Society, 1978).

Beyond this symbolic function, there was another side to the ambassador's social life: its role in the acquisition of intelligence, about which the authors of the treatises on diplomacy were explicit. On this point apparently the most 'strictly utilitarian', to borrow Betty Behrens' description, was Étienne Dolet.[101] For Dolet, munificence could suborn even the most upright men, and when it came to winning hearts and minds, nothing could surpass liberality, which should, therefore, be bestowed generally and not only on spies.[102] He went on to give a definition of liberality in the context of diplomacy:

Now by liberality I mean magnificence and splendour in his manner of living, and an abundance of food sufficient for the entertainment of many persons at the ambassador's table. By this practice of a lavish and splendid manner of living we place under obligation to ourselves both men of ample and men of slender means.[103]

The practical advantages of such a strategy are made even more explicit in Niccolò Machiavelli's advice to Raffaello Girolami on his appointment as ambassador to the Emperor. Pre-empting Hawkins' comment on the importance of 'inviting and being invited' by some ten years, Machiavelli wrote that 'the best means for getting information is to give it'. He went on:

I have seen entertainments given in the houses of very serious men, who thus offer such fellows a reason for visiting them, so that they can talk with them, because what one of them doesn't know another does, and much of the time they all together know everything.[104]

Lapo, too, noted the potential of informal social occasions for obtaining information with which to threaten or blackmail, though he did not use those terms. He wrote: 'Dinner parties, tavern life, pandering, bribes, thefts, adultery, sexual degradation, and shameful acts are publicly revealed [...] And so, if you ever need a favour from these people, the result is that, almost like a learned doctor, you have your medications ready and prepared.'[105] The key instrumental functions of sociability in the ambassador's house were, in short, to place guests under an obligation to reciprocate, and, more specifically, as a means of obtaining information. As with pillow talk, however, entertainment could work both ways: for every piece of information gleaned, another might have to be traded.

---

[101] Behrens, 'Treatises', p. 625.   [102] Dolet, 'De Officio Legati', p. 86.
[103] Ibid., p. 87.   [104] Machiavelli, 'Advice', p. 117.
[105] Lapo, De Curiae Commodis, p. 177.

Like Machiavelli's letter, Dolet's treatise is notable for its matter-of-fact approach to the ambassador's sociability; other treatises (of both earlier and later dates) paint a more idealised picture. Ermolao Barbaro concluded his earlier 'De Officio Legati' with the wish that the ambassador's enthusiasm for the arts should inspire the performance of entertainments, painting, writing and singing in his household, not to mention the playing of draughts and ball games.[106] Yet even Ottaviano Maggi's 'perfect ambassador' of 1566, in general a paragon of the virtues, was aware of the practical benefits of liberality, which, he wrote, would put men under an obligation for ever. Like Machiavelli and Dolet, he recommended that the ambassador should extend his liberality with a banquet in his palace.[107]

Liberality was not the only social virtue expected of envoys. Contemporary writers on diplomacy were also clear that the ambassador's lifestyle should be suitably splendid, splendour being the domestic counterpart to magnificence.[108] Étienne Dolet wrote that funds should be allocated to the ambassador according to the magnificence of the court to which he was posted, so that he should not be accused of offending majesty through an inappropriately parsimonious lifestyle.[109] That attitude is reflected in a comment from Stephen Gardiner to Henry VIII about Gregorio Casali:

> I assure your Highnes he lyveth here sumptuously and chargeably, to your Highnes honnour, and, in this gret skasete, must nedes be dryven to extremite, oonles your Highnes be gratious lord unto him in that behaulf.[110]

Cinzia Sicca's discussion of the London house of the Bardi and Cavalcanti company draws attention to the type of lavish furnishing that one might expect to find in a diplomatic house. Although Pierfrancesco Bardi and Giovanni Cavalcanti were not ambassadors, they acted as informal diplomatic representatives for the Medici in London from the first years of Henry VIII's reign through the pontificates of both Leo X and Clement VII. Among the items listed in an inventory of the house, taken in 1523, were 'sizeable quantities of silverware'.[111] The importance of

---

[106] Barbaro, 'De Officio Legati', p. 167.
[107] Ottaviano Maggi, *De Legato Libri Duo* (Venice, 1566), fol. 65r.
[108] James Lindow, 'Splendour', in Marta Ajmar-Wollheim and Flora Dennis (eds), *At Home* (London: Victoria & Albert Museum, 2006), pp. 306–7.
[109] Dolet, 'De Officio Legati', p. 84.
[110] Stephen Gardiner, *The Letters of Stephen Gardiner*, ed. James Arthur Muller (Cambridge: Cambridge University Press, 1933), p. 15 (*L&P*, Vol. IV, 5476).
[111] Sicca, 'Consumption and trade of art', pp. 186, 182. On tableware, see Valerie Taylor, 'Banquet plate and Renaissance culture: a day in the life', *Renaissance Studies* 19 (2005), 621–33.

silverware for entertaining is one aspect of diplomatic splendour borne out by significant documentation. Nicholas Hawkins' comment on the importance of inviting and being invited comes in the context of a letter to Thomas Cromwell on the apparently insignificant issue of his table service. At the time, late 1532, Hawkins was at the meeting of Clement VII and Charles V in Bologna, and one might suppose that he would have had other matters on his mind. Nonetheless, he complained:

Both Master Benet, and the Imbassators bothe with thEmperour and with the Pope, and all other Imbassators as wel smal as great, have ther meate vessel for ther tabul all of silver [...]

Hawkins, however, did not. He continued:

Now thei, whiche at home be daili servid in silver, divine yow, how thei be content, and what thei thinke both on the King and me, to be servid with me in tin or peuter, and that nocht as ye cnow in Itali.[112]

He therefore proposed to take some of the plate he had on loan from the king, and have it melted down and remade into a more appropriate form at his own expense, if Cromwell 'thocht it convenient' to so persuade Henry. Cromwell's reply is not, to my knowledge, extant, but the letter illustrates very clearly the importance of this particular type of domestic object in establishing social status: Hawkins' guests expect him to serve them on silver tableware, and if he fails to do so they will also think badly of the king. The 1523 Venetian *relazione* similarly emphasizes the presence of silverware on the ambassador's table:

Having arrived at court, many of these lords, gentlemen and prelates were invited to dinner. This was most beautiful and very honourable, with great plates of the most lavish food and with a huge sideboard of silverware, which took up the whole width of a large hall, and reached as high as the beams of the ceiling, packed with great pieces of silverware which stayed on it at all times, besides those which were in use; some pieces were borrowed, such as platters and plates, but only a very few, because each of the ambassadors had his own share of them.[113]

The passage highlights both the *credenza's* dual-purpose nature as serving table and means of display,[114] and the use of rented plates to create the required impression of splendour. Both Hawkins and the Venetians were engaged in particularly ceremonial embassies – the latter had been sent to pay homage to the new Pope Adrian VI – and such sumptuousness may not have been an everyday business, but even allowing for a certain degree of exaggeration, the descriptions demonstrate the value attached

---

[112] *St P*, Vol. VII, p. 406 (*L&P*, Vol. V, 1661).   [113] *Relazioni*, Series 2, Vol. III, p. 102.
[114] Taylor, 'Banquet plate', p. 623.

to silverware. In his treatise on splendour, Pontano highlighted the importance of tableware, noting that the Roman emperor Alexander Severus had faced censure for his lack of gold plate and mediocre goblets.[115] Writing on conviviality, Pontano described how the household's gold and silver should be displayed on sideboards and balustrades.[116] As Evelyn Welch comments in relation to *De splendore*, 'it should not be read as [...] a rigidly prescriptive text'; however, the diplomatic sources confirm the correlation she finds between some of Pontano's examples and contemporary preoccupations.[117]

Whether by reference to the Severan emperors or by invoking Constantine's victory, the city of Rome functioned as a theatre for diplomacy. From the moment of their entry, ambassadors engaged with its ancient and Christian symbolism. They sought to enhance the reputation of their nation in Rome both by attending its festivals at the many national churches in the city and by organising celebrations of events such as the birth of a new prince, or the signing of a treaty. These public occasions were a chance to perform their prince's honour before the Roman crowds, just as they did before a more select audience in the world of ceremony. Lavish accommodation functioned to convey a sense of courtly magnificence and to facilitate the hosting of events where envoys might acquire valuable information. In this social context, the ambassador's *persona mixta* is again apparent. He embodied his prince as he entertained in magnificent (and, sometimes, national) fashion, while as his familial 'self', he employed family property and social connections both to obtain accommodation and in the quest for information.

---

[115] Pontano, *Virtù Sociali*, pp. 228–31.   [116] Pontano, *Virtù Sociali*, pp. 260–1.

[117] Evelyn Welch, 'Public magnificence and private display: Giovanni Pontano's *De Splendore* (1498) and the domestic arts', *Journal of Design History* 15 (2002), 211–27 (220).

7 'Those who give are not all generous': The world of gifts

When Baldassarre Castiglione, a former resident ambassador in Rome, wrote in *Il Libro del Cortegiano* that 'those who give are not all generous', he might well have been thinking back to his experience as a diplomat.[1] Ambassadors in early modern Europe were frequent disbursers of tips, rewards and bribes, and usually expected something in return for their liberality. This chapter considers the conventions, both written and unwritten, that governed such activities in Renaissance Rome. In his handbook on ambassadors at the curia the papal master-of-ceremonies Paride Grassi included a chapter headed: 'How much ambassadors should give to papal officials, and who these officials are.'[2] It was not, he said, for him to set out how much ambassadors should give to jesters and musicians, but he went on to list those officials whom one *was* expected to tip, from himself, as master-of-ceremonies, to couriers, the gatekeeper and the man at the secret garden. In the case of those gratuities, the ambassador could expect advice from the ceremonial office on how to comport himself. For the most part, however, the protocol of gift-giving was uncodified.

In her life of Cardinal Soderini, Kate Lowe noted both the importance of 'perquisites, gifts and backhanders' at the papal court and the difficulty of finding evidence for them.[3] There are obvious problems with sources in this field: while official, ceremonial gifts were often recorded in writing, less licit payments were often not. However, there is enough of a paper trail to reconstruct at least some of the gift-giving practices at the papal court, and this chapter considers diplomatic letters, trial records and prescriptive treatises in order to do so. Its first section examines various types of official gifts, while the second assesses the extent to which gift-giving at the papal court was subject to regulation, where the

---

[1] Baldesar Castiglione, *The Book of the Courtier*, trans. George Bull (London: Penguin, 1976), p. 313. On the *Cortegiano* as advice for diplomats, see Woodhouse, 'Honourable dissimulation', pp. 28–30.
[2] BAV, MS Vat. Lat. 12270, fols. 70v–71v.   [3] Lowe, *Church and Politics*, p. 249.

boundary between legitimate and illegitimate gifts lay, and what constituted 'corruption' in this period, drawing in particular on evidence about the tipping of lower-ranking officials. The third section looks at the language used by diplomats to justify their gift-giving, in particular, the concept of liberality and the reciprocal pair 'reward' and 'service'. Here the discussion focuses on two instances in the course of negotiations over Henry VIII's 'divorce' from Catherine of Aragon when Henry's diplomats offered gifts to cardinals but subsequently encountered problems, enabling a consideration of the ways that gifts might, as Natalie Zemon Davis has put it, 'go wrong'.[4]

Many studies of early modern gift-giving have been heavily influenced by the work of the sociologist and anthropologist Marcel Mauss, nephew and student of Émile Durkheim, who published his 'Essai sur le don' in 1925.[5] Mauss made it clear, as Gadi Algazi has pointed out, that it was not his intention to provide a model for the use of historians[6]; nonetheless, his concepts have often been borrowed. Sharon Kettering, for example, has employed Mauss' theory in analysing French patron–client relationships in the later sixteenth and seventeenth centuries, and Maija Jansson has applied it to English diplomatic gifts in the seventeenth and eighteenth centuries.[7] Although wholehearted adherence to Mauss' theory is becoming increasingly less fashionable,[8] his ideas remain sufficiently influential in the field for some brief observations on their development to be necessary here. In summary, Mauss' *The Gift* is not a historical study, but draws on anthropological accounts of archaic societies, particularly those of the Pacific Rim, to posit the gift system as a 'total social phenomenon'. Every type of social institution in the societies Mauss discusses is expressed through gifts, he argues, which must be given, received and reciprocated as 'gift' and 'counter-gift'; the formal voluntary character of the gift conceals this obligation to reciprocate;

---

[4] Natalie Zemon Davis, *The Gift in Sixteenth-Century France* (Oxford: OUP, 2000), p. 165.

[5] Marcel Mauss, *The Gift: The Form and Reason for Exchange in Archaic Societies*, trans. W. D. Halls (London: Routledge, 1990). On the intellectual context of Mauss' work, see the foreword to that volume by Mary Douglas (pp. vii–xviii), and Patrick J. Geary, 'Gift exchange and social science modeling: the limitations of a construct', in Gadi Algazi, Valentin Groebner and Bernhard Jussen (eds), *Negotiating the Gift: Pre-Modern Figurations of Exchange* (Göttingen: Vandenhoeck & Ruprecht, 2003), pp. 129–40.

[6] Gadi Algazi, 'Doing things with gifts', in Algazi et al. (eds), *Negotiating the Gift*, pp. 9–27 (pp. 9–10).

[7] Sharon Kettering, 'Gift-giving and patronage in early modern France', *French History* 2 (1988), 131–51. Maija Jansson, 'Measured reciprocity. English ambassadorial gift exchange in the seventeenth and eighteenth centuries', *Journal of Early Modern History* 9 (2005), 348–70.

[8] Felicity Heal, 'Food gifts, the household and the politics of exchange in early modern England', *Past and Present* 199 (2008), 41–70.

there is no such thing as a 'free gift'.[9] Particularly relevant here is the question of language and the semantics of gift-giving.

On this point, Gadi Algazi, Valentin Groebner and Bernhard Jussen have challenged Maussian theory, questioning whether an overarching category of 'The Gift' is useful at all and arguing that it has led to 'unwarranted generalisations'. Instead, they emphasise the importance of studying the ways that gifts are named, represented and registered. For example, they suggest that it is often only the label applied to a gift, rather than any characteristic of the gift *per se*, that distinguishes its legitimacy or illegitimacy.[10] Such a semantic approach has usefully been employed by Valentin Groebner in his study of political presents in fifteenth- and sixteenth-century Basel. He describes the emergence of the word *miet*, which had connotations of bribery and the illicit, in fourteenth-century south Germany; this, he argues, 'appears to have been *the* key term for forbidden gifts to officials'.[11] Bernard Jussen's study of medieval religious discourse likewise considers the language of gifts to demonstrate that the terms *munus* and *remuneratio*, commonly referred to by scholars in Maussian terms as 'gift' and 'counter-gift', in fact, occur in 'significantly different contexts' and cannot be regarded as a conceptual pair.[12] Nonetheless, many historians have remained content to follow Mauss in grouping together a variety of differently-named 'gifts' for analysis, as he does in the case of the Trobriand Islanders, when he notes the 'proliferation of distinctive names for all kinds of total counter-services', only to follow by dismissing 'the strange refinements that are given to names'.[13] Among them is Davis, who downplays the differences between types of gift in sixteenth-century France: they were, she says, 'linked together by the categories and words used to describe them and by the virtues and values they were thought to express in the giver and arouse in the recipient'.[14] This chapter, however, begins from the premise that early modern diplomats did make distinctions between types of gift, that this was reflected in the terminology they used to describe them, and that lumping them all together into a single category is unlikely to be helpful.[15]

---

[9] Mauss, *The Gift*, pp. 3, 16–17.   [10] Algazi, 'Doing things with gifts', pp. 14, 18–19.
[11] Groebner, *Liquid Assets*, pp. 71–2.
[12] Bernhard Jussen, 'Religious discourses of the gift in the Middle Ages. Semantic evidences (second to twelfth centuries)', in Algazi et al. (eds), *Negotiating the Gift*, pp. 173–92 (p. 174).
[13] Mauss, *The Gift*, pp. 30–1.
[14] Davis, *The Gift*, pp. 14, 22–3. Ilana Krausman Ben-Amos, 'Gifts and favors: informal support in early modern England', *Journal of Modern History* 72 (2000), 295–338 similarly groups together a wide variety of 'reciprocal interactions' under the heading 'gift'.
[15] Algazi, 'Doing things with gifts', p. 21.

Scholarly consideration of gifts in the specific context of diplomacy is relatively rare. An alternative critique of Mauss, with specific reference to diplomacy, has been offered by Cutler, who places emphasis instead on the function of diplomatic gifts as 'signs'.[16] It is a valuable approach to the more ceremonial type of diplomatic gift, but its usefulness with respect to illegitimate gift-giving seems limited, for such gifts were emphatically not to be placed on public display. Groebner discusses diplomatic gifts in relation to city politics in Basel in his *Liquid Assets*, but while some of his findings have broad resonance, others are more contingent on that particular municipal environment. Levin cites a number of examples of pensions and 'bribes' offered by Spanish ambassadors in sixteenth-century Italy, but does not discuss the process of gift-giving in any depth.[17] Jansson, dealing with English diplomatic gifts in the seventeenth and eighteenth centuries, limits her analysis to ceremonial presents covered by the rules of precedence, leaving aside the backhanders discussed here.[18] Martin, writing about dowries and Muscovian diplomacy, likewise restricts his study to the more official type of gift.[19] Although there is a broad literature on the concept of corruption in the seventeenth century, most notably the work of Waquet, caution is necessary in applying this work to earlier periods.[20] Understandings of corruption, as the work of Groebner and others shows, undoubtedly changed over time and it would take a far larger study than this to make comparisons with confidence. In examining the less licit gifts given by ambassadors, this chapter considers the extent to which Mauss' theory of the gift and those arguments subsequently derived from it, or as alternatives to it, prove useful as tools for their analysis. In particular, drawing on the work of Algazi, Jussen and Groebner, it suggests that by paying close attention to both the labels given to gifts and the rhetoric attached to the process of gift-giving, it is possible to gain important insights into contemporary attitudes.

a.   Presents and presentations

Fantoni has argued that in the framework of court politics, the ostentation of the gift and publicity about it were particularly important.[21] Some

---

[16] Anthony Cutler, 'Significant gifts: patterns of exchange in late antique, Byzantine and early Islamic diplomacy', *Journal of Medieval and Early Modern Studies* 38 (2008), 79–101, especially pp. 87–91.

[17] Levin, *Agents of Empire*, pp. 150, 169–70.   [18] Jansson, 'Measured reciprocity', p. 352.

[19] Russell E. Martin, 'Gifts for the bride: dowries, diplomacy, and marriage politics in Muscovy', *Journal of Medieval and Early Modern Studies* 38 (2008), 119–45.

[20] Jean-Claude Waquet, *Corruption: Ethics and Power in Florence, 1600–1770*, trans. Linda McCall (Cambridge: Polity Press, 1991).

[21] Marcello Fantoni, *La Corte del Granduca: Forma e Simboli del Potere Mediceo fra Cinque e Seicento* (Rome: Bulzoni, 1994), p. 128.

diplomatic gifts, in short, worked by virtue of their public nature. Like ceremony, they were a means of symbolic communication. Presentations of gifts occurred in a variety of contexts in the course of diplomacy: in formal occasions at court, as diplomats travelled to their postings, and at the conclusion of a particular ambassador's service. This section of the chapter will consider these three types of gift-giving in turn, noting the similarities and differences in the descriptions of gifts and the circumstances in which they were presented.

i.   Gifts between princes

In the early part of the sixteenth century, all sorts of gifts were exchanged between European princes. King Manuel I of Portugal famously sent Pope Leo X an elephant.[22] This was particularly extravagant, but lavish gifts were usual. 'Competitive magnificence' was the order of the day.[23] On 28 June 1505, Johannes Burchard feared 'horrendous scandal' at court because the orators of both France and Spain planned to present to the Pope a palfrey (in Italian *chinea*) as tribute for the Realm of Naples, which both their kings claimed. The Spanish orator, in Burchard's words 'a most importunate man, lacking modesty and eloquence', managed to sneak his *chinea* into the palace, and Julius finally agreed to receive both horses, without prejudice.[24] Most of the time the rivalries were played out more subtly. In 1521, John Clerk, an English resident in Rome, presented Henry VIII's pamphlet against Martin Luther, the *Assertio Septem Sacramentorum*, to Pope Leo X, giving a sermon against Luther in the course of the presentation.[25] The presentation of course underlined Henry's princely orthodoxy, but it was also a step in a sequence of diplomatic exchanges. Later the same month, Leo returned the favour, granting Henry the title 'Defender of the Faith'.[26] Such titles were among the boons popes could grant in alliance-building: Henry's equivalents in France and Spain were 'Most Christian' and 'Catholic' kings respectively. This exchange is obviously reciprocal, but it did not stand alone. Earlier gift exchanges between the papacy and the Tudor dynasty included the grant of a Golden Rose by Julius II in 1510. In 1513, after the English defeat of the French at Tournai, Henry was given the Holy

---

[22] Christopher Hibbert, *The Rise and Fall of the House of Medici*, p. 226.

[23] The phrase is from Glenn J. Richardson, 'Anglo-French political and cultural relations during the reign of Henry VIII' (unpublished doctoral thesis, University of London, 1995), p. 312.

[24] Burchard, Vol. II, p. 487.

[25] BAV, MS Vat. Lat. 12276, fol. 14v. Ellis (ed.), *Original Letters*, 3rd series, Vol. I, pp. 262–9 (*L&P*, Vol. III, 1654); ASV, Arch. Concist., Acta Misc. 31, fol. 130r.

[26] *L&P*, Vol. III, 1659; ASV, Arch. Concist., Acta Misc. 31, fol. 131r.

Sword and Cap of Maintenance by Leo X (who had just enjoyed the support of England's ally Spain in returning his family to power in Florence).[27] Henry also accorded favours to other Medici men: Giulio de' Medici (the future Clement VII) became cardinal-protector of England; Giuliano de' Medici, Pope Leo's brother, joined the Order of the Garter.[28] These gifts clearly illustrate the functioning of a reciprocal system with the Maussian characteristics that the gifts are formally voluntary but some return is clearly expected. Unlike the gifts discussed elsewhere in this chapter, however, many of them had a spiritual significance which added an extra rhetorical dimension to the process of exchange.

While the gifts cited above would have involved some public ceremony in the giving, and some had religious connotations, this was not true of all gifts between princes and popes. There were also presents of luxury items. In 1459, Francesco Sforza sent Pius II a gift of 'three very fat steers which had been fed on turnips', sufficient to divide among numerous members of Pius' court including the ambassadors there, who got one to share.[29] Besides those discussed above, papal gifts to Henry VIII included 'a hundred Parmesan cheeses and barrels of wine' (from Julius II); Leo X had a role in commissioning a tomb design for the king.[30] Sforza, as we have seen in earlier chapters, was a relatively new prince, and had reason to consolidate his relationship with Pius, a relatively new pope. Gift-giving was a means of doing that. The Medici-Tudor gifts are perhaps more ambiguous, especially given the very personal interests of the Medici popes in establishing their relatives as rulers of Florence, for which they sought the backing of diplomatic allies. These exchanges were, for the most part, arranged via the London offices of the Florentine merchant Giovanni Cavalcanti. He held no official diplomatic position in the papal service, but acted as a representative of Medici family interests.[31] It will become apparent that all sorts of diplomatic gifts embody such multiple meanings.

---

[27] Margaret Mitchell, 'Works of art from Rome for Henry VIII. A study of Anglo-Papal relations as reflected in papal gifts to the English king', *Journal of the Warburg and Courtauld Institutes* 34 (1971), 178–203 (pp. 179–80). On the Golden Rose, see Burke, *Historical Anthropology*, p. 170.

[28] *Ibid.*   [29] Pius, *Commentarii*, Vol. I, pp. 628–9 (*Secret Memoirs*, p. 137).

[30] Chambers, *Cardinal Bainbridge*, p. 37; Mitchell, 'Works of art', and, for a more recent treatment, see Cinzia Sicca, 'Pawns of international finance and politics: Florentine sculptors at the court of Henry VIII', *Renaissance Studies* 20 (2006), 1–34.

[31] Cinzia Sicca, 'Consumption and trade of art', and 'Pawns of international finance'; Mitchell, 'Works of art'.

ii.   Presents on the road

ᵃs we saw in the case of the *Assertio*, certain gifts would be given in a
highly ceremonial context, where the ambassador would make his presentation in what was, in effect, the persona of his prince. Diplomats
could also receive gifts in the persona of their masters, and this is
particularly apparent in the case of the gifts that were customarily given
in the course of their journeys to and from a posting. Special ambassadors travelling at relatively leisurely speeds were most commonly
involved in such presentations: as noted in Chapter 3, those ambassadors
who were travelling for urgent negotiations often bypassed such ceremony. The post road could be an important space for political activity,
and this included gift exchange. The English envoy Sir Francis Bryan
was given wine by the mayor of Boulogne while on his way to Rome in
1528.[32] The term 'present' is used in the English diplomatic correspondence of this period to describe this and other such gifts, and it offers a
useful distinguishing category with which to understand this particular
variety of gift-giving. Travelling to Bologna for the coronation of Charles
V in 1529–30, Sir Nicholas Carew and Richard Sampson were also given
wine in several French towns.[33] In Turin, the duke of Savoy sent a more
extravagant gift: 'A goodly present of Rawe wyldfoule that is to wytte. vj
capons iiij. fesant[es] / xij wodcock[es] / xij partriches / xij qwayles. and vj
rabett[es].'[34] On their subsequent arrival at Reggio nell'Emilia, they
received from the duke of Ferrara: 'xx. capons xx. pertryches / foure
hares / two cheses parmesanes / xij botteilles of wyne / two barylles of
olyues / vj boxes of marmelade and comfitures / vj torchett[es] and xxiiij
ca[n]del[es] of virgin waxe'.[35] Arriving in Lucca in 1528, Stephen
Gardiner and Edward Fox were given a similarly generous 'presente'
including twenty 'gret pykes', borne on four men's heads in basins of
silver, confectionary and wines. It was said to have filled a 'gret cham-
bre'.[36] Venetian ambassadors arriving in Ancona *en route* to Rome in
June 1509 received a gift of fish and fruit,[37] while when Enea Silvio
Piccolomini arrived in Rome as Imperial ambassador in 1447, he
received from Tommaso Parentucelli, the future Nicholas V, 'a boar,
partridges, pheasants and excellent wine'.[38] The number of instances in

---

[32] *St P*, Vol. VII, p. 93 (*L&P*, Vol. IV, 4661).   [33] Wall, *Voyage*, pp. 46–7, 51.

[34] Wall, *Voyage*, p. 56.   [35] Wall, *Voyage*, p. 58.

[36] *St P*, Vol. VII, p. 60 fn.; TNA, SP 1/47, fols. 117–18 (*L&P*, Vol. IV, 4078).

[37] *Dispacci*, p. 14.

[38] Paschini, 'Ambasciate', p. 48. That night (i.e. on the night of their arrival), the Cardinal
of Bologna (Tommaso Parentucelli, future Nicholas V) sent them as a gift 'un cinghiale,
pernici, fagiani e vino prelibato, il procuratore dei cavalieri Teutonici confetture, cera
e vino'

which wine was given tallies with Groebner's finding that it was the preferred diplomatic gift in Basel and other cities in eastern France, southern Germany and Switzerland.[39]

The *presentation* of presents was important because they worked by virtue of their highly symbolic and public nature. Their particular imagery varied: it might be quite literal, as in the case of the Lucca present, which was decorated with the arms of Henry VIII, those of the city, and those of the Holy Roman Emperor. Such symbolism allowed the republic to point to its political alliances and to allude to a preference for an Anglo-Imperial alliance over an Anglo-French one, without straightforwardly criticising the king of England.[40] The gift of wild fowl to Carew and Sampson has a symbolism less obvious today, but which would have been clearly understood at the time. Wild fowl had a particular cultural significance in late medieval and Renaissance Italy.[41] For most people, the consumption of fowl was regarded as unhealthy: it was thought to heat the blood, and consequently to lead to the sin of lust. For princes, however, and others who exercised political power, fowl was a suitably noble food; in Florence, members of the Signoria were required to eat it.[42] The fact that in Lucca, Gardiner and Fox received a present not of wild fowl but rather of pike might reflect their ecclesiastical status, but is more likely to be due to the timing: it was Lent. (Sampson, who did receive wild fowl, was a cleric too.) Such large fish were, like fowl, regarded as suitable gifts for people of high social standing.[43]

This gift-giving was an important part of diplomatic ceremonial, allowing the various towns, the two dukes, and the city of Lucca, to demonstrate their friendship and liberality towards the king of England, and thereby to underline their own status as givers. There is clearly a close relationship between this type of gift-giving and the liberal diplomatic entertaining discussed in Chapter 6, both of which characterise the giver/host as noble and honourable. As we saw in Chapter 1, 'honour' was a constant motif in the diplomatic correspondence of this period, and was central to contemporary understandings of nobility. Likewise, 'honour' is often referred to in the literature on gift-giving: Marcel Mauss

---

[39] Groebner, *Liquid Assets*, pp. 22–30.
[40] On the use of art objects in such symbolic ways, see Anthony Colantuono, 'The mute diplomat: theorizing the role of images in seventeenth-century political negotiations', in Elizabeth Cropper (ed.), *The Diplomacy of Art. Artistic Creation and Politics in Seicento Italy* (Nuova Alfa Editoriale: Milan, 2000), pp. 51–76.
[41] Allen J. Grieco, 'Food and social classes in late medieval and Renaissance Italy', in Jean-Louis Flandrin and Massimo Montanari (eds), *Food: A Culinary History from Antiquity to the Present* (New York: Columbia University Press, 1999), pp. 302–12.
[42] *Ibid.*, p. 305.   [43] *Ibid.*, p. 306.

wrote that in the primitive societies he studied, honour was expressed through gifts, but also in many other ways.[44] Alain Derville comments that the study of the gift invites the scholar to reflect on the centrality of honour, and Natalie Zemon Davis argues that for a local seigneur in sixteenth-century France, his gifts to superiors functioned to establish him in their 'noble world of honor'.[45]

iii.   Leaving gifts

The concept of the *persona mixta*, borrowed from Valentin Groebner's study of the ways that municipal officeholders received gifts in the fifteenth and sixteenth centuries,[46] offers a useful starting point from which to consider a second type of present which ambassadors regularly received: that given on their departure from a particular posting. Although this type of gift shares with the present certain ceremonial elements, and undoubtedly had a similar function of honouring the ambassador's master, it included a greater element of 'reward' for the individual ambassador (that is, for his non-princely, private persona). It may also have had the function of partially defraying those costs of his mission that should have been covered by the host court.[47] At this relatively early stage of resident diplomacy the formalities of such arrangements were not yet fully worked out. Such gifts could add substantially to a diplomat's income, or at least make good the expenses incurred through his work.[48]

One typical gift to a departing ambassador was the gold chain. Following his special embassy to the coronation of the Holy Roman Emperor at Bologna, Sir Nicholas Carew, the chief ambassador and a gentleman of the king's privy chamber, received a gold chain weighing 2,000 ducats, while the other English ambassador, Richard Sampson, dean of the Chapel Royal, also received a chain, but of half the weight. Their herald and secretary, Thomas Wall, was presented with 100 crowns of Venice.[49] As Marcello Fantoni has pointed out one of the advantages of the chain as a gift was its easy conversion to cash: it is for this reason, he suggests, that its precise weight and number of links was often

---

[44] Mauss, *The Gift*, pp. 37–8.

[45] Alain Derville, 'Pots de Vin, Cadeaux, Racket, Patronage. Essai Sur les Mécanismes de Décision dans L'Etat Bourguignon', *Revue du Nord* 56 (1974), 341–64 (p. 345); Davis, *The Gift*, p. 63.

[46] Groebner, *Liquid Assets*, p. 68.

[47] On some problems experienced by ambassadors in this regard see Mattingly, *Renaissance Diplomacy*, pp. 33, 141.

[48] MacMahon, 'Ambassadors of Henry VIII', p. 239.   [49] Wall, *Voyage*, p. 84.

specified.[50] Indeed, it is possible that Nicholas Carew cashed in his chain, for in a list of royal plate three years later is the entry: 'Received of the King a great chain of gold, bought by him of Sir Nic. Carewe, with 101 links.'[51] Such gifts clearly involved an element of personal reward, but were also part of the systemic exchange that went on between European courts and their representatives. That their presentation was an international convention is clear from numerous cases that can be cited: for example, on his departure from England in May 1526, the chief French ambassador received a chain weighing 2,500 ducats.[52] The chain was not, however, the only acceptable gift: money was also given. Although, as we will see, cash gifts were not always perceived to be appropriate for men of higher rank, Valentin Groebner has pointed out that gifts of gold money, as distinct from those of silver or copper, might also be regarded as 'costly treasures'.[53] In March 1535, on his departure from Venice after almost ten years there as English ambassador, the Senate agreed to give Giambattista Casali 'silver, gold or money' to the value of 500 ducats, and his secretary, fifty ducats' worth of cloths of silk or money.[54] On their respective departures from England in February and December 1529, Vicenzo Casali, acting as a diplomatic messenger, received a gift of seventy-two crowns of the sun, at 4s 8d, while the Imperial ambassador received two hundred crowns of the sun, at 4s 4d.[55] These leaving gifts functioned in a circular system of reciprocity in which every court (or republic) was expected to give appropriately, even if the return might not be direct or immediate.

The case of Carew, Sampson and Wall demonstrates that such leaving presents might be given with some ceremony. A gentleman of the emperor's privy chamber, the chamber treasurer and another gentleman usher came to Carew's lodging with four torches burning before them. Sampson's gift was accompanied by 'very goodly wourd[es]', as was the gift to the embassy herald, Thomas Wall.[56] The case also illustrates how presents to ambassadors were framed within the social order, confirming

[50] Fantoni, *La Corte del Granduca*, p. 105. Although Fantoni's study deals with a somewhat later period (late sixteenth to early seventeenth century), the similarity in the gifts is striking.

[51] *L&P*, Vol. VI, 339.

[52] Letter of Uberto Gambara to Francesco Guicciardini, Lambeth Palace Library, MS 4434, fol. 273v.

[53] Groebner, *Liquid Assets*, p. 5.

[54] *CSP Ven*, Vol. V, pp. 38, 40. The rate of exchange is noted in this decision as six livres and four soldi per ducat.

[55] *L&P*, Vol. V, 309, 316. Note the variation between the rates, and from the official exchange rate.

[56] Wall, *Voyage*, p. 84.

Fantoni's observation of later Medici court practice that the intrinsic or symbolic value of the gift rose in direct proportion to the rank of the recipient.[57] Alain Derville, writing on bribery in fifteenth-century Lille and Saint-Omer, similarly found that social hierarchy was meticulously respected in the exchange of gifts.[58] The careful observance of such distinctions is confirmed in the case of Carew by the fact that the presentations were made by a gentleman of the Emperor's privy chamber, his equal in rank.[59] MacMahon, however, has qualified this point in his study of Henry VIII's ambassadors, arguing that while social status was indeed the central factor in determining the leaving gift, the diplomat's popularity at the receiving court and his length of service were also relevant.[60]

b.   Regulation and registration

The authors of fifteenth- and sixteenth-century treatises on diplomacy were rather coy about discussing gifts. Étienne Dolet, a secretary to the French ambassador to Venice in the late 1520s, referred in his *De Officio Legati* to 'shrewd men not of one's household, who have been inveigled by our liberality'.[61] Inveigling may or may not have involved bribery, of course, but the implication was that they had been persuaded to do something they would not have done otherwise. Later in his treatise, however, Dolet specified that by 'liberality' he meant 'magnificence and splendor in [the ambassador's] manner of living'.[62] Even among those who were willing to emphasise the instrumental functions of liberality in general, there was a marked reticence to discuss explicitly the advantages to be obtained through gift-giving. Donald Queller's study of a later Venetian document on the ambassador, probably from the 1570s, finds an implicit reference to the role of gift-giving in cultivating contacts at court in the phrase 'to satisfy everyone according to his rank'.[63] Queller is

---

[57] Fantoni, *La Corte del Granduca*, pp. 97, 102–5.   [58] Derville, 'Pots de Vin', p. 345.
[59] On the diplomatic functions of the Privy Chamber, and the development of an internationally-recognised rank of 'Gentleman of the Privy Chamber', see David Starkey, 'Intimacy and innovation: the rise of the Privy Chamber, 1485-1547', in Starkey (ed.), *The English Court from the Wars of the Roses to the Civil War* (London: Longman, 1987), pp. 71–118.
[60] MacMahon, 'Ambassadors of Henry VIII', pp. 239–40.
[61] Dolet, 'De Officio Legati', p. 86.   [62] *Ibid.*, p. 87.
[63] Donald E. Queller, 'How to succeed as an ambassador: a sixteenth-century Venetian document', in Joseph R. Strayer and Donald E. Queller (eds), *Post Scripta: Essays on Medieval Law and the Emergence of the European State in Honor of Gaines Post (= Studia Gratiana* 15 (1972)), pp. 655–71 (p. 661, 668). The Italian wording is: 'sodisfare à ciascuno secondo il grado suo'.

keen to interpret this as an injunction to offer bribes, but he is over-hasty in assuming that such gifts were necessarily illegitimate. They had the *potential* to corrupt, but that gifts were given is not, in and of itself, evidence of corruption. Many courtiers of early modern Europe received 'pensions' from foreign crowns; the practice was openly acknowledged, and little expectation was placed upon the payments beyond a hope that they would contribute to the maintenance of friendly relations between the realms in question.[64]

Those gifts *received* by ambassadors were the subject of some more discussion. Guicciardini observed 'that ambassadors often take the side of the prince at whose court they are. That makes them suspected either of corruption or of seeking rewards, or at least of having been bedazzled by the endearments and kindnesses shown them.' He thought their bias might also be due to an overestimation of the importance of the court to which they were posted.[65] Likewise, Dolet was aware of the anxieties gifts aroused and wrote that an ambassador would be 'deserving of capital punishment' if:

Won over by gifts or suborned by the promise of wealth and honors, you favor the interests of your enemy, and urge your king to a course which you know is to his disadvantage.[66]

Venice, where Dolet served as secretary to the French ambassador, was one of the states that did impose regulations in this regard. Laws of 1403 and 1406, reiterated in 1482, barred Venetian ambassadors from accepting gifts, including benefices. The Venetian diplomat Ermolao Barbaro, referred to the proscription in his own *De Officio Legati*, but ironically fell foul of it himself in 1491, when he was made patriarch of Aquileia by Pope Innocent VIII while on embassy to Rome.[67] Venice was not alone in its desire for regulation: in Basel, gifts received by envoys had to be handed over to the city, a requirement which, according to Groebner, provoked 'a certain disquiet'. The city council passed resolutions on the subject repeatedly, and eventually relaxed the rules, suggesting that their effectiveness in preventing the practice was limited.[68] In the context of princely diplomacy, however, strict rules about the acceptance or registration of gifts were, at this stage, rare. The sort of detailed record-keeping of diplomatic gifts apparent in later fourteenth- and fifteenth-century Basel was not established in England until the

[64] Potter, 'Foreign policy', p. 129.   [65] Guicciardini, *Maxims and Reflections*, p. 80.
[66] Dolet, 'De Officio Legati', 89.
[67] Barbaro, 'De Officio Legati', p. 164. For background, see Biow, *Doctors, Ambassadors, Secretaries*, p. 105.
[68] Groebner, *Liquid Assets*, pp. 117, 126.

seventeenth century.[69] This reflects a more general pattern, in which republics were rather quicker to standardise and regulate diplomatic practices than were principalities, which relied for longer on a more personalised form of representation based on a relationship of service between ambassador and prince. Yet while the rules of diplomatic gift-giving may not have been written, there is plenty of evidence to suggest that clear shared conventions existed. How did contemporaries understand them? How did they distinguish between what was an acceptable and what an unacceptable gift?

One of the difficulties facing any traveller abroad is the need to negotiate the local conventions of tipping. The same was surely true at the sixteenth-century court of Rome, where diplomats from across Europe and beyond had to work out how much to pay to whom and when. In an effort to protect new ambassadors from greedy officials' extravagant requests, the papal master-of-ceremonies Paride Grassi set out a list of court personnel to be tipped by the visiting diplomat, and the sums to be given.[70] Such payments, he wrote, were a means of expressing gratitude and not a matter of obligation or law, but it was the convention that the ambassador of a king should usually give a total of one hundred and fifty gold ducats, while a ducal representative should give one hundred ducats in total and those of marquises, republics and other princes could usually give a little less, as they wished.[71] There were, in short, very clear expectations about what should be given. Grassi's treatise offers useful guidance with which to interpret other evidence about gratuities, such as comments like that of the Mantuan ambassador who wrote in 1529 to his master that:

This poor man at the gates recommends himself to Your Excellency for some money that he says he would receive from you as a singular gift and grace and for alms.[72]

The precise identity of the 'poor man' is not known, nor is it possible to be definitive about the location of the gates. However, in the context of the detailed conventions for tipping described by Grassi, in which he specified that a ducal ambassador should give 'four or five ducats' at the 'iron gate', this request for a gift takes on a rather different character than it might in a situation where no such conventions existed. It may just as well be an assertion of entitlement as a plea for charity.

---

[69] Groebner, *Liquid Assets*, p. 18; Jansson, 'Measured reciprocity', p. 369.
[70] BAV, MS Vat. Lat. 12270, fols. 70v–71r.   [71] BAV, MS Vat. Lat. 12270, fol. 70v.
[72] 'Questo povero homo dalle porte se raccomanda a S. Ex^ia di qualche denari che dice che li recevera in singulare dono et gratia et per elemosina.' ASMn, Archivio Gonzaga 878, c. 235r.

Tipping was a highly-organised system at the court of Rome, the efficient functioning of which relied on ambassadors and others giving appropriate sums to the appropriate people. On 1 January 1528, William Knight, then an English ambassador at the papal court, wrote to Cardinal Thomas Wolsey about his attempts to offer a 'reward' of 2,000 crowns to Cardinal Lorenzo Pucci and thirty crowns to Pucci's secretary.[73] As I discuss below, the cardinal subsequently refused to accept the money; not so the secretary, who kept his thirty crowns.[74] Presumably he thought it a reasonable tip for his assistance. In his study of political presents in sixteenth-century Basel, Valentin Groebner outlined the concept of an 'access fee': the expected gift to a junior official for expediting access to his superiors.[75] It seems probable that Pucci's secretary, like the Basel officials, would have supplemented his income through the receipt of regular tips, and that this would not have been perceived as corrupt. The papal master-of-ceremonies Biagio Martinelli regularly recorded in his diary the tips he received from visiting ambassadors and how he shared them with his colleagues in the office of ceremonies. For example, on 22 June 1520, they received fifty gold ducats from the secretary of the duke of Albany (ambassador of the king of Scotland), of which Martinelli had twenty-five crowns; in 1523, they received forty large ducats to share between them from a group of Venetian ambassadors.[76] Martinelli also recorded cases in which the expected tips were not forthcoming. On the occasion of a presentation to the pope by the Imperial ambassador in 1521, he noted: 'For that our office is owed jewels, but up until now we've had nothing but fine words.'[77] Furthermore, a system of tip-sharing was in place between the staff of the ceremonial office and their colleagues in the papal chamber, in which the latter would pass on to the former, one-third of any 'emoluments and jewels' they received.[78]

The institutionalised nature of these arrangements makes clear that gift-giving was an integral and acknowledged diplomatic practice at Rome. These gratuities, like that received by Cardinal Pucci's secretary, can also be conceptualised as 'access fees' in the sense that the ceremonialists were facilitating diplomats' access to the ritual world of the curia.

---

[73] Burnet, *History of the Reformation*, Vol. IV, p. 36 (*L&P*, Vol. IV, 3751).

[74] Pocock, *Records*, Vol. I, p. 102 (*L&P*, Vol. IV, 4120).

[75] Groebner, *Liquid Assets*, p. 62.   [76] BAV, MS Vat. Lat. 12276, fols. 11v, 30r.

[77] 'Pro Qua Debentur Officio Nostro Jocalia, Sed Adhuc Nihil Habuimus Nisi Bona Verba.' *Ibid.*, fol. 13v. On ceremonialists' tips, see DeSilva, 'Ritual negotiations', pp. 103–5.

[78] 'cum quibus Cubicularijs conventum est per nos Magistros Cermoniarum quod sic teneantur de quibuscunque emolumentis et iocalibus per eos percipiendis, quod detur nobis tertia pars.' *Ibid.*, fol. 27r.

In this regard, Martinelli's recording of tips is particularly notable. Groebner has pointed to the increasingly stringent requirements placed on Basel city officials to report gifts received, and it is arguable that such registration of gifts offered a means of legitimising them and guarding against accusations of favouritism or corruption.[79] This view is confirmed by the evidence regarding illicit gifts, which suggests that one of their most important characteristics was that they were given in secret.

When Henry VIII sent Sir Francis Bryan and Pietro Vanni on embassy to Rome in early 1529, one of their tasks was to search the papal registers to try and prove that the brief produced by Catherine of Aragon establishing the legitimacy of her marriage was a forgery. Their instructions included the advice to find a trustworthy individual in the scribes' office, whom they could assure of 'a sufficient rewarde, be it in redy money. . . or contynuall enterteynment', and to handle the arrangement secretly.[80] In contrast to the 'official' tips that an ambassador was expected to offer to the ceremonialists, in this case, the 'reward' was clearly aimed at persuading individuals to do something beyond their normal, day-to-day work. The fact that the arrangement was to be kept secret confirms that this gift was illicit. Unlike regular tips, these rewards were not to be registered or recorded. Bryan wrote to the king on 26 January 1529 to report that not only had Vanni been searching the papal registers for relevant books and copying them; but that they had 'founde the menys to have those bokys to our logyng privily'.[81] It would be surprising if those means had not included the 'ready money' on offer. The relatively codified character of tipping at the papal court suggests that it would rapidly become apparent to an official when he was being offered a larger reward than expected. That, in turn, would raise questions about whether some additional service would be required too. Indeed, the system relied on a shared understanding of the reciprocal nature of the reward–service exchange, which I discuss further below.

What do these cases tell us about the environment in which diplomats might give gifts? First, although the process of regulating diplomatic gift-giving was more clearly codified in republican contexts than in principalities, documentation from the court of Rome indicates that registration of gifts was important. This arguably acted as a means of legitimising them. Gifts that might be perceived to be corrupting had to be given secretly. All of the gifts cited here bear out Mauss' idea that there is no such thing

---

[79] Groebner, *Liquid Assets*, pp. 15–22 on the extensive recording of gifts; p. 69 on the duty to report them.
[80] BL, Cotton MSS, Vit. B, vol. x, fol. 170r (*L&P*, Vol. IV, 4977).
[81] *St P*, Vol. VII, p.150 (*L&P*, Vol. IV. 5213).

as a 'free gift'. However, the Maussian theories do not shed light on the question of what constituted 'corruption'. That idea requires an analysis of other elements in gift-giving, in particular, the ways that gifts were labelled as acceptable or unacceptable.

c.   Rhetorics of reward

In her study of gifts in early modern France, Natalie Zemon Davis shows that gift relationships could be 'the source of intolerable obligation and of accusations of corruption'.[82] What was it, though, that made a gift corrupt? Algazi argues that it is not any characteristic of the gift itself that defines it as such, but rather the way it is labelled or represented.[83] In relation to the court of Rome, D. S. Chambers suggests that the criterion for distinguishing acceptable rewards might be when they were given for 'the performance of just and necessary services in good conscience, for which the laborer was worthy of his hire – in distinction from manipulating the machine and silencing consciences to assist sinister ends'.[84] His hypothesis is borne out by the issue in May 1530 by Clement VII of a mandate forbidding – on pain of excommunication – anyone from writing or advising on the question of Henry VIII's marriage to Catherine of Aragon, 'contrary to his conscience, in the hope of rewards, prayers, hatred, fear or favour'.[85] This mandate was a response to the extensive offers of 'reward' being made by both sides in the divorce in return for the support of university faculties, but it is revealing for the way it draws the line between acceptable and unacceptable practice. Clement did not outlaw reward altogether, and probably could not have done without great difficulty: princes and their representatives had long paid for academic opinion on questions of politico-legal importance. The Pope chose instead to rule that while it was unacceptable to act against one's conscience, it was acceptable to take a reward for doing what one believed to be right. That begs the question: who or what determined whether a gift was taken in 'good conscience'? We thus return to the

---

[82] Davis, *The Gift*, p. 165.   [83] Algazi, 'Negotiating the gift', p. 18.
[84] D. S. Chambers, 'The economic predicament of Renaissance cardinals', *Studies in Medieval and Renaissance History* 3 (1966), 289–313 (p. 310).
[85] 'Sub excommunicationis latae sententiae pena, a qua ab alio quam a Romano pontifice nisi in mortis articulo nequeant absolutionis beneficium obtinere, mandamus, ne in dicti matrimoniali causa contra conscientiam spe premii, aut prece, odio, vel timore, aut gratia ducti verbo aut scriptis aliquid allegare, scribere aut consulere.' *Vetera Monumenta Hibernorum et Scotorum: Historiam Illustrantia*, ed. Augustinis Theiner (Rome: Typis Vaticanis, 1864), p. 592 (*L&P*, Vol. IV, 6549).

importance of the representation and labelling of gifts, and the rhetoric that had to accompany them.

Given the anxieties that surrounded diplomatic gift-giving, strategies were needed to situate particular gifts in the context of socially-accepted norms, and two rhetorical devices dominate contemporary discussions of gift-giving. The first drew on the classically-inspired virtue of liberality to make the gift appear honourable, voluntary and disinterested. The second device, the pairing of 'reward' and 'service', drew on ideas relating to feudal relationships of allegiance or their degenerated forms, patronage and clientage. In the rhetoric of liberality, the need for reciprocity is dissimulated: in that of reward/service, it is acknowledged. We now turn to see how this rhetoric was used in two prominent cases during Henry VIII's divorce negotiations, when the English ambassadors to Rome offered substantial gifts to cardinals from whom they were soliciting support. There was, of course, nothing exceptional about a prince offering money or benefices to one or other cardinal; nonetheless, there is evidence of a certain level of anxiety at the papal court in relation to gift-giving,[86] a suggestion borne out by Grassi's reference to officials' greed.

Cardinal Lorenzo Pucci was a close advisor to Pope Clement VII and had a key role in the decision-making related to Henry VIII's marriage.[87] In an early set of diplomatic instructions concerning the divorce negotiations, the cardinal was specifically named. The English ambassadors were to solicit his friendship and favour; on receiving a positive response, they were to offer him a reward.[88] It is notable that the friendship and favour were to be established first. Sharon Kettering has argued in relation to gifts between patrons and clients in sixteenth- and seventeenth-century France that one of the characteristics of acceptable patronage (as opposed to illegitimate bribery) was that it should be situated in the context of a personal relationship.[89] A similar mentality is expressed in this case. Gregorio Casali, Henry's resident ambassador at the curia, replied a few weeks later. He advised that Pucci was acting 'most lovingly' in all matters, and he and his colleagues proceeded to offer Pucci a gift of two thousand crowns.[90] (His secretary, as we saw above, was given thirty.) Casali used the word *munificentia*, meaning

---

[86] See the discussion of reform proposals in Chambers, 'Economic predicament', pp. 301 and 309.

[87] *St P*, Vol. VII, p. 63 (*L&P*, Vol. IV, 4118). Pocock, *Records*, Vol. I, p. 97 (*L&P*, Vol. IV, 4120). *St P*, Vol. VII, p. 144 (*L&P*, Vol. IV, 5152).

[88] Burnet, *History*, Vol. IV, p. 31 (*L&P*, Vol. IV, 3641).

[89] Kettering, 'Gift-giving and patronage', p. 150.

[90] Pocock, *Records*, Vol. I, p. 38 (*L&P*, Vol. IV, 3715). Burnet, *History*, Vol. IV, p. 36 (*L&P*, Vol. IV, 3751).

'munificence' or 'liberality' to describe the reward: in doing so, he positioned the offer in the context of the social virtues, as a disinterested, honourable and voluntary gift. However, nearly three months later, it became clear that the cardinal was refusing to take the money.[91] Whether he had refused it all along, or whether he had accepted it and then changed his mind, is not discernable from the surviving letters. Such problems with gifts are well-documented in historical studies: Kettering points out that in patron–client relationships, 'to refuse to give or receive a gift is to refuse a personal relationship, which may be interpreted as a hostile act',[92] and it is clear that this is the ambassadors' view. Similarly, Ben-Amos has argued that 'obligations to reciprocate could be involuntary and disliked'.[93] Here, despite the rhetoric of liberality, the cardinal clearly believed that in taking the money, he would incur an undesirable obligation to reciprocate: the case demonstrates the shared understanding of what such a reward meant.

Further light is shed on attitudes towards gift-giving by a subsequent discussion between Cardinal Wolsey and Casali, six months later, about whether some other gift might be given to Cardinal Pucci.[94] First of all, Wolsey said that the king would not rest until the cardinal accepted one, implying that the refusal was an insult and underlining the role of honour in gift exchanges. He then asked Casali to find out, by means of some conversation with the cardinal's intimates, what sort of gift would suit best, and hinted that the initial offer had perhaps been insufficiently generous. He suggested a gift of hangings, gold plate or horses and further proposed a contribution towards the building of the new St Peter's, which he situated in the context of the 'liberality of Christian princes'. These references to non-cash gifts hint at a belief that perhaps the *type* of gift – money – rather than the fact of the offer had prompted the refusal. Casali wrote back recommending a gift of silver plate, which as well as being fashionable might have been perceived as a less obviously coercive and thus more acceptable gift than cash. (It may also have reflected a view that Pucci had not, in fact, proved particularly helpful.) Fantoni has observed that at the Medici court of the later sixteenth and early seventeenth centuries, gentlemen were given such things as precious objects or titles, while food and cash gifts were perceived to be appropriate for servants.[95] The discussion here may reflect a similar set of values.

---

[91] Pocock, *Records*, Vol. I, p. 102 (*L&P*, Vol. IV, 4120).
[92] Kettering, 'Gift-giving and patronage', p. 131.
[93] Ben-Amos, 'Gifts and favors', p. 333.
[94] *St P*, Vol. VII, p. 100 (*L&P*, Vol. IV, 4813).
[95] Fantoni, *La Corte del Granduca*, especially section III.a. 'Il dono: liberalità e potere', pp. 97–137 (pp. 102–5).

In discussions of Cardinal Pucci's gift, the concepts of 'liberality' and 'reward' were both used. Yet the case also demonstrates the limits to labels' power. Despite the rhetoric of liberality, Pucci clearly believed that it would be unacceptable to take a gift without offering something in return. As an influential advisor to the pope, the cardinal was acting, in a certain sense, as a 'gatekeeper', and the decision to offer him a reward fits rather well with Groebner's scheme of 'access fees' mentioned above in relation to the cardinal's secretary: Pucci, in turn, was expediting access to *his* superior. However, it would be a mistake to regard him only in that sense: he was, in his own right, a prince of the Church, and contemporaries believed the Pope would respect his advice.[96] Like the tips to the servants, the behaviour of Pucci and the ambassadors is best explained by their mutual awareness of the reciprocal nature of gifts. When the cardinal refused the reward, he extracted himself from the duty to provide a service in return.

Two years later, in an effort to win the support of Pietro Accolti, cardinal of Ancona, in Henry VIII's divorce case, the English ambassadors offered large 'rewards' in the form of benefices and pensions to Accolti and his nephew Benedetto, the cardinal of Ravenna. This was a classic 'gift-gone-wrong', for Benedetto Accolti double-crossed Henry and took similar payments from his opponents. A rich collection of material about the affair survives in documents from the cardinal's 1535 trial for abuse of power in his role as Legate to the Marches (in which his corruption by the king of England was a side-issue). During the process, members of his household were interrogated and Accolti corresponded with his lawyer about the English dealings. Combined with the diplomatic correspondence, it provides a significant insight into understandings of 'bribery' at the papal court.[97]

The idea that it is legitimate to offer rewards to ensure that 'justice' and 'truth' prevail is clearly expressed in the documents. When Henry VIII wrote to William Benet, ambassador in Rome, with instructions concerning a 'princely reward' for the cardinal of Ancona, the king explained:

And this offer the king's highness maketh unto him, not to corrupt him, whose integrity, his grace knoweth well, neither would admit it, nor his highness' honour, most addicted to truth and justice, would be persuaded so to do; but

---

[96] *St P*, Vol. VII, p. 144 (*L&P*, Vol. IV, 5152).
[97] For background to the trial, see Enea Costantini, *Il Cardinal di Ravenna al governo d'Ancona e il Suo Processo Sotto Paolo III* (Pesaro: Federici, 1891). The case is discussed briefly in Chambers, 'Economic predicament', p. 310, and in greater detail in his thesis, 'English representation', pp. 81–2 and 559–69.

only to animate and encourage him to defend and sustain the truth, and to let and empech such injury and wrong, as is enterprised against his highness, in this his grace's matter.[98]

Whether this flowery explanation can be considered an accurate account of what the ambassadors thought they were doing must be doubtful. It does demonstrate, however, the variety of linguistic devices that might be applied to pretend that a bribe was not a bribe. The idea of 'justice' was also used by the cardinal in a note, probably to his lawyer, about the affair. He wrote that although Gregorio Casali 'tempted me many times with the greatest of offers', Casali:

Sought nothing from me on the king's part, except that my uncle and I should be content not to go headlong against the king, and that we should consider well the good justice which this king required.[99]

The cardinal was, of course, attempting to defend himself against the accusation of corruption, and it seems improbable that Casali asked for so little from Accolti, although it is possible that he couched his request in such terms. However, it is Accolti's rhetoric that is of interest. As we have seen, it would have been acceptable for him to receive a gift in return for his conscientious conduct. Accolti went on to say of Henry's offer to nominate him to an English bishopric that:

I thanked the king for the great courtesy and liberality which he employed, but told him that I had done him no service, neither I, nor my uncle, for which we would merit such a thing.[100]

Here Accolti employs both the concept of 'liberality' and the pairing of reward and service discussed above to explain why he turned down the bishopric: he could not accept the reward because he had not provided service. He does so with the polite rhetoric conventionally used to hedge around such requirements of reciprocity, just as concepts of liberality were employed in the case of Cardinal Pucci.

Accolti then contradicts himself. Aware that his claim of having turned down a bishopric may not be sustainable (a number of his servants would testify that he had, in fact, accepted it), he tries to characterise the nomination as a voluntary, disinterested gift:

---

[98] Pocock, *Records*, Vol. II, p. 144 (*L&P*, Vol. V, 611).

[99] 'El cavalier predetto adunque piu volte mi tentò con grandissime offerte, ne mi ricercava d'altro da parte del Re, se non che fussimo contenti et mio zio et io, di non andar precipiti contro al Re, et che volessimo considerar bene la bona justitia che esso Re pretendeva.' ASF, Fondo Accolti 9, no. 30, fol. 2r.

[100] 'Ringratiai il Re della molta cortesia et liberalità che usava, ma li dissi ch'io non li havevo fatto servitio alcuno ne io, ne mio zio per il quale meritassimo tal cosa.' *Ibid.*, fol. 2v.

And [Casali] told me that the king had said to him... that even though he was
certain not to be able to make use of me in his cause, that nonetheless he wanted
to employ this liberality towards me, for the good qualities, etc.[101]

To a contemporary, well aware of the rules of reciprocity, this would
surely seem rather unlikely. Nonetheless, because the concept of liberality implied a free, voluntary gift, and denied the reciprocal nature of
the transaction, this was a plausible line of argument for Accolti to
employ.

In contrast, however, the men who questioned Accolti's servants
about their master's activities were quite sure that no-one gave something for nothing. An early exchange in the interrogation of Flavio
Crisolino, one of the cardinal's agents in Rome, reveals the interrogator's implicit pairing of reward and service, to which Flavio responds in
kind:

(INTERROGATOR): To what end and effect was the said money given to the said
                Reverend Lord and the said promises made?
(FLAVIO): They were made and given in respect of having him favour the king's
          matrimonial cause in the presence of his uncle the Reverend
          Cardinal of Ancona.[102]

The interrogator's question effectively eliminates the possibility that the
money might have been given freely with no expectation of recipro-
cation, and the documents in this case make it abundantly clear that all
concerned shared a conception that rewards should be reciprocated.
Even while Cardinal Accolti dressed up his self-justification with the
rhetoric of liberality and imputed to Henry VIII the possibility that the
king would give something for nothing, he claimed that he refused to
accept rewards precisely because he was providing no service. Indeed,
this was the crux of the case against him: if it could be proven that he
did take the rewards, he surely must have provided the service
requested.

The Accolti documents also confirm the observation made in relation
to Bryan and Vanni's rewards to the scribes, that secrecy was an important concomitant of illicit gifts. When Casali and his colleague William
Benet went to Accolti's house to discuss their offers, they went on their

---

[101] '[Casali] mi disse che il re li haveva detto in presentia del dottor Stephano, che se bene
era certo di non si poter servir di me in la sua causa che pur voleva usar questa liberalita
verso di me, per le bone qualita ec.' *Ibid.*, fol. 3r.
[102] '[Int.] ad quem finem et effectum fuerunt date? dicto pecunis dicto Reverendissimo
domino et fatte promissiones predicte. Respondit furno fatte et date respattive havesse
afavorire apresso suo zio Reverendissimo Cardinale dancona la causa matrimoniale di
ipso re.' ASR, Tribunale del Governatore di Roma, Processi 3, 2 1, fol. 64r.

own and used the back door.[103] Furthermore, when Benet went to London to organise a 'princely reward' for the Accolti cardinals, he purported that he went on private business, exploiting his 'private' persona in his prince's interests.[104] The need for secrecy was also a problem that the ambassadors encountered in their attempt to obtain benefices with which to bribe the Accolti cardinals. It was, wrote Henry VIII, not possible for the gift to be made secretly, because of the number of court officials who would be involved in drawing up the documentation. A temporary compromise involving unofficial payments therefore had to be found.[105] The reticence about making public offers to the cardinals underlines the illicit nature of the transaction. After all, it was not so unusual to grant bishoprics to foreigners in this period: Cardinal Lorenzo Campeggio and Girolamo Ghinucci held Salisbury and Worcester and both provided service to the English in their respective roles as cardinal-protector and ambassador. There was something different about the promises being made here.

The diplomatic gift-giving detailed in this chapter amply demonstrates Castiglione's maxim that 'those who give are not all generous'. The gifts given by, and to, ambassadors, required a return. Rewards and gifts of all sorts were important tools in diplomatic practice. Presents were an open, symbolic expression of friendship and liberality: their giving was a part of the noble world of honour in which the envoy personified his prince. Tips would ease an ambassador's way through the stages of ceremony at the court of Rome, while bribery could find him politically useful friends. Gift-giving was also a means through which the social virtue of liberality could be expressed. Accusations of corruption were not usually prompted by any intrinsic quality of a particular reward. *Corruption*, like *bribe*, was rather a label with which to declare gift transactions improper or illicit. In short, a gift became a bribe when someone cried 'corruption!' In the campaign for Henry VIII's first divorce, all sorts of gifts were deemed to be corrupting: and they were defended heartily by their givers as entirely legitimate. In illicit gift-giving, ambassadors would use much the same rhetoric – that of liberality and reward – that they employed in more legitimate cases. By labelling gifts in this way they hoped to avoid

---

[103] 'Vedeva andare monsignor Benetto et il cavaliare Casale per la porta dirieto in casa del cardinale de Ravenna secretamente lor due senza altri.' ASR, Tribunale del Governatore di Roma, Processi 3; 2 II; 3 May 1535.

[104] Theiner, *Vetera Monumenta*, p. 598 (*L&P*, Vol. V, 511). Pocock, *Records*, Vol. II, p. 144 (*L&P*, Vol. V, 611).

[105] *St P*, Vol. VII, p. 364 (*L&P*, Vol. V, 887).

being accused of bribery. Underlying the rhetoric was a shared under-standing – in these cases based on or reinforced by the papal decree – that offering inducements to act against one's conscience was unacceptable. But when conscience, essentially unknowable, was the determinant of the legitimate gift, the justification for the gift's presentation became all-important.

Conclusion

In 1527, mutinous Imperial troops sacked the city of Rome. The ambassadors of rival powers scattered. Those of England and France found themselves holed up, under siege, in the Castel Sant'Angelo with Pope Clement VII. Those of Venice and Mantua fled to the protection of Isabella d'Este's city palazzo. Those of Spain tried to negotiate themselves out of their embarrassing political advantage. If any single event marked the rise of Spanish power on the Italian peninsula, the Sack was it. The fall of Florence to imperial troops in 1530 and the establishment of the Spanish-backed Medici duchy shortly afterwards only confirmed Charles V's role as arbiter of Italian politics. Matters had shifted decisively away from the balance that had characterised the peninsula's politics in the later fifteenth century.

There are two ways of looking at what happened next. Historians of diplomacy, concerned with innovations in the institutions and practice of international relations, tend to shift their attention to the impact of religious reform. The Reformation was a harbinger of new developments in European diplomatic practice: what Mattingly called the embassies of 'ill-will'. It gave a new dimension to the development of diplomatic institutions. Now, the key question for the resident ambassador was how he, as a Protestant, might operate in a Catholic country that regarded him as a heretic (or indeed, vice versa). The rise of the confessional state changed the rules and was undoubtedly significant in the working-out of ideas about exterritoriality and immunity.

For the Catholic powers of Europe, however, Rome kept its role as a diplomatic centre. They had to deal with Protestant rulers separately, via bilateral negotiations, but then they had always dealt with the Ottomans that way, and perhaps it was not so different. The same language of crusading was used in Rome against Henry VIII of England as was used against the Ottoman Turks.[1] That the power of the popes was under

---

[1] Susan Brigden, 'Henry VIII and the crusade against England', in Betteridge and Lipscomb (eds), *Henry VIII and the Court*, pp. 215–34.

attack from Protestants gave them considerable incentive to reinvigorate their court as a centre for information and negotiation for the representatives of Catholic Europe who remained. Even after his break with Rome, Henry VIII ensured that, via informal routes, he received news from there.[2] Both as a supranational centre for this side of the confessional divide, and as a large feudal power on the Italian peninsula, Rome maintained an important role in international relations. Conflicts continued over the order of precedence. The new Grand Duchy of Tuscany fought it out with Savoy; the Spanish sought elevation over the French.[3] The ceremonial world of the later sixteenth and seventeenth century was grander still than what had gone before.[4] A thorough study of the extent to which Rome was a site for innovation in diplomatic practice after the mid-sixteenth century has yet to be done: it would be a worthy project.

What is certain is that between the middle of the fifteenth century and the 1530s, Rome had been central to developments in European diplomacy. At the papal court, ceremonial texts were rewritten to accommodate the emergence of a new institution: the resident ambassador. Though the ceremonialists were careful to appeal to tradition, they oversaw substantial innovation during this period. The personnel of diplomacy changed as peace in Italy broke down, and by the 1520s, the envoys resident in Rome were increasingly professional, many with military experience. Yet while traditional accounts of Renaissance diplomacy have found in it the origins of 'modern' diplomatic practice, many of its characteristics seem highly alien to the twenty-first century observer. Sixteenth-century diplomats were regarded as the personification of their prince's honour. In the symbolic world of the court they fought to defend that honour through assertion of their place in the order of precedence. An ambassador's lifestyle was expected to be liberal, magnificent and splendid, thereby reflecting the virtues of his prince. Diplomacy drew heavily on private resources and family connections. Newsgathering was an important task for the resident ambassador, but by no means his only function. He had significant roles, too, in negotiation, as a 'fixer' for special ambassadors, and in the symbolic world of the court of Rome, where the liturgical ceremonies provided a space in which the rivalries of the European powers symbolically played out. This book has illuminated the social networks that underpinned these processes, emphasising the role of family ties and sociability in the efficient operation of diplomacy. Exigencies of distance and difficulty of communication meant that resident diplomats sometimes enjoyed considerable freedom of manoeuvre,

---

[2] Fletcher, *Our Man in Rome*, p. 203.
[3] Osborne, 'The surrogate war'; Levin, 'A New World Order'.   [4] See Chapter 3.

or, to put it another way, resigned themselves to taking responsibility for risky decisions. Yet while distance could pose problems it also created spaces for political activity along the post routes.

It is impossible to draw a clear line between what was 'public' and what was 'private' in the diplomatic practice of this period. The ambassador's house, for example, acted as an embassy building: his servants and associates functioned as embassy staff. The authors of treatises on diplomacy were concerned with ensuring the proper conduct of household members, because the ambassador's authority over his household reflected the king's good governance of his realm. When he entertained at home, he not only acquired information but demonstrated the liberality appropriate to his status as a princely representative. Diplomatic gift-giving could also demonstrate liberality, but it was surrounded by anxieties. Contemporaries were well aware of the potential of gifts to corrupt; offers of reward had to be hedged around with the appropriate rhetoric. Practices of gift-giving also draw our attention to the dual persona of the Renaissance ambassador as both private individual and royal representative. It is not always straightforward – nor was it intended to be – to discern for which of these two selves a gift was intended.

In assessing the figure of the ambassador in both aspects of his official role – the practical politics of newsgathering and negotiation, and the symbolism of ceremony – and in his personal capacity as a gentleman or a member of family networks, this study has aimed to give a holistic picture of resident diplomacy as it became established at its largest centre. In Rome, the 'theatre of the world', the two selves of the diplomat made him a particular type of performer. He played his own role and that of his prince. In symbolic performance or in conversation the ambassador acted at once as his master and on his own behalf. In the liminal space between these two selves, he was a figure of whom one could never be quite sure. In diplomacy, however, ambiguity is very useful. The indistinct boundary allowed the ambassador to acknowledge the merits of a proposal 'as a private gentleman' while denying (truthfully or not) that he was empowered to agree to it. It allowed him to float an initiative of his own, implying it was sanctioned by his home state, in order to explore the reaction of the pope or cardinals. These practices of constructive ambiguity are perhaps why the joke about ambassadors 'lying abroad' has such purchase. It is not so much that envoys were deceitful, though on occasion they were. It is more that the figure of the Renaissance ambassador, as a performer of two roles, institutionalised the possibility that they might be.

Bibliography

Primary sources (manuscript)

Archivio dei Casali di Monticelli d'Ongina
    Cassetta I (1420–1547)
Archivio di Stato di Firenze
    Fondo Accolti b. 9
    Dieci di Balia, Responsive, 139
Archivio di Stato di Mantova
    Archivio Gonzaga 871, 873, 876, 877, 878, 880 (letters from
        Rome), 1463, 1464 (letters from Venice)
Archivio di Stato di Modena
    Archivio Estense
        Carteggio Ambasciatori, Italia, Roma, b. 32
Archivio di Stato di Roma
    Tribunale del Governatore di Roma, Processi 3
Archivio di Stato di Siena, Balia
Archivio Segreto Vaticano
    Archivio Concistoriale
        Acta Miscellanea, Vol. 31
    Segretaria di Stato
        Francia, Vol. 1
Biblioteca Apostolica Vaticana
    MSS Barberini Latini
        2452: Paride Grassi, *De Oratoribus Curiae Romanae*
        2799: Biagio Martinelli da Cesena, *Diario 1518–1540*
        3567: Lettere e negotiationi del Cardinale Volsey
        Inglese
    MSS Vaticani Latini
        12270: Paride Grassi, *De Oratoribus Curiae Romanae*
        12276: Biagio Martinelli da Cesena, *Diario
        1518–1532*
        12409: Paride Grassi, *De Oratoribus Curiae Romanae*
Biblioteca del Museo Correr, Codice Cicogna 3473, Ducali di A. Gritti
  a F. Contarini

Biblioteca Nazionale Marciana, Venice
    Codices Italiani VII, 1043 (=7616) Lettere di Gasparo Con-
    tarini (1528–1529)
    Codices Italiani VII 802 (=8219) Lettere di Francesco
    Contarini
Bibliothèque Nationale de France
    MSS Français 3040, 19751
British Library
    Additional MS 28572
    Cotton MSS: Vitellius B VII, VIII, IX, X, XI
    Harleian MS 419
Lambeth Palace Library
    MS 4434, Letter book of the papal mission to England,
    1526–1527
National Archives
    State Papers series 1: 1/53

Primary sources (printed)

Barbaro, Ermolao, 'De Officio Legati', in ed. Vittore Branca, *Nuova Collezione di Testi Umanistici Inediti o Rari XIV* (Florence: Olschki, 1969), pp. 157–67.

Billon, François de, *Le Fort Inexpugnable de l'Honneur du Sexe Femenin, Construit Par Françoys de Billon, Secretaire* (Paris: Jean d'Allyer, 1555).

Biondo, Flavio, *Roma Trionfante*, trans. Lucio Fauno (Venice: Tramezzino, 1544).

Bufalini, Leonardo and Giambattista Nolli, *Plan of Rome 1551/1748*, eds Jim Tice et al. http://vasi.uoregon.edu/bufalini.htm.

Burchard, Johann, *Liber Notarum*, ed. Enrico Celani, 2 vols (Città di Castello: Lapi, 1906).

Burnet, Gilbert, *History of the Reformation of the Church of England*, ed. Nicholas Pocock, 7 vols (Oxford: Clarendon Press, 1865).

Carteggi Diplomatici fra Milano Sforzesca e la Bologna, ed. E. Sestan (Rome: Istituto Storico Italiano per l'Età Moderna e Contemporanea, 1985).

Carteggio degli Oratori Mantovani Alla Corte Sforzesca (1450–1500), ed. Isabella Lazzarini (Rome: Ministero per i beni e le attività culturali, 1999).

Castiglione, Baldesar, *The Book of the Courtier*, trans. George Bull (London: Penguin, 1976).

Cellini, Benvenuto, *My Life*, trans. Julia Conaway Bondanella and Peter Bondanella (Oxford: Oxford University Press, 2002).

Chigi, Agostino, *The Correspondence of Agostino Chigi (1466–1520)*, ed. Ingrid Rowland, Studi e Testi 399 (Vatican City: BAV, 2001).

Correspondenz des Kaisers Karl V, ed. Karl Lanz, 3 vols (Leipzig: Brockhaus, 1844).

Descriptio Urbis: The Roman Census of 1527, ed. Egmont Lee (Rome: Bulzoni, 1985).

De Vascho, Antonio, *Il Diario della Citta' di Roma*, ed. Giuseppe Chiesa (Città di Castello: Lapi, 1911).

del Piombo, Sebastiano, *L'Opera Completa* (Milan: Rizzoli, 1980).

Dispacci degli Ambasciatori Veneziani Alla Corte di Roma Presso Giulio II, 25 Guigno 1509–9 Gennaio 1510, ed. Roberto Cessi (Venice, 1932) *degli Ambasciatori Veneziani Alla Corte di Roma Presso Giulio II, 25 Guigno 1509–9 Gennaio 1510*, ed. Roberto Cessi (Venice: Deputazione di storia patria per le Venezie, 1932).

Dolet, Étienne, *De Officio Legati* (Lyons: Dolet, 1541).

'Étienne Dolet on the functions of the ambassador, 1541', ed. Jesse S. Reeves, *American Journal of International Law* 27 (1933), 80–95.

Dykmans, Marc (ed.), *Le Cérémonial Papal de la Fin du Moyen Age à la Fin de la Renaissance*, 4 vols (Brussels: Institut Historique Belge de Rome, 1977–85).

Ellis, Henry (ed.), *Original Letters Illustrative of English History*, 11 vols (London: Dawsons, 1969).

Erasmus, Desiderius, 'Convivium Religiosum', in *Opera Omnia*, Series 1, Vol. 3 (Amsterdam: North-Holland Publishing Company, 1972), pp. 231–66.

Collected Works of Erasmus (Toronto: University of Toronto Press, 1974–).

Freeling, George Henry (ed.), *Informacõn for Pylgrymes unto the Holy Londe* (London: Roxburghe Club, 1824 [1498]).

Gardiner, Stephen, *The Letters of Stephen Gardiner*, ed. James Arthur Muller, (Cambridge: Cambridge University Press, 1933).

Grassi, Paride, *Botschafterzeremoniell am Papsthof der Renaissance: Der Tractatus de Oratoribus des Paris de Grassi*, Stenzig, Philipp (ed.), (Frankfurt: Peter Lang, 2014).

Guicciardini, Francesco, *Maxims and Reflections of a Renaissance Statesman (Ricordi)*, trans. Mario Domandi (Gloucester: Smith, 1970).

Habitatores in Urbe: The Population of Renaissance Rome, ed. Egmont Lee (Rome: La Sapienza, 2006).

Hrabar, V. E., *De Legatis et Legationibus Tractatus Varii* (Dorpat, 1905).

Jean-Claude Waquet, *Corruption: Ethics and Power in Florence, 1600–1770*, trans. Linda McCall (Cambridge: Polity Press, 1991).

Lapo da Castiglionchio the Younger, *De Curiae Commodis*, in ed. Christopher S. Celenza, *Renaissance Humanism and the Papal Curia* (Ann Arbor: University of Michigan Press, 1999).

Le Huen, Nicole, *Le Grant Voyage de Jherusalem* (Paris: François Regnault, 1517).

Lettere di Principi, ed. Girolamo Ruscelli, 3 vols (Venice: Ziletti, 1581).

Machiavelli, Niccolò, 'Memoriale a Raffaello Girolami', eds., Rinaldo Rinaldi, A. Montevecchi, F. Gaeta and Luigi Blasucci, in *Opere*, 4 vols (Torino: Unione tipografico-Editrice Torinese, 1971–1999), Vol. 2, pp. 223–7.

'Advice to Raffaello Girolami when he went as ambassador to the Emperor', in *The Chief Works and Others*, trans. Allan Gilbert, 3 vols (Durham: Duke University Press, 1965), Vol. I, pp. 116–19.

Maggi, Ottaviano, *De Legato Libri Duo* (Venice, 1566).

Molini, Giuseppe (ed.), *Documenti di Storia Italiana*, 2 vols (Florence: Tipografia all'Insegna di Dante, 1836–37).

More, Thomas, *Utopia (1516)*, ed. Henry Morley (London: Cassell, 1901, online at www.gutenberg.org/files/2130/2130-h/2130-h.html).

Nolli, Giambattista. *The 1748 Map of Rome*, eds Jim Tice et al. http://nolli.uoregon.edu., (2005).

Patrizi Piccolomini, Agostino, *L'Oeuvre de Patrizi Piccolomini, ou, Le Cérémonial Papal de la Premiere Renaissance*, ed. Marc Dykmans, 2 vols (Vatican City: Biblioteca Apostolica Vaticana, 1980–82).

Pius II (Aeneas Sylvius Piccolomini), *I Commentarii*, ed. Luigi Totaro, 2 vols (Milan: Adelphi, 1984).

  Secret Memoirs of a Renaissance Pope, ed. Leona C. Gabel, trans. Florence A. Gragg (London: The Folio Society, 1988).

Pocock, Nicholas (ed.), *Records of the Reformation: The Divorce 1527–1533*, 2 vols (Oxford: Clarendon Press, 1870).

Pontano, Giovanni, *Ioannis Ioviani Pontani Opera Omnia Soluta Oratione Composita* (Venice: Aldo Manuzio, 1518).

  I Libri delle Virtù Sociali, ed. Francesco Tateo (Rome: Bulzoni, 1999).

Priscianese, Francesco, *Del Governo della Corte d'un Signore in Roma* (Città di Castello: S. Lapi Editore, 1883).

Relazioni degli Ambasciatori Veneti al Senato, ed. Eugenio Albèri, 15 vols (Florence: Società editrice fiorentina, 1839–63).

Sanuto, Marin, *I Diarii*, eds Rinaldo Fulin, Federico Stefani, Nicolò Barozzi, Guglielmo Berchet and Marco Allegri, 59 vols (Bologna: Forni, 1969).

State Papers Published under the Authority of Her Majesty's Commission: King Henry the Eighth, 11 vols (London: Record Commission, 1832–50).

Vetera Monumenta Hibernorum et Scotorum: Historiam Illustrantia, ed. Augustinis Theiner (Rome: Typis Vaticanis, 1864).

Wall, Thomas, *The Voyage of Sir Nicholas Carewe to the Emperor Charles V in the Year 1529*, ed. R. J. Knecht (Cambridge: Cambridge University Press, 1959).

Weil-Garris, Kathleen and John F. D'Amico, 'The Renaissance Cardinal's ideal palace: a chapter from Cortesi's *De Cardinalatu*', in Henry A. Millon (ed.), *Studies in Italian Art and Architecture 15th through 18th Centuries* (Rome: Edizioni dell'Elefante, 1980), pp. 45–123.

Secondary literature

Adair, E. R., *The Exterritoriality of Ambassadors in the Sixteenth and Seventeenth Centuries* (London: Longmans, Green, 1929).

Adams, Robyn and Rosanna Cox (eds), *Diplomacy and Early Modern Culture* (Basingstoke: Palgrave, 2011).

Ajmar-Wollheim, Marta and Flora Dennis (eds), *At Home in Renaissance Italy* (London: Victoria & Albert Museum, 2006).

Algazi, Gadi, Valentin Groebner and Bernhard Jussen (eds), *Negotiating the Gift: Pre-Modern Figurations of Exchange* (Göttingen: Vandenhoeck & Ruprecht, 2003).

Algazi, Gadi, 'Doing things with gifts', in Algazi et al. (eds), *Negotiating the Gift*, pp. 9–27.

Allen, E. John B., *Post and Courier Service in the Diplomacy of Early Modern Europe* (The Hague: Martinus Nijhoff, 1972).

Anciaux, Robert, 'Évolution de la Diplomatie de l'Empire Ottoman et de sa Perception de l'Europe aux XVIIe e XVIIIe Siècles', in Servantie (ed.), *L'Empire Ottoman*, pp. 151–66.

Ansani, Michele, 'La Provvista dei Benefici (1450–1466): Strumenti e Limiti dell'Intervento Ducale', in Chittolini (ed.), *Gli Sforza*, pp. 1–113.

Argegni, Corrado, *Condottieri, Capitani, Tribuni*, Enciclopedia Biografica e Bibliografica "Italiana", Serie XIX, 3 vols (Milan: Istituto Editoriale Italiano Bernardo Carlo Tosi, 1937).

Armellini, Mariano, *Le Chiese di Roma dalle Loro Origini Sino al Secolo XVI* (Rome: Tipografia Editrice Romana, 1887).

Austin, J. L., *How to Do Things with Words*, eds J. O. Urmson and Marina Sbisà, 2nd edition (Oxford: Oxford University Press, 1976).

Babcock, Robert, *The Spinelli Family: Florence in the Renaissance 1430–1535: Guide to an Exhibition at the Beinecke Library* (New Haven: Beinecke Rare Book and Manuscript Library, 1989).

Bazzoli, Maurizio, 'Ragion di Stato e Interessi degli Stati. La Trattatistica sull'Ambasciatore dal XV al XVIII Secolo', *Nuova Rivista Storica* 86 (2002), 283–328.

Beard, Mary, *The Roman Triumph* (Cambridge, MA: Harvard University Press, 2007).

Behrens, Betty, 'The office of the English resident ambassador: its evolution as illustrated by the career of Sir Thomas Spinelly, 1509–22', *Transactions of the Royal Historical Society*, 4th series, 16 (1933), 161–95.

'Origins of the office of English resident ambassador in Rome', *English Historical Review* 49 (1934), 640–58.

'Treatises on the ambassador written in the fifteenth and early sixteenth centuries', *English Historical Review* 51 (1936), 616–27.

Bell, Catherine, *Ritual: Perspectives and Dimensions* (New York and Oxford: Oxford University Press, 1997).

Bell, Gary M., 'Tudor-Stuart diplomatic history and the Henrician experience', in Robert L. Woods et al. (eds), *State, Sovereigns and Society in Early Modern England: Essays in Honour of A. J. Slavin* (Stroud: Sutton, 1998), pp. 25–43.

A Handlist of British Diplomatic Representatives, 1509–1688 (London: Royal Historical Society, 1990).

Bély, Lucien (ed.) *L'Invention de la Diplomatie. Moyen Age-Temps Modernes* (Paris: Presses Universitaires de France, 1998).

'La Naissance de la Diplomatie Moderne', *Revue d'Histoire Diplomatique* 3 (2007), 271–94.

Ben-Amos, Ilana Krausman, 'Gifts and favors: informal support in early modern England', *Journal of Modern History* 72 (2000), 295–338.

Betteridge, Thomas and Suzannah Lipscomb (eds), *Henry VIII and the Court: Art, Politics and Performance* (Aldershot: Ashgate, 2013).

Beverley, Tessa, 'Venetian ambassadors 1454–94: an Italian elite' (unpublished doctoral thesis, University of Warwick, 1999).

Biow, Douglas, *Doctors, Ambassadors, Secretaries: Humanism and Professions in Renaissance Italy* (Chicago: University of Chicago Press, 2002).

Bisaha, Nancy, 'Pope Pius II and the crusade', in Housley (ed.), *Crusading in the Fifteenth Century*, pp. 39–52.

Bölling, Jörg, *Das Papstzeremoniell der Renaissance: Texte, Musik, Performanz* (Frankfurt am Main: Peter Lang, 2006).

Borello, Benedetta, 'Strategie di Insediamento in Città: i Pamphilj a Roma nel Primo Cinquecento', in Visceglia (ed.), *La nobiltà*, pp. 31–61.

Brady, W. Maziere, *Anglo-Roman Papers* (London: Gardner, 1890).

Branca, Vittorio, 'Ermolao Barbaro and late quattrocento Venetian humanism', in J. R. Hale (ed.), *Renaissance Venice* (London: Faber & Faber, 1973), pp. 218–43.

Branchi, Andrea, *'Alexander VI's plans for Rome'*, in Prebys (ed.), *Early Modern Rome*, pp. 548–55.

Braudel, Fernand, *The Mediterranean and the Mediterranean World in the Age of Philip II*, trans. Siân Reynolds (London: Fontana, 1975).

Brigden, Susan, '"The shadow that you know": Sir Francis Bryan and Sir Thomas Wyatt at court and in embassy', *Historical Journal* 39 (1996), 1–31.

and Jonathan Woolfson, 'Thomas Wyatt in Italy', *Renaissance Quarterly* 58 (2005), 464–511.

'Henry VIII and the crusade against England', in Betteridge and Lipscomb (eds), *Henry VIII and the Court*, pp. 215–34.

Brown, Andrew and Graeme Small, *Court and Civic Society in the Burgundian Low Countries c. 1420–1530* (Manchester: Manchester University Press, 2007).

Bryce, Judith, '"Fa Finire Uno Bello Studio et Dice Volere Studiare," Ippolita Sforza and her books', *Bibliothèque d'Humanisme et Renaissance* 64 (2002), 55–69.

Bullard, Melissa Meriam, 'The language of diplomacy in the Renaissance', in Bernard Toscani (ed.), *Lorenzo de' Medici: New Perspectives* (New York: Peter Lang, 1993).

Burke, Peter, *The Historical Anthropology of Early Modern Italy: Essays on Perception and Communication* (Cambridge: Cambridge University Press, 1987).

'Varieties of performance in seventeenth-century Italy', in Gillgren and Snickare (eds), *Performativity and Performance in Baroque Rome*, pp. 15–23.

Byatt, Lucinda M. C., 'The concept of hospitality in a cardinal's household in Renaissance Rome', *Renaissance Studies* 2 (1988), 312–20.

Calendar of Letters, Despatches and State Papers Relating to the Negotiations between England and Spain, 13 vols (London: Longman, 1862–1916).

Carter, C. H. (ed.), *From the Renaissance to the Counter-Reformation: Essays in Honor of Garrett Mattingly* (New York: Random House, 1965).

Casanova, Cesarina, *Gentilhuomini Ecclesiastici: Ceti e Mobilità Sociale Nelle Legazioni Pontificie (secc. XVI–XVIII)* (Bologna: CLUEB, 1999).

Cerioni, Lydia, *La Diplomazia Sforzesca Nella Seconda Metà del Quattrocento e i Suoi Cifrari Segreti*, 2 vols (Rome: Il centro di ricerca editore, 1970).

Chambers, D. S., 'English representation at the court of Rome in the early Tudor period' (unpublished doctoral thesis, University of Oxford, 1961–62).

Cardinal Bainbridge in the Court of Rome (Oxford: Oxford University Press, 1965).

'The economic predicament of Renaissance cardinals', *Studies in Medieval and Renaissance History* 3 (1966), 289–313.

'The enigmatic eminence of Cardinal Sigismondo Gonzaga, *Renaissance Studies* 16 (2002), 330–54.

Popes, Cardinals and War: The Military Church in Renaissance and Early Modern Europe (London: I. B. Tauris, 2006).

Chaplais, Pierre, *English Diplomatic Practice in the Middle Ages* (London: Hambledon and London, 2002).

Chastel, André, *The Sack of Rome, 1527*, trans. Beth Archer (Princeton: Princeton University Press, 1983).

Chittolini, Giorgio, 'The "private", the "public", the state', in Julius Kirshner (ed.), *Origins of the State*, pp. 34–61.

Gli Sforza, la Chiesa Lombarda, la Corte di Roma: Strutture e Pratiche Beneficiarie nel Ducato di Milano (1450–1535) (Naples: Liguori, 1989).

Christie, Richard Copley, *Étienne Dolet: The Martyr of the Renaissance* (London: Macmillan, 1880).

Clough, Cecil H., 'Three Gigli of Lucca in England during the fifteenth and early sixteenth centuries: diversification in a family of mercenary merchants', *The Ricardian* 13 (2003), 121–47.

Cockram, Sarah, *Isabella d'Este and Francesco Gonzaga: Power Sharing at the Italian Renaissance Court* (Aldershot: Ashgate, 2013).

Colantuono, Anthony, 'The mute diplomat: theorizing the role of images in seventeenth-century political negotiations', in Elizabeth Cropper (ed.), *The Diplomacy of Art: Artistic Creation and Politics in Seicento Italy* (Nuova Alfa Editoriale: Milan, 2000), pp. 51–76.

Connell, William J. (ed.), *Society and Individual in Renaissance Florence* (Berkeley: University of California Press, 2002).

Costantini, Enea, *Il Cardinal di Ravenna al Governo d'Ancona e il Suo Processo Sotto Paolo III* (Pesaro: Federici, 1891).

Creighton, Mandell, *A History of the Papacy from the Great Schism to the Sack of Rome*, 5 vols (London: Longmans, Green & Co, 1892–94).

'The Italian bishops of Worcester', in *Historical Essays and Reviews* (London: Longmans, Green, 1911), 202–34.

Cutler, Anthony, 'Significant gifts: patterns of exchange in late antique, Byzantine and early Islamic diplomacy', *Journal of Medieval and Early Modern Studies* 38 (2008), 79–101.

D'Amico, John F., *Renaissance Humanism in Papal Rome: Humanists and Churchmen on the Eve of the Reformation* (Baltimore and London: Johns Hopkins University Press, 1983).

Dandelet, Thomas, *Spanish Rome 1500–1700* (New Haven and London: Yale University Press, 2001).

Davis, Natalie Zemon, *The Gift in Sixteenth-Century France* (Oxford: Oxford University Press, 2000).

Della Gattina, F. Petruccelli, *Histoire Diplomatique des Conclaves*, 2 vols (Paris: Librarie Internationale, 1864).

Derville, Alain, 'Pots de Vin, Cadeaux, Racket, Patronage. Essai Sur les Mécanismes de Décision dans l'Etat Bourguignon', *Revue du Nord* 56 (1974), 341–64.

DeSilva, Jennifer Mara, 'Ritual negotiations: Paris de' Grassi and the office of ceremonies under Popes Julius II and Leo X' (unpublished doctoral thesis, University of Toronto, 2007).

'Senators or courtiers: negotiating models for the College of Cardinals under Julius II and Leo X', *Renaissance Studies* 22 (2008), 154–73.

'Official and unofficial diplomacy between Rome and Bologna: the de' Grassi family under Pope Julius II, 1503–13', *JEMH* 14 (2010), 535–57.

De Strobel, Anna Maria and Fabrizio Mancinelli, 'La Sala Regia e la Sala Ducale', in Pietrangeli (ed.), *Il Palazzo Apostolico Vaticano*, pp. 73–9.

De Vivo, Filippo, *Information and Communication in Venice: Rethinking Early Modern Politics* (Oxford: Oxford University Press, 2007).

Diccionari Biogràfic (Barcelona: Alberti, 1969).

Dickinson, G., *Du Bellay in Rome* (Leiden: Brill, 1960).

Dizionario Biografico degli Italiani (Rome: Enciclopedia Italiana, 1960–).

Dover, Paul M., 'Royal diplomacy in Renaissance Italy: Ferrante d'Aragona (1458–1494) and his ambassadors', *Mediterranean Studies* 14 (2005), 57–94.

'"Saper la Mente della Soa Beatitudine": Pope Paull II and the Ambassadorial Community in Rome (1464–71)', *Renaissance and Reformation* 31, no. 3 (2008), 3–34.

'The economic predicament of Italian Renaissance ambassadors', *Journal of Early Modern History* 12 (2008), 137–67.

Dykmans, Marc, 'Paris de Grassi', *Ephemerides Liturgicae* 96 (1982), 407–82.

'Paris de Grassi II', *Ephemerides Liturgicae* 99 (1985), 383–417.

'Paris de Grassi III', *Ephemerides Liturgicae* 100 (1986), 270–333.

Esposito, Anna, '"Li Nobili Huomini di Roma": strategie Familiari Tra Città, Curia e Municipo', in Gensini (ed.), *Roma Capitale*, pp. 373–88.

Fantoni, Marcello, *La Corte del Granduca: Forma e Simboli del Potere Mediceo fra Cinque e Seicento* (Rome: Bulzoni, 1994).

Feci, S., 'Manetti, Latino Giovenale', *Dizionario Biografico degli Italiani* (Roma: Enciclopedia Italiana, 1960 'Manetti, Latino Giovenale', *Dizionario Biografico degli Italiani* (Roma: Enciclopedia Italiana, 1960

Fedele, Clement and Mario Gallenga, *Per Servizio di Nostro Signore: Strade, Corrieri e Poste dei Papi dal Medioevo al 1870 (= Quaderni di Storia Postale* 10 (Modena: Mucchi, 1998)).

Ferguson, John, *English Diplomacy 1422–1461* (Oxford: Clarendon Press, 1972).

Fernández, Henry Dietrich, 'The patrimony of St Peter: the papal court at Rome c.1450–1700', in John Adamson (ed.), *The Princely Courts of Europe: Ritual, Politics and Culture under the Ancien Régime 1500–1750* (London: Weidenfeld & Nicolson, 1999), pp. 141–63.

Ferrajoli, Alessandro. 'Il Ruolo della Corte di Leone X', *Archivio della R. Società Romana di Storia Patria* 36 (1913), 519–84.

Fletcher, Catherine, 'Renaissance diplomacy in practice: the case of Gregorio Casali, England's ambassador to the papal court 1525–33' (unpublished doctoral thesis, University of London, 2008).

'"Furnished with gentlemen": the ambassador's house in sixteenth-century Italy', *Renaissance Studies* 24 (2010), 518–35.

'War, diplomacy and social mobility: the Casali family in the service of Henry VIII', *Journal of Early Modern History* 14 (2010), 559–78.

and Jennifer M. DeSilva, 'Italian ambassadorial networks in early modern Europe: an introduction', *Journal of Early Modern History* 14 (2010), 505–12.

Our Man in Rome: Henry VIII and His Italian Ambassador (London: Bodley Head, 2012).

'Performing Henry at the court of Rome', in Betteridge and Lipscomb (eds), *Henry VIII and the Court*, pp. 179–96.

The Spanish Presence in Sixteenth-Century Italy: Images of Iberia (Farnham: Ashgate, 2015).

'The altar of Saint Maurice and the invention of tradition in Saint Peter's', in McKitterick et al. (eds), *Old Saint Peter's, Rome* (Cambridge: Cambridge University Press, 2013).

'Mere emulators of Italy: The Spanish in Italian diplomatic discourse, 1492–1550', in Piers Baker-Bates and Miles Pattenden (eds), *Imagining Iberia* (Ashgate, in press).

Fosi, Irene, 'Court and city in the ceremony of the possesso in the sixteenth century', in Signorotto and Visceglia (eds), *Court and Politics*, pp. 31–52.

Fragnito, Gigliola, 'Cardinals' courts in sixteenth-century Rome', *Journal of Modern History* 65 (1993), 26–56.

Frati, Lodovico, *La Vita Privata di Bologna* (Rome: Bardi, 1968).

Frazee, C. A., *Catholics and Sultans: The Church and the Ottoman Empire* (Cambridge: Cambridge University Press, 1983).

Frey, Linda S. and Marsha L. Frey, *The History of Diplomatic Immunity* (Columbus: Ohio State University Press, 1999).

Frigo, Daniela, *Il Padre di Famiglia: Governo della Casa e Governo Civile Nella Tradizione dell' "Economica" tra Cinque e Seicento* (Rome: Bulzoni, 1985).

'Corte, Onore e Ragion di Stato: Il Ruolo dell'Ambasciatore in Età Moderna', in Frigo (ed.), *Ambasciatori e Nunzi. Figure della Diplomazia in Età Moderna (= Cheiron* 30 (Rome: Bulzoni, 1998)), pp. 13–55.

(ed.), *Politics and Diplomacy in Early Modern Italy: The Structure of Diplomatic Practice, 1450–1800* (Cambridge: Cambridge University Press, 2000).

'"Small states" and diplomacy: Mantua and Modena', in Frigo (ed.), *Politics and Diplomacy*, pp. 147–75.

'Principe e Capitano, Pace e Guerra: Figure del 'Politico' tra Cinque e Seicento', in Marcello Fantoni (ed.), *Il "Perfetto Capitano": Immagini e realtà (secoli XV–XVII)* (Rome: Bulzoni, 2001), pp. 273–304.

Frommel, Christoph Luitpold, *Der Römische Palastbau der Hochrenaissance*, 3 vols (Tübingen: Wasmuth, 1973).

Fubini, Riccardo, 'L'Ambasciatore nel XV Secolo: Due Trattati e Una Biografia (Bernard de Rosier, Ermolao Barbaro, Vespasiano da Bisticci)', *Mélanges de l'Ecole Française de Rome. Moyen Age* 108 (1996), 645–65.

'La "Résidentialité" de l'Ambassadeur Dans le Mythe et Dans la Réalité: Une Enquête Sur les Origines', in Lucien Bély (ed.), *L'Invention de la Diplomatie. Moyen Age-Temps Modernes* (Paris: Presses Universitaires de France, 1998), pp. 27–35.

'Diplomacy and government in the Italian city-states of the fifteenth century (Florence and Venice)', in Frigo (ed.), *Politics and Diplomacy*, pp. 25–48.

Gasquet, Cardinal, *A History of the Venerable English College, Rome* (London: Longmans, 1920).

Geary, Patrick J., 'Gift exchange and social science modeling: the limitations of a construct', in Algazi et al. (eds), *Negotiating the Gift*, pp. 129–40.

Geertz, Clifford, *Negara: The Theatre-State in Nineteenth-Century Bali* (Princeton: Princeton University Press, 1990).

Gensini, Sergio (ed.), *Roma Capitale (1447–1527)* (Pisa: Pacini Editore, 1994).

Gershoy, Leo, 'Garrett Mattingly: a personal appreciation', in Carter (ed.), *From the Renaissance*, pp. 7–12.

Gillett, Andrew, *Envoys and Political Communication in the Late Antique West, 411–533* (Cambridge: Cambridge University Press, 2003).

Gillgren, Peter and Mårten Snickare, *Performativity and Performance in Baroque Rome* (Farnham: Ashgate, 2012).

Giry-Deloison, Charles, 'Le Personnel Diplomatique au Début du XVIe Siècle. L'Exemple des Relations Franco-Anglaises de l'Avènement de Henry VII au Camp du Drap d'Or (1485–1520)', *Journal des Savants* (1987), 205–53.

Gleason, E. G., *Gasparo Contarini: Venice, Rome and Reform* (Berkeley and Los Angeles: University of California Press, 1993).

Goldthwaite, Richard A., *Wealth and the Demand for Art in Italy* (Baltimore and London: Johns Hopkins University Press, 1993).

Gouwens, Kenneth and Sheryl E. Reiss (eds), *The Pontificate of Clement VII: History, Politics, Culture* (Aldershot: Ashgate, 2005).

Grendler, Paul F., *The Universities of the Italian Renaissance* (Baltimore and London: Johns Hopkins University Press, 2002).

Grieco, Allen J., 'Food and social classes in late medieval and Renaissance Italy', in Jean-Louis Flandrin and Massimo Montanari (eds), *Food: A Culinary History from Antiquity to the Present* (New York: Columbia University Press, 1999), pp. 302–12.

Groebner, Valentin, *Liquid Assets, Dangerous Gifts: Presents and Politics at the End of the Middle Ages*, trans. Pamela E. Selwyn (Philadelphia: University of Pennsylvania Press, 2002).

Hale, J. R., *War and Society in Renaissance Europe 1450–1620* (Leicester: Leicester University Press, 1985).

Hallman, Barbara McClung, 'The "disastrous" pontificate of Clement VII: disastrous for Giulio de' Medici?', in Gouwens and Reiss (eds), *Pontificate of Clement VII*, pp. 29–40.

Hampton, Timothy, *Fictions of Embassy* (Ithaca: Cornell University Press, 2009).

Harvey, Margaret, *England, Rome and the Papacy 1417–1464: The Study of a Relationship* (Manchester: Manchester University Press, 1993).

Heal, Felicity, *Hospitality in Early Modern England* (Oxford: Clarendon Press, 1990).

'Food gifts, the household and the politics of exchange in early modern England', *Past and Present* 199 (2008), 41–70.

Hervey, Mary F. S., *Holbein's "Ambassadors": The Picture and the Men. An Historical Study* (London: George Bell and Sons, 1900), pp. 53–5.

Hexter, J. H., 'Garrett Mattingly, historian', in Carter (ed.), *From the Renaissance*, pp. 13–28.

Hibbert, Christopher, *The Rise and Fall of the House of Medici* (Harmondsworth: Penguin, 1979).

Hildebrant, Esther, 'Christopher Mont, Anglo-German Diplomat', *Sixteenth Century Journal* 15 (1984), 281–92.

Hillgarth, J. N., *The Spanish Kingdoms 1250–1516*, 2 vols (Oxford: Clarendon Press, 1976–78).

Hook, Judith, *The Sack of Rome, 1527* (London: Macmillan, 1972).

Housley, Norman (ed.), *Crusading in the Fifteenth Century: Message and Impact* (Basingstoke: Palgrave Macmillan, 2004).

Huelsen, Christian, *Le Chiese di Roma nel Medio Evo* (Florence: Olschki, 1927).

Huffman, Joseph P., *The Social Politics of Medieval Diplomacy: Anglo-German Relations (1066–1307)* (Ann Arbor: University of Michigan Press, 2000).

Hurtubise, Pierre, 'L'Implantation d'Une Famille Florentine à Rome au Début du XVIe Siècle: Les Salviati', in Gensini (ed.), *Roma Capitale*, pp. 253–71.

Ilardi, Vincent, 'The first permanent embassy outside Italy: the Milanese embassy at the French court, 1464–1483', in Thorp and Slavin (eds), *Politics, Religion and Diplomacy*, pp. 1–18.

Isom-Verhaaren, Christine, 'Shifting identities: foreign state servants in France and the Ottoman empire', *Journal of Early Modern History* 8 (2004), 109–34.

Jacobsen, Helen, *Luxury and Power: The Material World of the Stuart Diplomat, 1660–1714* (Oxford: Oxford University Press, 2012).

James, Mervyn, *English Politics and the Concept of Honour (1485–1642)*, Past and Present Supplement 3 (Oxford: Past and Present Society, 1978).

Jansson, Maija, 'Measured reciprocity. English ambassadorial gift exchange in the seventeenth and eighteenth centuries', *Journal of Early Modern History* 9 (2005), 348–70.

Jeanneret, Michel, *A Feast of Words: Banquets and Table Talk in the Renaissance* (Cambridge: Polity Press, 1991).

Jussen, Bernhard, 'Religious discourses of the gift in the Middle Ages. Semantic evidences (second to twelfth centuries)', in Algazi et al. (eds), *Negotiating the Gift*, pp. 173–92.

Jusserand, J. J., 'The school for ambassadors', *American Historical Review* 27 (1922), 426–64.

Kahn, David, *The Codebreakers: The Story of Secret Writing* (New York: Scribner, 1996).

Kempers, Bram, 'Epilogue: A hybrid history: the antique basilica with a modern dome', in McKitterick et al. (eds), *Old Saint Peter's*, pp. 386–403.

Kettering, Sharon, 'Gift-giving and patronage in Early Modern France', *French History* 2 (1988), 131–51.

Kidwell, Carol, *Pontano: Poet and Prime Minister* (London: Duckworth, 1991).

King, Margaret L., 'Caldiera and the Barbaros on marriage and the family: humanist reflections of Venetian realities', *Journal of Medieval and Renaissance Studies* 6 (1976), 19–50.

Kirkwood, Kenneth P., *The Diplomat at Table: A Social and Anecdotal History through the Looking-Glass* (Metuchen: Scarecrow Press, 1974).

Kirshner, Julius (ed.), *The Origins of the State in Italy, 1300–1600* (Chicago and London: University of Chicago Press, 1995).

Lazzarini, Isabella, *Fra Un Principe e Altri Stati: Relazioni di Potere e Forme di Servizio a Mantova nell'Età di Ludovico Gonzaga* (Rome: Istituto Storico Italiano per il Medio Evo, 1996).

Letters and Papers, Foreign and Domestic, of the Reign of Henry VIII, eds. J. S. Brewer, J. Gairdner and R. H. Brodie, 22 vols (London: HMSO, 1862–1932).

Leverotti, Franca, *Diplomazia e Governo dello Stato: I "Famigli Cavalcanti" di Francesco Sforza (1450–1466)* (Pisa: Gisem-ETS, 1992).

Levin, Michael J., 'A New World Order: the Spanish campaign for precedence in early modern Europe', *Journal of Early Modern History* 6 (2002), 233–64.

Agents of Empire: Spanish Ambassadors in Sixteenth-Century Italy (Ithaca and London: Cornell University Press, 2005).

Lindow, James, 'Splendour', in Ajmar-Wollheim and Dennis (eds), *At Home*, pp. 306–7.

Lowe, K. J. P., *Church and Politics in Renaissance Italy: The Life and Career of Cardinal Francesco Soderini, 1453–1524* (Cambridge: Cambridge University Press, 1993).

'"Representing" Africa: ambassadors and princes from Christian Africa to Renaissance Italy and Portugal, 1402–1608', *Transactions of the Royal Historical Society*, 6th series, 17 (2007), 101–28.

Luzio, Alessandro, 'Isabella d'Este e il Sacco di Roma', *Archivio Storico Lombardo*, Series 4, 10 (1908), 5–107 and 361–425.

MacCulloch, Diarmaid (ed.), *The Reign of Henry VIII: Politics, Policy and Piety* (Basingstoke: Macmillan, 1995).

McKitterick, Rosamond, John Osborne, Carol M. Richardson and Joanna Story (eds), *Old Saint Peter's, Rome* (Cambridge: Cambridge University Press, 2013).

McLean, Paul D., *The Art of the Network: Strategic Interaction and Patronage in Renaissance Florence* (Durham and London: Duke University Press, 2007).

MacMahon, Luke, The ambassadors of Henry VIII: the personnel of English diplomacy, c.1500–c.1550' (unpublished doctoral thesis, University of Kent, 1999).

Mallett, Michael, *Mercenaries and Their Masters: Warfare in Renaissance Italy* (London: Military Book Society, 1974).

The Borgias: The Rise and Fall of a Renaissance Dynasty (London: Paladin, 1969).

'The emergence of permanent diplomacy in Renaissance Italy', *DSP Discussion Papers* no. 56 (Leicester: Centre for the Study of Diplomacy, 1999).

'I Condottieri nelle Guerre d'Italia', in Mario del Treppo (ed.), *Condottieri e Uomini d'Arme nell'Italia del Rinascimento* (Naples: Liguori, 2001), pp. 347–60.

'The transformation of war, 1494–1530', in Shaw (ed.), *Italy and the European Powers*, pp. 3–21.

and Christine Shaw, *The Italian Wars 1494–1559* (Harlow: Pearson, 2012).

Margaroli, Paolo, *Diplomazia e Stati Rinascimentali: Le Ambascerie Sforzesche Fino Alla Conclusione della Lega Italica (1450–1455)* (Florence: La Nuova Italia, 1992).

Marriott, Wharton, *Vestiarium Christianum* (London: Rivingtons, 1868).

Martin, John, 'Inventing sincerity, refashioning prudence: the discovery of the individual in Renaissance Europe', *American Historical Review* 102 (1997), 1309–42.

Myths of Renaissance Individualism (Basingstoke: Palgrave Macmillan, 2006).

Martin, Russell E., 'Gifts for the bride: dowries, diplomacy, and marriage politics in Muscovy', *Journal of Medieval and Early Modern Studies* 38 (2008), 119–45.

Masson, Georgina, *Courtesans of the Italian Renaissance* (London: Secker & Warburg, 1975).

Mattingly, Garrett, *Renaissance Diplomacy* (Harmondsworth: Penguin, 1973).

Mauss, Marcel, *The Gift: The Form and Reason for Exchange in Archaic Societies*, trans. W. D. Halls (London: Routledge, 1990).

Mazzei, Rita, 'Quasi un Paradigma: "Lodovicus Montius Mutinensis" fra Italia e Polonia a Metà del Cinquecento', *Rivista Storica Italiana* 115 (2003), 5–56.

'La Carriera di un Lucchese Segretario del re di Polonia a Metà del Cinquecento', *Archivio Storico Italiano* 164 (2006), 419–56.

Meek, Edward L., 'The conduct of diplomacy during the reign of Edward IV (1461–1483)' (unpublished doctoral thesis, University of Cambridge, 2001).

Mellano, Maria Franca, *Rappresentanti Italiani della Corona Inglese a Roma ai Primi del Cinquecento* (Rome: Istituto di Studi Romani, 1970).

Meserve, Margaret, 'Italian humanists and the problem of the crusade', in Housley (ed.), *Crusading in the Fifteenth Century*, pp. 13–38.

Miller, Anthony, *Roman Triumphs and Early Modern English Culture* (Basingstoke: Palgrave, 2001).

Minnich, Nelson H., 'The participants at the Fifth Lateran Council', *Archivum Historiae Pontificiae* 12 (1974), 157–206, list of ambassadors on pp. 205–6, reprinted in Nelson H. Minnich, *The Fifth Lateran Council (1512–17)* (Aldershot: Ashgate Variorum, 1993).

'The "Protestatio" of Alberto Pio (1513)', in Rino Avesani et al. (eds), *Società, Politica e Cultura a Carpi ai Tempi di Alberto III Pio: Atti del Convegno Internazionale (Carpi, 19–21 maggio (1978)*, (*Medioevo e Umanesimo* 46), Vol. 1 (Padua: Studio Bibliografico Antenore, 1981), pp. 261–89, reprinted in Minnich, *Fifth Lateran Council*.

Miranda, Salvador, 'The Cardinals of the Holy Roman Church', www2.fiu.edu/~mirandas/cardinals.htm.

Mitchell, Margaret, 'Works of art from Rome for Henry VIII. A study of Anglo-Papal relations as reflected in papal gifts to the English king', *Journal of the Warburg and Courtauld Institutes* 34 (1971), 178–203.

Modigliani, Anna, '"Li Nobili Huomini di Roma". Comportamenti Economici e Scelte Professionali', in Gensini (ed.), *Roma Capitale*, pp. 345–72.

Molho, Anthony, 'The Italian Renaissance, made in the USA', in Antony Molho and Gordon S. Wood (eds), *Imagined Histories: American Historians Interpret the Past* (Princeton: Princeton University Press, 1998), pp. 263–94.

Mozzarelli, Cesare, 'Onore, Utile, Principe, Stato', in Adriano Prosperi (ed.), *La Corte e il "Cortegiano"*, 2 vols (Rome: Bulzoni, 1980), Vol. II, pp. 241–53.

Murphy, Caroline P., *The Pope's Daughter* (London: Faber & Faber, 2006).

Nesselrath, Arnold and Fabrizio Mancinelli, 'Gli Appartamenti del Palazzo Apostolico Vaticano da Giulio II a Leone X', in Pietrangeli (ed.), *Il Palazzo Apostolico*, pp. 107–17.

Nussdorfer, Laurie, 'The politics of space in early modern Rome', *Memoirs of the American Academy in Rome* 42 (1997), 161–86.

Oldrini, Paolo, 'Debolezza Politica e Ingerenze Curiali al Tramonto della Dinastia Sforzesca: Il Carteggio con Roma al Tempo di Francesco II Sforza (1530–1535)', in Giorgio Chittolini (ed.), *Gli Sforza, la Chiesa Lombarda, la Corte di Roma: Strutture e Pratiche Beneficiarie nel Ducato di Milano (1450–1535)* (Naples: Liguori, 1989).

Olin, Martin, 'Diplomatic performances and the applied arts in seventeenth-century Europe', in Gillgren and Snickare (eds), *Performativity and Performance in Baroque Rome*, pp. 25–45.

Oliva, Anna Maria, 'Gli Oratori Spagnoli a Roma tra Fine Quattrocento e Primo Cinquecento', in Prebys (ed.), *Early Modern Rome*, pp. 706–11.

O'Malley, John W., *Trent: What Happened at the Council* (Cambridge, MA: Belknap Press, 2013).

Orsini, Luciano, *La Sacrestia Papale: Suppellettili e Paramenti Liturgici* (Milan: Edizioni San Paolo, 2000).

Osborne, Toby, *Dynasty and Diplomacy in the Court of Savoy: Political Culture and the Thirty Years' War* (Cambridge: Cambridge University Press, 2002).

'The surrogate war between the Savoys and the Medici: sovereignty and precedence in early modern Italy', *The International History Review* 29 (2007), 1–21.

'The house of Savoy and the theatre of the world: performances of sovereignty in early modern Rome', in Vester (ed.), *Sabaudian Studies*, pp. 167–90.

Oxford Dictionary of National Biography: From the Earliest Times to the Year 2000, eds H. C. G. Matthew and Brian Harrison (Oxford: Oxford University Press, 2004).

Partner, Peter, *Renaissance Rome 1500–1559: A Portrait of a Society* (Berkeley: University of California Press, 1976).

The Pope's Men: The Papal Civil Service in the Renaissance (Oxford: Clarendon Press, 1990).

Paschini, Pio, 'Ambasciate e Ambasciatori a Roma dal Quattro al Cinquecento', in Ugo Ojetti (ed.), *Ambasciate e Ambasciatori a Roma* (Milan: Bestetti e Tumminelli, 1927), pp. 47–74.

Tre Illustri Prelati del Rinascimento: Ermolao Barbaro, Adriano Castellesi, Giovanni Grimani (= *Lateranum* new series 23 (Rome: Facultas Theologica Pontificii Athenaei Lateranensis, 1957)).

Pecchiai, Pio, *Roma nel Cinquecento* (Bologna: Licinio Cappelli, 1948).

Pellegrini, Marco, 'A turning-point in the history of the factional system in the sacred college: the power of Pope and Cardinals in the age of Alexander VI', in Signorotto and Visceglia (eds), *Court and Politics in Papal Rome*, pp. 8–30.

Penn, Thomas, *Winter King: The Dawn of Tudor England* (London: Penguin, 2012).

Petruccelli della Gattina, F., *Histoire Diplomatique des Conclaves*, 2 vols (Paris: Librarie Internationale, 1864).

Picot, Émile, *Les Français Italianisants aux XVIe Siècle*, 2 vols (Paris: Honoré Champion, 1906–7).

Pietrangeli, Carlo (ed.), *Il Palazzo Apostolico Vaticano* (Florence: Cardini, 1992).

Pistarino, Geo, 'La Sede di Roma nell'Apertura del Nuovo Mondo', in Gensini (ed.), *Roma Capitale*, pp. 541–79.

Polanyi, Karl, *The Livelihood of Man* (New York and London: Academic Press, 1977).

Poncet, Olivier, 'The cardinal-protectors of the crowns in the Roman Curia during the first half of the seventeenth century: the case of France', in Signorotto and Visceglia (eds), *Court and Politics*, pp. 158–76.

Potter, David, 'Foreign policy', in Diarmaid MacCulloch (ed.), *The Reign of Henry VIII: Politics, Policy and Piety* (Basingstoke: Macmillan, 1995), pp. 101–33.

Prajda, Katalin, 'The Florentine Scolari family at the court of Sigismund of Luxemburg in Buda', *Journal of Early Modern History* 14 (2010), 513–33.

Prebys, Portia (ed.), *Early Modern Rome: 1341–1667* (Ferrara: SATE/AACUPI, 2011).

Prodi, Paolo, *Diplomazia del Cinquecento: Istituzioni e Prassi* (Bologna: Prof. Riccardo Pàtron, 1963).

The Papal Prince. One Body and Two Souls: The Papal Monarchy in Early Modern Europe, trans. Susan Haskins (Cambridge: Cambridge University Press, 1987).

Queller, Donald E., *Early Venetian Legislation on Ambassadors* (Geneva: Droz, 1966).

The Office of Ambassador in the Middle Ages (Princeton: Princeton University Press, 1967).

'How to succeed as an ambassador: a sixteenth-century Venetian document', in Joseph R. Strayer and Donald E. Queller (eds), *Post Scripta: Essays on Medieval Law and the Emergence of the European State in Honor of Gaines Post' (= Studia Gratiana* 15 (Rome: 1972)), pp. 655–71.

Ramsey, P. A. (ed.), *Rome in the Renaissance: The City and the Myth* (Binghamton: Center for Medieval and Renaissance Studies, 1982).

Read, Conyers, 'The social responsibilities of the historian', *American Historical Review* 55 (1950), 275–85.

Richardson, Carol, 'The housing opportunities of a Renaissance cardinal', *Renaissance Studies* 17 (2003), 607–27.

Reclaiming Rome: Cardinals in the Fifteenth Century (Leiden: Brill, 2009).

'Francesco Todeschini Piccolomini (1439–1503), Sant'Eustachio and the Consorteria Piccolomini', in Mary Hollingsworth and Carol M. Richardson (eds), *The Possessions of a Cardinal: Politics, Piety and Art, 1450–1700* (University Park: Pennsylvania State University Press, 2009), pp. 46–60.

Richardson, Glenn, 'Anglo-French political and cultural relations during the reign of Henry VIII' (unpublished doctoral thesis, University of London, 1995).

Renaissance Monarchy: The Reigns of Henry VIII, Francis I and Charles V (London: Arnold, 2002).

The Field of Cloth of Gold (New Haven: Yale University Press, 2013).

Rietbergen, Peter, *Power and Religion in Baroque Rome: Barberini Cultural Policies* (Leiden: Brill, 2006).

Romano, Dennis, *Housecraft and Statecraft: Domestic Service in Renaissance Venice, 1400–1600* (Baltimore and London: Johns Hopkins University Press, 1996).

Roosen, William, 'Early modern diplomatic ceremonial: a systems approach', *Journal of Modern History* 52 (1980), 452–76.

Russell, Joycelyne G., *Peacemaking in the Renaissance* (London: Duckworth, 1986).

Diplomats at Work: Three Renaissance Studies (Stroud: Sutton, 1992).

Schwoebel, Robert, *The Shadow of the Crescent: The Renaissance Image of the Turk (1453–1517)* (Nieuwkoop: B. De Graaf, 1967).

Senatore, Francesco, *"Uno Mundo de Carta": Forme e Strutture della Diplomazia Sforzesca* (Naples: Liguori, 1998).

Servantie, Alain (ed.), *L'Empire Ottoman dans l'Europe de la Renaissance* (Leuven: Leuven University Press, 2005).

Setton, Kenneth M., *The Papacy and the Levant (1204–1571)*, 4 vols (Philadelphia: American Philosophical Society, 1976–84).

Shaw, Christine, *Julius II: The Warrior Pope* (Oxford: Blackwell, 1993).

'The papacy and the European powers', in Shaw (ed.), *Italy and the European Powers: The Impact of War, 1500–1530* (Leiden: Brill, 2006), pp. 107–26.

The Political Role of the Orsini Family from Sixtus IV to Clement VII. Barons and Factions in the Papal States (Rome: Istituto Storico Italiano per il Medio Evo, 2007).

Sicca, Cinzia M., 'Consumption and trade of art between Italy and England in the first half of the sixteenth century: the London house of the Bardi and Cavalcanti company'. *Renaissance Studies* 16 (2002), 163–201.

'Pawns of international finance and politics: Florentine sculptors at the court of Henry VIII', *Renaissance Studies* 20 (2006), 1–34.

Signorotto, Gianvittorio and Maria Antonietta Visceglia (eds), *Court and Politics in Papal Rome, 1492–1700* (Cambridge: Cambridge University Press, 2002).

Snyder, Jon R., *Dissimulation and the Culture of Secrecy in Early Modern Europe* (Berkeley: University of California Press, 2009).

Sola, Emilio, 'La Frontera Mediterránea y la Información: Claves Para el Conocimiento del Turco a Mediados del Siglo XVI', in Servantie (ed.), *L'Empire Ottoman*, pp. 297–316.

Soykut, Mustafa, *The Image of the "Turk" in Italy* (Berlin: Klaus Schwarz Verlag, 2003).

Starkey, David, 'Representation through intimacy: a study in the symbolism of monarchy and Court office in early modern England', in John Guy (ed.), *Tudor Monarchy* (New York: Arnold, 1997), pp. 42–78.

'Intimacy and innovation: the rise of the Privy Chamber, 1485–1547', in Starkey (ed.), *The English Court from the Wars of the Roses to the Civil War* (London: Longman, 1987), pp. 71–118.

Stinger, Charles L., *The Renaissance in Rome* (Bloomington: Indiana University Press, 1985).

'Roma triumphans: triumphs in the thought and ceremonies of Renaissance Rome', *Medievalia et Humanistica* 10 (1981), 189–201.

Stollberg-Rilinger, Barbara, 'Le Rituel de l'Investiture dans le Saint-Empire de l'Epoque Modern: Histoire Institutionelle et Pratiques Symboliques', *Revue d'Histoire Modern et Contemporaine* 56 no. 2 (2009), 7–29.

'The impact of communication theory on the analysis of the early modern statebuilding processes', in Wim Blockmans, André Holenstein and Jon Mathieu (eds), *Empowering Interactions: Political Cultures and the Emergence of the State in Europe 1300–1900* (Farnham: Ashgate, 2009), pp. 313–18.

Storey, Tessa, *Carnal Commerce in Counter-Reformation Rome* (Cambridge: Cambridge University Press, 2008).

Tabacci, Stefano, 'Olimpia Maidalchini', in *Dizionario Biografico degli Italiani* at www.treccani.it/enciclopedia/olimpia-maidalchini_%28Dizionario-Biografico%29/ [accessed 24 June 2014].

Taylor, Valerie, 'Banquet plate and Renaissance culture: a day in the life', *Renaissance Studies* 19 (2005), 621–33.

Thompson, James Westfall and Saul K. Padover, *Secret Diplomacy: Espionage and Cryptography 1500–1815* (New York: Frederick Ungar, 1963).

Thorp, Malcolm R. and Arthur J. Slavin (eds), *Politics, Religion and Diplomacy in Early Modern Europe: Essays in Honor of De Lamar Jensen* (Kirksville: Sixteenth Century Journal Publishers, 1994).

Tomas, Natalie, *The Medici Women: Gender and Power in Renaissance Florence* (Aldershot: Ashgate, 2005).

'All in the family: the Medici women and Pope Clement VII', in Gouwens and Reiss (eds), *Pontificate of Clement VII*, pp. 41–53.

Tomassetti, Giuseppe, *La Campagna Romana Antica, Medioevale e Moderna*, eds Luisa Chiumenti and Fernando Bilancia, 7 vols (Florence: Olschki, 1979).

Trexler, Richard C. (ed.), *Persons in Groups: Social Behavior as Identity Formation in Medieval and Renaissance Europe* (Binghamton: Center for Medieval & Early Renaissance Studies, 1985).

Triff, Kristin Adrean, 'Patronage and public image in Renaissance Rome: three Orsini palaces' (Ann Arbor: UMI, 2000). PhD dissertation, Brown University, 2000.

Tronzo, William (ed.), *St Peter's in the Vatican* (Cambridge: Cambridge University Press, 2005).

Vasoli, Cesare, 'Il Cortigiano, il Diplomatico, il Principe: Intellettuali e Potere nell'Italia del Cinquecento', in Adriano Prosperi (ed.), *La Corte e il "Cortegiano"*, 2 vols (Rome: Bulzoni, 1980), Vol. II, pp. 173–93.

Vatin, Nicolas, 'The Hospitallers at Rhodes and the Ottoman Turks, 1480–1522', in Norman Housley (ed.), *Crusading in the Fifteenth Century: Message and Impact* (Basingstoke: Palgrave Macmillan, 2004).

Vedovato, Giuseppe, 'I Giovani nelle Ambascerie della Repubblica Fiorentina', Estratto dagli', *Scritti in Onore di Niccolò Rodolico* (Florence, 1944).

Note sul Diritto Diplomatico della Repubblica Fiorentina (Florence: Sansoni, 1946).

Vester, Matthew (ed.), *Sabaudian Studies: Political Culture, Dynasty and Territory, 1400–1700* (Kirksville: Truman State University Press, 2013).

Visceglia, Maria Antonietta, 'Il Cerimoniale Come Linguaggio Politico', in M. A. Visceglia and Catherine Brice (eds), *Cérémonial et Rituel à Rome (XVIe–XIXe siècle)* (Rome: École Française de Rome, 1997), pp. 117–76.

(ed.), *La Nobiltà Romana in Età Moderna: Profili Istituzionali e Pratiche Sociali* (Rome: Carocci, 2001).

Watkins, John, 'Toward a new diplomatic history of medieval and early modern Europe', *Journal of Medieval and Early Modern Studies* 38 (2008), 1–14.

Weissman, Ronald F. E., 'The importance of being ambiguous: social relations, individualism and identity in Renaissance Florence', in Susan Zimmerman and Ronald F. E. Weissman (eds), *Urban Life in the Renaissance* (Newark: University of Delaware Press, 1989), pp. 269–80.

Welch, Evelyn, 'Public magnificence and private display: Giovanni Pontano's *De Splendore* (1498) and the domestic arts', *Journal of Design History* 15 (2002), 211–27.

Wilkie, William E., *The Cardinal Protectors of England: Rome and the Tudors before the Reformation* (Cambridge: Cambridge University Press, 1974).

Williams, Megan K., '"Dui Fratelli... Con Dui Principi": family and fidelity on a failed diplomatic mission', *JEMH* 14 (2010), 579–611.

Wodka, Josef, *Zur Geschichte der Nationalen Protektorate der Kardinäle an der Römische Kurie* (Innsbruck and Leipzig: Verlag Felizian Rauch, 1938).

Woodhouse, J. R., 'Honourable dissimulation: some Italian advice for the Renaissance diplomat', *Proceedings of the British Academy* 84 (1994), 25–50.

Zimmermann, T. C. Price and Saul Levin, 'Fabio Vigile's Poem of the Pheasant: humanist conviviality in Renaissance Rome', in Ramsey (ed.), *Rome in the Renaissance*, pp. 265–78.

Index

Made in the USA
Middletown, DE
08 April 2025